Russian-Jewish Given Names
Their Origins and Variants

RUSSIAN-JEWISH GIVEN NAMES

BY
BORIS
FELDBLYUM

AVOTAYNU, INC.
Teaneck, NJ
1998

Avotaynu, Inc.
P.O. Box 900
Teaneck, NJ 07666

Library of Congress Cataloging in Publication Data

Feldblyum, Boris, 1951–
Russian-Jewish given names: their origins and variants / by Boris Feldblyum.
  p cm.
Includes bibliography
ISBN 1-886223-07-6
1. Names, Personal—Jewish—Russia (Federation) I. Title
CS3010.F45 1998
929.4'089924—dc21   97-49485
                                                    CIP

To all those named Israel and Sarah, Isaac and Esther, Moishe, Chava, Basya, Feiga, Chaim, and Nathan, whose lives were cut short in every generation, yet whose names are immortal and will be with us forever

Contents

List of Tables

Introduction

Throughout history, Jewish given names have been of interest to ordinary people, to scholars and to governments. Ordinary people usually focus on choosing a newborn baby's name or on making a genealogical connection with an ancestor. Scholars study the linguistic aspects of names and their origins. Governments register their citizens for such purposes as taxation, military service and the dispensation of benefits.

With the recent growth of interest in Jewish history in general, and in genealogy in particular, the subject of Jewish given names is attracting the attention of many new researchers. Many books have been written on this subject in many languages, but no practical guide concentrates solely on the Jewish given names specific to Eastern Europe and Russia, the ancestral homelands of most Western Jews of today. The importance of scholarly information on Jewish names of Russian origin cannot be overestimated by those who study Russian history. Jewish names have evolved over time in the countries where Jews have lived; Russia is no exception. By the time of the great Jewish emigration at the turn of the twentieth century, the pool of names used by Russian Jews exceeded four thousand.

The possibility of writing a Russian-Jewish name guide occurred to me many years ago, when I was attracted to a book published in 1911 in the city of my birth, Zhitomir, Ukraine. The book's long and hard-to-translate title, *Sbornik dlya soglasovaniya raznovidnostej imen—biblejskikh, natsional'nykh, talmud-icheskikh, zaimstvovannykh i drugikh, upotreblyaemykh evreyami v Rossii*, literally means "Collection to reconcile variations of names: Biblical, ethnic, talmudic, adopted and others—as used by the Jews of Russia." It was written by Iser Kulisher. Although not the ultimate answer to all name-related questions, Kulisher's book is invaluable today as the most comprehensive known treatment of the origin of Jewish given names published in the Russian language. Making it accessible now to English-speaking readers makes it possible to understand better the names as they were pronounced, written and used in Russia. This information is especially important to those family historians, genealogists and other researchers who have recently gained unprecedented access to Jewish records in the archives of the former Soviet Union.

Iser Kulisher, who held the official title of "Learned Jew in the Office of the Volhynia Governor," did a remarkable job in his 1911 work of compiling and categorizing several thousand Jewish given names from the many primary and secondary sources available to him. His motivation to write the book was his desire to alleviate the hardships experienced by Russian Jews because of what he and his contemporaries called a "confusion of names." It is hard for us, living at the turn of the twenty-first century, to comprehend how a name could have created such severe problems 100 years ago. The root of this issue was that the Russian Jews were strangers in a strange land. They became unwilling Russian subjects during the three Partitions of Poland from 1772 through 1795, when

Russia annexed eastern Poland. The resident Jews' strange customs, strange language and a plethora of names did not fit conveniently the structure of the Russian language. The Russian government, historically anti-Semitic, was not eager to understand the lives and the needs of its several hundred thousand newly acquired subjects. Regulations pertaining to Jews that were promulgated in Imperial Russia were particularly onerous. For example, with regard to names, once officially recorded at birth, Jews were forbidden to change their names in any way. This law created enormous problems when it clashed with centuries-old Jewish naming customs and the errors and other vagaries of local clerks and official "crown rabbis" who were responsible for registering the Jews.

The Russian government insisted that every variation in the spelling of an individual's name in every official register or list actually represented a different individual. No consideration was given to the fact that errors were bound to occur as a result of transliteration/translation from the Jews' mother tongue to Russian.

By the beginning of the twentieth century, interaction between Jews and their government on the matter of given names can only be described as chaotic. The government was both ignorant of and oblivious to the fact that Mojshe, Moshe, Moisej, Moshka and Movsha, as listed in various official documents, could in fact be the same person. It wanted to tax, draft and fine poor Mojshe five times over.

Contemporary family history researchers, although far more knowledgeable about Jewish history than the Russian bureaucrats of the early 1900s, are often puzzled by the same discrepancies and variations in the Russian-Jewish alphabet soup of names. It is ironic that a reference book intended to enlighten czarist government officials by demonstrating that Mojshe, Moshe, Moisej, Moshka and Movsha were simply variant spellings of the same name has become almost a century later a valuable source for descendants of Russian Jews now dispersed throughout the world.

This book is designed primarily to help family history researchers understand the patterns of Jewish names in Russia at the turn of the twentieth century.

It is limited in its discussion of Yiddish onomastics; the Soviet period is not discussed at all (this work is planned for the future, along with the study of name changes from Russian-Yiddish to Anglicized Yiddish names created during the period 1890–1920).

This book is organized into three sections: a historical overview, a list of Hebrew sacred names and their sources, and a cross-index of familiar Jewish names to the original Hebrew. The first section provides a historical overview of the evolution of Jewish names. It covers biblical times through the early twentieth century. Although based on the introductory section of Kulisher's book, the text has been edited to soften the polemic tone of his writing, which is largely irrelevant today. It has also been expanded to include background information needed for a better understanding of the evolution of Jewish names' in their historical context. In addition to discussing name development, Section One presents a number of tables that contain Jewish names used in various time periods and geographical regions of Europe and the Middle East.

Kulisher's essay was an important first step in the study of Jewish given names, although the need has quickly arisen to verify and understand better both the sources cited by Kulisher himself and other works published later in the twentieth century. The first early work, on which Kulisher relied heavily, was the 1893 monograph in Russian entitled *Evrejskie imena sobstvennye* (Jewish given names) by Meshel Pogorel'skij. An earlier source, which retains its value to this day, is the work of Leopold Zunz entitled *Die Namen der Juden* (Jewish names) written in 1837. It is significant that these two books were published for the same reason given by Kulisher, namely to resolve the confusion over Jewish given names. Pogorel'skij stated the problem as a *misunderstanding* of the use of Jewish given names. This misunderstanding was one cause of many of the problems Jews faced in the early 1890s in their relations with the Russian government. Zunz was prompted to write his monograph by the Prussian decree limiting the choice of Jewish names. Although important in their discussions of biblical to medieval times in the development of Jewish names, neither work focused on the Jewish names used in Russia (although Pogorel'skij cited a limited number of the Yiddish versions of some biblical names).

The linguistic aspect of Russian-Jewish names was discussed only superficially by Kulisher. More than sixty years after Kulisher, this subject was carefully examined by E. Stankiewicz (1969) in his article, "The Derivational Pattern of Yiddish Personal (Given) Names." This article is essential reading for a better understanding of the phonetics and morphology of Russian-Jewish names. It has also been considered by Alexander Beider (1993) in his *Dictionary of Jewish Surnames from the Russian Empire*.

The second section of the book, "Jewish Names Used in Russia, Including Their Known Derivations, Abbreviations and Distortions," contains all the names organized by their root names, biblical or Talmudic or adopted by the Jews from other peoples. Because this book is intended to help the reader understand and read the names in their Russian spellings, the Russian phonetic transliteration, rather than the English, is presented here—for example, Khaim instead of Chaim. Every root name is accompanied by its *kinnui* (folk name), as well as by all known variants and changes. In order to preserve consistency in translating names, the transliteration guide was adopted from the Alexander Beider's (1993) book on Russian surnames, except as noted. All Russian-Jewish names are transliterated according to their Russian spelling.

Section Three of the book, "List of Secular Names and Their Roots," is a reference table that makes it possible to identify the original Hebrew name (in its Russian translation) when only the familiar form of a given name is known. Sections two and three combine to form a valuable research tool. For example, if an ancestor's name was Zelik in Russia, the reference table indicates that this name was a derivative of many sacred names: Aaron, Asor, Avraam, Azriil, Efrem, Eleazar, Eliakim, Girson, Iakov, Iekufiil, Isaak, Iuda, Meshuilam, Meshuilom, Nafan, Ruvim, Shimariya, Shneur and Solomon. Consulting with Section Two makes it possible to establish other variants of Aaron, Isaac or

Solomon and to analyze a given name pattern inherent in a family being researched.

The inventory of several thousand given names based on Kulisher's book and augmented from other sources is a unique reference tool. It allows a researcher to find a sacred name that corresponds to a commonly used Yiddish name and also helps to trace many names throughout history. In many cases, it allows a researcher to tie a name to a specific geographical area. However, the list by itself does not solve all the problems that may arise in the course of research. Without understanding the evolution of Jewish names through history, it is difficult to analyze why a certain name was given to a person and why some forms of a given name did not look and sound at all like the sacred name.

Acknowledgements

This book was developed with the generous help and cooperation of a number of people. Sallyann Amdur Sack was instrumental in designing the book concept, and Harold Rhode reviewed the historical background section and helped with reconciling the Hebrew names. Max Tiktin of the George Washington University in Washington, D.C., offered invaluable suggestions and critiques regarding the books concept and Hebrew name usage. Peggy Pearlstein and Harry Leich of the Library of Congress helped me greatly in researching old, obscure sources. Irene Saunders Goldstein served as editor and helped put the book in its final form. I am deeply indebted to my sons, Joshua and Jeremy, who typed all the Hebrew names, verified biblical references, transliterated many thousands of Russian-Jewish names and typed several portions of the manuscript. I am especially grateful to my wife, Tamara, for her understanding and patience during the last two years.

И. И. Кулишеръ,

Ученый Еврей при Волынскомъ Губернаторѣ.

———

СБОРНИКЪ

ДЛЯ СОГЛАСОВАНІЯ РАЗНОВИДНОСТЕЙ ИМЕНЪ:

библейскихъ, національныхъ, талмудическихъ, заимствованныхъ

и другихъ,

УПОТРЕБЛЯЕМЫХЪ ЕВРЕЯМИ въ РОССІИ.

Издано при матеріальномъ участіи
С. Р. Варшавера.

Житоміръ.
Типографія и Переплетная Ш. Хорожанскаго, Михайловская, 12.
1911.

Title page of the 1911 work by Iser Kulisher *Sbornik dlya soglasovaniya raznovidnostej imen—biblejskikh, natsional'nykh, talmudicheskikh, zaimstvovannykh i drugikh, upotreblyaemykh evreyami v Rossii* (Collection to reconcile variations of names: Biblical, ethnic, talmudic, adopted and others—as used by the Jews of Russia).

Origins of Russian-Jewish Given Names

This section presents an edited and expanded version of the introduction to the
Collection to Reconcile Variations of Names *by Iser Kulisher published in 1911*
in Zhitomir, Russia. It is a unique opportunity for the contemporary reader to
look at the problem of the confusion about Russian-Jewish given names that
existed at the beginning of the twentieth century from the perspective of a person
who lived then.

The collection of names offered here addresses one of the many perplexing
issues of Jewish lives, a matter of great importance to us: the question of which
given names are used by Jews. In the first place, this question has practical
value in the civil and legal situation of many Jews. The laws and regulations in
force today do not pamper us with many rights, but even this modicum of civil
good is unavailable to many Jews because of the situation concerning Jewish
given names. It is sufficient to remember that unreconcilable names result every
year in ruined lives for many young people and in the financial destruction that
many unfortunate Jewish families suffer at times of military draft.

The following are examples of distorted Jewish names that illustrate the dire
consequences for draftees in one small *shtetl* during one year only. Note that all
draftees had died before the draft; regardless, in each case, the deceased were
considered to be draft dodgers and their families were fined.

Names from Draft List	Names from Death Records Book
Trut, Shlioma Ojzer Itskov	Trut, Shlioma Ejzer Itskov
Baranchuk, Mojsej Lejbovich	Baranchuk, Mojshe Lejbovich
Burilo, Itskhok-Ajzik Khaimov	Burilo, Ajzik Khaimov
Sukholetko, Iosif Yankelev	Sukholetko, Iosel' Yankelev
Bilogolov, Mojshe Iosif Shoelev	Bilogolov, Mojshe Shoil' Iosifov
Tsigan, Khaim Getsel'	Chigan, Khaim Getsel'
Erlikhman, Vol'f Ishiev	Erlikhman, Vol'f Ovseyev
Kantor, Yankel' Aron Duvidov	Kantor, Yankel' Aronov
Pavolotskij, Lejb-Gersh Shimonov	Favolotskij, Lejb-Gersh Simonov

(Note: The Hebrew letter פ reads as both *p* and *f* in the last example in the list, hence the
confusion.)

In another case, a Jew identified as Mojshe was drafted into the army, but he
was also fined 300 rubles for a supposed brother Moisej, who was said to have
evaded the draft because this Mojshe had been listed as Moisej in one of the lists.

Other examples include the family of a Yankel' Korotkin, executed in Vilna,
who was fined because the deceased was accused of draft evasion; Letichev
resident Yankel' Rozenblat was murdered during a pogrom, yet his family was
fined; another family was fined because a girl named Sima was entered by
mistake as Simkha. Hundreds of cases such as these occur every year, making
the lives of many ordinary Jews unbearable because of the consequences of

inconsistent spelling of names in official records and the resulting confusion of names.

In addition to conscription nightmares, other areas of Jewish life are made difficult due to confusion regarding Jewish names, so the question of Jewish names is important to both the Jewish people and to the government. It is especially important to the latter. The government has made repeated attempts to solve this issue, most recently in the statute of 1893. Nevertheless, confusion regarding Jewish names continues, with the legal consequences becoming more complicated with every passing day.

This situation may be rectified in only one way: to give government institutions, rabbis, and all official and private individuals a list of all the names that the Jews in Russia use today with their variants, and to reconcile all existing Jewish documents with such a list.

The Rabbinical Council of the Ministry of the Interior created in 1910 was charged with preparing such a list. More than a year has passed, but we are unaware of any attempt to meet the requirements of the Ministry of the Interior. The primary goal of the current collection of names is to meet those requirements.

In your hand is the complete collection of all names used by Jews in Russia—root names, derivatives, and nicknames (*kinnuim*). The names are cited in transliterated Hebrew [in this book, transliterated to Russian—the Cyrillic alphabet—from Hebrew, and then from the Russian to the English form] and translated according to their meaning. Every name is accompanied by all its *kinnuim*, as well as by all its known variants. This part of the collection, in my opinion, can fulfill the first task of helping the government. In addition, the book aims to help both Jews and Christians to form a proper view of Jewish names. We meet with many prejudices in this area, committed by both sides, stimulated by the profusion of Jewish names, which total roughly 3,000. One must note, however, that other peoples' onomastic lists have just as many names; for example, there are 7,000 German given names, but this deluge of names causes no disaster or misfortune to anyone. It is known, for instance, that Poles and Germans have not only just double or triple names, but occasionally longer names, and they are listed under all these names in vital records and other documents; in everyday life, however, their bearers are called by just one name, as the following examples show.

Such double and triple names as Theodor-Gustav, Sophie-Marie, Ivan-Kazimir-Adam, Ludviga-Marie-Serafina, Karl-Marian, Joseph-Lui-Arman-Blank, Arthur-Stanislaw-Florentin, and many, many others have never caused a government to demand from a mother one more child, Iozef, in addition to Joseph, or an Arthur in addition to Artur. Even if such an innocent act had been committed, a draft board would never demand Yozef in addition to Joseph, as it demanded to produce Moishe in addition to the already-drafted Moisej, or Iosel in addition to deceased Iosif.

Complete anarchy with regard to Jewish names is fed in no small part by their complete and utter disregard by the Jews themselves. The fact of the matter is that the Jewish religion allows every Jew free choice in names, even if the names are taken from pagans; in addition, Jews, like many other people, customarily give a child a folk name, a *kinnui*, besides a root or sacred given name. The arbitrary approach to name-giving and the absence of any regulating principle led to the formation of multiple names; this was further complicated by area-specific pronunciation and diminutive name patterns. In some instances, such a practice leads to the complete substitution of the principal given name by a local pet name. The Middle Ages proved disastrous for Jewish names. On one hand, Jews often adopted local names during forced migrations from country to country and adjusted them in their everyday life; Christians, on the other hand, altered hard-to-understand Hebrew names to ease pronunciation. This confusion led to the creation of many new names phonetically similar to Jewish names. Societal hatred of the Jews, which induced the creation of an excess of scornful and pejorative distortions of Jewish names, restricted the Jews to adopt supposedly Christian, but really biblical and ancient, names. All this led to false notions about Jewish names that prevailed among the Jewish people themselves. Humiliating nicknames that clearly mocked the Jewish people became accepted not only among Christians but, regrettably, among Jews themselves. Any attempt on the part of a more conscientious and dignified people to relieve the burden of this shame—that of bearing a nickname instead of a name—met with resistance on the part of both Jews and Christians. The former were accused of assimilationism; the latter charged us with the theft of Christian names. To dispel prejudices on both sides is a pressing necessity, not only for practical reasons, but also to find the truth. The search for truth is the second goal of the present collection. As a reference book, it contains not only all sacred names (*shem ha-kodesh*) and their secular variations (*kinnuim*), but also combinations of names, as are common among Jews in various areas of Russia. The main sources of names were vital records and religious books.[1]

This collection of Jewish given names is far from an exhaustive source. My work is just a compilation from many sources. I do not solve the problem, but merely pose a question and bring to my aid all I could collect among the existing materials. I only want to paint a picture of the situation concerning Jewish names—the picture we have observed both historically and at the present time. The problem demands thorough and comprehensive analysis, which is absent in this book. I merely want to state the necessity of such analysis and will be satisfied if this collection eases the task of studying Jewish names by all those who wish to do so.

This book admittedly suffers from shortcomings: incomplete materials, insufficiently developed subject matter when discussing certain historical periods. Jewish onomastics is still awaiting its scholars, and if my collection serves them even partially, my goal is fulfilled. As for justification of the omissions from which my work suffers, I must admit to have hurried, as I thought it was necessary to publish the collection as soon as possible in our hard times.

---

[1] Kulisher's list of reference books is reproduced in the Bibliography.

Jewish Names Throughout History: An Overview

Given names are an indication of the cultural level of a people. Their advent signified a transition from indifference to an individual's character among members of a tribe to the formation of personality. One can clearly see the beginnings of the contrast between the concepts of *me* and *not me*. However, this contraposition was not absolute, because *me* developed in the tribal, societal environment, when all previous tribal life went into forming the personality. All tribal history can be traced here; a national character of each individual personality is created that infuses an individual given name. To quote George Kerber (1897), in a given name "we find a reflection and monument of the spiritual qualities, morals and customs of the whole people."

To ancient peoples, given names were not just a random mark or sign, but an indication of the character of either their bearers or those who had given the names. They believed that the name affected a man's fate. Greek names, for example, clearly reflected the qualities of the ideal man: chivalry, bravery, strength, political views, religiosity. The names of Germanic people, on the other hand, represented forces of nature, for example, Eberhard (boar), Wolfhard (wolf), Bernhard (bear), Hildebrand (one who burns with desire to fight), Arnulf (eagle-wolf), Kunrat (brave horseman), etc.; in parallel with these names, one also finds names that reflect admirable qualities of the soul, such as good nature: Friedrich, Friedebald Heinrich. Names of religious character (theophoric names) prevail among ancient Jews, although one can often see among them names that were derived from the names of various animals and forces of nature. When the Jewish nomads broke with the ancient Semites and the worship of nature, they retained their adoration of מלך (*melekh*) and בעל (*ba'al*) which personified the sun. To the sun they brought their sacrifices. It is here that the biblical custom to sacrifice the firstborn—בכור (*bakhor*)—is rooted.

Tanakh as Prime Source of Names

A large majority of the 2,800 personal names (which refer to about 15,000 persons) found in the *Tanakh* (which the Christians call the Old Testament) convey special meanings apart from their personal applications. The meanings of the remainder of the names have been obscured, probably by textual corruption or the insufficient resources of comparative philology (*Jewish Encyclopedia* 1905). Early nature worship by the Israelites found its expression in reverence for sacred rocks, rivers, trees, animals, etc:

- Numerous examples of rock worship are found in the *Tanakh*. One example is Jacob's rock of Bethel (Genesis 28:11–19). Sacred rocks were kept at the altar up to the post-biblical Mishnaic period. Trees, mainly oaks and palms, were considered to be expressions of the vital strength of the Holy Spirit. For a long time after, the Israelites worshiped God by rivers and trees.

- Passages in the *Tanakh* indicate that the Israelites considered certain springs to be sacred; this is reflected in some local place names: באר שבע (*beer sheva*, or spring of the oath, in Genesis 26:33); קדש ברנע (*kadesh barne'a*, in Genesis 14:7); עין דור (*eyn dor*, or source of homestead, in Joshua 17:11); בעל באר (*ba'al be'er*, or owner of a well, in Joshua 19:8) and עין שמש (*eyn shemesh*, or source of the sun, in Joshua 15:7).
- Snakes—personifying youth, prosperity and health—held a prominent place in the mythology of all peoples. They were worshiped by the Egyptians and the people of classical antiquity, as dedicated to Aesculapius, the Greco-Roman god of medicine. A snake-like scepter, the caduceus, was considered an attribute of God the healer. Among the ancient Phoenicians, snakes personified kind souls. Israelites also worshiped the snake images until the third century B.C.E.
- The name of Joshua's associate כלב (Kalev) meaning dog suggests that the Egyptians and the Semites honored dogs; כלבים (*kelevim*) were supported from the Temple's income; among other revered dogs was Isis (Sothis); among Phoenician names, one given name כלב אלם (*kelev ilem*) is found that means the same as עבד אלם (*eved olam*, trusted associate or servant to God) and כלבא (*kalba*, or bitch). From these examples, several given names of Israelites derive: כלאב (Kilav) from כלב (Kelev) and שנאב (Shena'av) from שנב (Shanav).
- The cult of the horse is similar to that of the dog. Thus we find in the second book of Kings that Yoshia (יאשיה) killed the Temple horses that had been dedicated to the sun and kept by the entrance to the Temple. There are possible traces of a similar cult in given names mentioned in Numbers 13:11, סוסי (*susi*, or horse).

To summarize, nature worship was common among the Israelites and other Semitic people, as was the worship of tribal gods. The concept of God as the absolute God is a sign of the later times of the prophet Jeremiah; until that period יקוק (YHWH) was the God of the Israelites,[2] while other gods belonged to other peoples.

The general development of religion among the Israelites can be described broadly as a transition from general animism regarding objects of nature and animals to the concept of the tribal god and then to absolute monotheism. These stages of religious development are reflected in the development of given names.

The Semites granted their gods their favorite epithets: בעל (*ba'al*) or מלך (*melekh*), that is, king, master. These words are components of many given names. The name בעל (*ba'al*) refers to the name of a deity; likewise do the names אבימלך (Avimelekh) and the Phoenician אביבעל (Aviba'al) and אבבעל (Avba'al). God's names, such as מלך (*melekh*), בעל (*ba'al*) and אדן (*adon*) were brought by the Jews from their prehistoric settlement. When the Israelites accepted יקוק (YHWH) as God, מלך (*melekh*) was considered by them to be a

---

[2] To honor the Jewish custom not to write God's name in vain (that is, other than in religious texts), the Hebrew letter ה is replaced with ק in this book.

pagan concept, as was later בעל (*ba'al*); God was called יקוק (YHWH), while מלך (*melekh*) was now reserved for *king*. A surname, מלכם (Malkhim), from the tribe of Benjamin, is cited in I Kings 8:9; before the time of Moses and later in the time of Kings, מלך (*melekh*) was God of pagans to the Ammonitians; מלכם (*malkhim*) was the idol of the Ammonites and Moabites (II Kings 23:3; Jeremiah 12:12); Joshua 10:1 mentions the Canaanite king אדני צדק (Adonai Tsedek). The theophoric element אל (*el*) which was commonly used by Jews as well as Assyrians and Phoenicians, is found in the Hebrew and Southern Arabic languages, and in Aramaic and Ethiopian dialects as an element of given names. It is used in both singular and plural forms, and in poetic and prophetic forms of speech colored by epithets: עליון (*Elyon*), עולם (*Olam*), יה (*Yah*), ראי (*Roi*), אל (*El*). Many names constructed with אל (*el*) are found in the period before Samuel, for example, משותאל (Meshotal), מהויאל (Mehuyel), מהללאל (Mahalalel), and, in the *Tanakh*, the name הלל (Hillel) is an incomplete name for God and is presented as a supplement. The other ancient name for God, צור (Tsur), is as old as אל (El); it is found in old given names such as אליצור (Elitsur), פריהו (Prihu), פדהאל (Padahel), צורישדי-ברצור (Tsurishadai-Bartsur). צסר (Tsur) is God's son and later is the epithet of God's name. Gradually, and in opposition to these generally accepted names of God, יקוק אל (YHWH El) became the exclusive given name of God among the Israelites. The God of Israel is the living God, unlike the false and nonliving gods of the pagans. He is the Source and Creator of life. The oath חי יקוק (*chai YHWH*) or "as God lives," supports this notion. It was logical that the mandatory abbreviated forms of God's name, יהו (*yeho*) and יו (*yo*) at the beginning of the word, and יהו (*yahu*) and יה (*yah*) at the end, constitute an integral component of many given names.

Such names as אביה (Aviyah, or God is my Father), יואח (Yoach, or God is Brother) and יואב (Yoav, or God is Father) further prove that all stages in the religious development of the Jewish people were reflected in their given names. However, not only did this spiritual aspect of life contribute to the creation of Jewish given names, family life and political developments did as well.

Biblical names have been the main foundation of Jewish names from ancient to modern times. They compose the most important segment of Hebrew onomastics and have served as the focus of studies for many Jewish scholars.

Several methods were used to classify biblical names to help understand their formation. Kulisher followed George Kerber's (1897) classification and divided biblical names in two large groups: elementary (names based on one Hebrew word) and compound (names based on more than one Hebrew word).

Elementary names
- Names devoid of religious content and based on subjects with no cultural meaning, for example, גשם (Geshem, or rain), שפן (Shafan, or badger)
- Names related to body and soul, for example, קרח (Kareach, or bold)
- Single-syllable roots with characteristic endings:
  - עזרי (Ezri) in I Chronicles 27:26, זבדי (Zavdi) in I Chronicles 8:19, and פלטי (Palti) in I Samuel 25:44
  - עדלי (Adlai), עתלי (Atli), and אחזי (Achazai).

- Names ending with א, such as גרא (Gera) in Genesis 46:21 and עבדא (Abda) in I Kings 4:6

Compound names

- Names with the theophoric element אל (*el*), for example, פלטיאל (Paltiel) in Numbers 34:26
- Phoenician names such as עבדאל (Avda'al, or servant of God), and other names with the prefix עבד (*eved*, or servant)
- Names that form a sentence:
  - הננאל (Hananel, or God is compassionate) in Jeremiah 31:38; צוריאל (Tsuriel, or God is my rock), מלכיאל (Malkiel, or God is my king) in Genesis 46:17 and נריה (Neriyah, or Light of the Lord) in Jeremiah 32:12
  - Names formed from two sacred names, as in אליהו (Eliyahu, or the Lord is my God)
  - Names such as שאר ישׁוּב (Shear Yashuv, or remnant will return) in Isaiah 7:3 and חפצי-בה (Hephzibah, or she is my desire) in II Kings 21:1
- Names formed with אבי (Avi) at the beginning or end of a name, as in אביאל (Avial), אליאב (Aliav)

Quite numerous are names that incorporate a verb in the perfect tense and those that define God as a giver, helper, liberator, judge, defender, as one who is both mighty and graceful, as in גדליהו (Gedaliahu, or God is great); or when hopes or expectations are expressed, as in ישׁמעאל (Yishmael, or God heeds).

The Israelites' captivity in Egypt also influenced the development of Jewish names. Suffice it to mention the name of the Jewish leader משׁה (Moshe, or Moses, in English) who brought the Jewish people out of slavery in Egypt and led them to the land of Israel. The name Moshe has an Egyptian (Coptic) root, discussed below.

Moses' assistant was named חור (Chur). This name belonged also to the Medianite king. Kerber (1897) explained this name as a transformation of Horus, the Egyptian god of light. Kerber also suggested that the name אסיר (Asir) was derived from the Egyptian god Osiris.

Classification of Biblical Names by Pogorel'skij

An earlier approach to the classification of biblical names was developed by Dr. Meshel Pogorel'skij (1893), who served as a rabbi in Kherson, Ukraine. His efforts to alleviate the government-inspired problems associated with Russian-Jewish names predated Kulisher's by nearly 20 years.

According to Pogorel'skij, biblical names may be divided into five classes: names that reflect the circumstances of birth, names that refer to a known event, names that reflect varying degrees of blood relation, names that reflect a concept of God, and names that carry other symbolic messages.

Names That Reflect Circumstances of Birth

The most famous example of this class of names is the Roman name Caesar, from the Latin *caedere,* or cut. The name was given to a future emperor, Julius

Gaius. The well-known legend states that he was extracted from his mother's womb by what is known today as Caesarean section. Another example of this class of name was Agrippa (for boys) or Agrippina (for girls). The name was given to a child born feet first (breach birth). Such names were common in ancient Rome and in Judea. The etymology of the name Agrippa goes back to the biblical name יעבץ (Yabets, or pain, I Chronicles 4:9).

The Bible explains the formation of the names of almost all tribal forefathers and other historically significant persons by the circumstances of their births:

- קין (Cain). ". . .[Eve said] I've gotten a man from the Lord." (Genesis 4:1)
- שת (Shet, or Seth in its Anglicized form). "[Adam] begot a son . . . and called his name Shet." (Genesis 5:3)
- נח (Noach, or Noah in its Anglicized form). "And [Lamech] called his name Noach, saying 'This name shall comfort us'." (Genesis 5:29)
- ישמעאל (Ishmael). "The angel of the Lord said unto [Hagar]: 'thou shalt call his name Ishmael'" (Genesis 16:11)
- יצחק (Isaac). "Abraham called the name of his son . . . Isaac." (Genesis 21:3)
- עשו (Esau). "The first came forth ruddy . . . and they called his name Esau." (Genesis 25:25)
- יעקב (Jacob). "And after that came forth his brother . . . and his name was called Jacob." (Genesis 25:26)
- ראובן (Reuben). ". . . and [Leah] called his name Reuben, for she said: 'Because the Lord hath looked upon my affliction, for now my husband will love me'." (Genesis 29:32)
- שמעון (Simeon). - ". . . the Lord . . . hath therefore given me this son also." (Genesis 29:33)
- לוי (Levi). ". . . I have born him three sons. Therefore was his name called Levi." (Genesis 29:34)
- יהודה (Judah). "This time will I praise the Lord. Therefore she called his name Judah." (Genesis 29:35)
- דן (Dan). "God hath judged me. . . . Therefore called she his name Dan." (Genesis 30:6)
- נפתלי (Naphtali). ". . . have I wrestled with my sister . . . . And she called his name Naphtali." (Genesis 30:8)
- גד (Gad). "And Leah said: 'Fortune is come!' And she called his name Gad." (Genesis 30:11)
- אשר (Asher). "And Leah said: 'Happy am I! . . .' And she called his name Asher." (Genesis 30:13)
- יששכר (Issachar). "And Leah said: 'God hath given me my hire'. . . And she called his name Issachar." (Genesis 30:18)
- זבלון (Zebulon). "And Leah said: '. . . now will my husband dwell with me'. And she called his name Zebulon." (Genesis 30:20)
- יוסף (Joseph). "And she called his name Joseph, saying: 'The Lord add to me another son'." Genesis 30:24
- בנימין (Binyamin). When she was dying, Rachel named him בן אני (Ben-Oni), son of my sorrow; but the father named him Binyamin, the son of

the right hand. (Genesis 35:18)

- פרץ (Peretz). ". . . and she said: 'Wherefore hast thou made a breach for thyself?' Therefore his name was called Perez." (Genesis 38:29)
- משה (Moshe). "And she called his name Moses and said: 'Because I drew him out of the water'." (Exodus 2:10)[3]

Names That Refer to a Known Event

- פלג (Peleg, or channel). ". . . the name of the first one was Peleg for in his days the earth was divided." (Genesis 10:25)
- גרשׂום (Gershom, or stranger). "She bore a son whom he named Gershom, for he said: I have been a stranger in a foreign land." (Exodus 2:22).
- אליעזר (Eliezer, or my God has helped). ". . . and the other was named Eliezer, meaning, the God of my father was my help and He delivered me from the swords of Pharaoh." (Exodus 18:4)
- בריעה (Beriya, or evil). "And she named him Beriyah, because it occurred when there was misfortune in his house." (I Chronicles 7:23)
- איכבוד (Ikavod, or without glory). "She named the boy Ichavod, meaning . . . the glory is gone from Israel . . . for the Ark of God has been captured." (I Samuel 4:21)

Names That Reflect Varying Degrees of Blood Relation

These names are called patronymics in the broadest sense of the word, and they consist of two parts: a prefix that expresses the degree of relation and a relative's given name. Such names can be divided into several groups according to the prefixes:

- Names formed with the paternal prefix אב (av), or according to phonetic requirements, אבי (avi)
  – אב-רהם (Ab-raham), "father of a mighty nation" (Genesis 11:26)
  – אבי-הוד (Abi-hud), "my father is majestic" (I Chronicles 8:3)
  – אבי-טל (Avi-tal), "father of dew" (I Chronicles 3:3); also used as a feminine name
  – אב-נר (Avner), "father of light" (I Samuel 17:55)
  – אבשלם (Avishalom), "father of peace" (I Kings 15:2)
  It should be noted that in several examples, the father is honored after the son (for example, Avi-shalom) instead of the son being honored after the father. In addition, the prefix ab/av does not always mean *father*; it is used often in a broader sense as *forefather,* as of a tribe or clan. The name of the patriarch, אברהם (Abraham), and his original name, אברם (Abram), must be understood in this context.
- Names formed with the maternal prefix אם (em), or according to the

---

[3] Some linguists note, with good reason, that Pharaoh's daughter would not have given a baby a Jewish name. They therefore derive the name Moses from the Coptic word מוש (musch), meaning *water*; the correct translation of the name is not *taken from the water,* but *water sprite.*

phonetic requirements, אמי (Emi), were seldom used. One biblical name with this prefix is אמ־נון (Amnun), or Navin's mother. This name, אמנון (Amnon), appears in II Samuel 3:2.

Both prefixes אב (av) and אם (em) could be used in combination with the prefix אח (ach) to form names such as אחיאם (Achiam) (II Samuel 23:33), which means uncle, as in mother's brother, and אחאב (Achav), which means uncle, as in father's brother.

- Names formed from בן (ben, or son) and בת (bat, or daughter) include:
  – בן־ימין (Ben-yamin); בת שבע (Bat-Sheba). Influenced by the Chaldean language during the Babylonian exile, the word בן (ben) was gradually replaced by the Aramaic word, בר (bar). The names בר־הנה (Bar-Hanah), בר־תלמי (Bar-Talamey) בר־אבא דנא (Barabba) exist in both the *Tanakh* and the Christian New Testament.
  – בן־ישי (Ben-Yishai) in I Samuel 20:27
  – בן־אחיטוב (Ben-Ahitub) instead of אחימלך (Akhimelech) in I Samuel 22:12[4]

  In poetic expressions, בן (ben) is often replaced by the feminine בת (bat). Thus, in the Book of Lamentations, the following forms are used almost exclusively: בת ציון (Bat Tsion), בת ירושלים (Bat Yerushalayim), בת יהודה (Bat Yehuda).

- Names formed from אחי (achi, or brother) include:
  – אחי־מלך (Achimelekh) in I Samuel 21:2
  – אחיתפל (Achitofel) in II Samuel 15:22

  Closely related to the names that express this degree of relationship are the names that symbolize the relationship to a people or nation. They begin with the prefixes עם (am) or עמי (ami).
  – עמינדב (Aminadab, or my nation is noble) in Exodus 6:23
  – עמרם (Amram, or mighty nation) in Exodus 6:18

  Prefixes איש (ish, or man) with its variation אש (esh), signify man's qualities
  – איש בשת (Ish Boshet, or man of Ba'al) in II Samuel 2:8
  – איש הוד (Ish Hod, or man of glory) in I Chronicles 7:18
  – אשחור (Askhur) I Chronicles 2:24
  – אשבן (Eshban) I Chronicles 1:41
  – אשבל (Ashbel) I Chronicles 8:1

Names That Reflect the Concept of God

A large class of biblical names features prefixes and suffixes that reflect the concept of God. The addition of these elements to a name infers that the person either is devoted to God or takes God as his protector.

- אל (el). This suffix, which means God in Hebrew, must not be confused

---

[4] It should be noted that the form Akhimelech preceded the patronymic form Ben Ahitob. The custom of creating children's names from the elements of the names of parents was sufficient in biblical times to identify a person uniquely.

with the Arabic suffix *al*, which is common in given names adopted from the Arabic. This caution must be considered particularly when reading Jewish names of the Middle Ages, such as אלקבץ (Al-Kabats) and אלפסי (Alfasi). It must also be taken into account that these names are not given names, but are early examples of what we know today as surnames.

- י (*ye*), יה (*yah*) or יהו (*yeho*), and יו (*yo*). These additions are identical and often interchangeable. The name יהושע (Yehoshua/Joshua) is one of the earliest given names constructed with יהו. We do not find such names with יהו among the tribal names formed after Israelites crossed into the Promised Land.

- בעל (Ba'al). This prefix is rarely encountered in Jewish names. A few examples: King David's son, called בעל-ידע (Beeliada) in I Chronicles 14:7, was also called אל-ידע (Eliada) in II Samuel 5:16. Likewise, ירו-בעל (Yeru-Ba'al) was only a nickname of Gideon (Judges 6:32). Other examples of this group include אש-בעל (Eshba'al) in I Chronicles 9:39, מריב-בעל (Merib-Ba'al) in I Chronicles 9:40 and simply בעל (Ba'al) in I Chronicles 9:36. All these names indicate Philistinian influence.

  The name Ba'al is also encountered, although seldom, in another orthography, בל (Bal), as in אש-בל (Ash-Bel) in I Chronicles 8:1, which clearly is the same as אש-בעל (Esh-Baal). Lastly, it is replaced occasionally by the word בשת (Boshet) which is the same as בעל (Ba'al), as in the following examples: ירובעל (Yeruba'al) in Judges 6:32 is a variant form of ירובשת (Yerubeshet) in II Samuel 11:21; אש-בעל (Esh-Baal) in I Chronicles 9:39 is a variant form of איש-בשת (Ish-Boshet) in II Samuel 2:8; מריב-בעל (Merib-Ba'al) in I Chronicles 9:40 is a variant form of מפיבשת (Mefiboshet) in II Samuel 4:4.

- Besides the above-mentioned names of God, other divine names were used in given names such as אדניקם (Adonikam), or "my God is exalted," in Ezra 2:13, אדנירם (Adoniram), or "God is exalted," in I Kings 4:6 and the latter's short form, אדרם (Adoram), in II Samuel 20:24; and אדניה (Adoniyah), or "the Lord is my God" in II Samuel 3:4.

  Often a name is stripped of prefixes and suffixes, leaving just its root. Examples include שמע (Sh'ma) in I Chronicles 5:8, from שמע-יה (Sh'mayeh) in I Chronicles 5:4; זכר (Zekher) in I Chronicles 8:31, from זכריה (Zekhar-iyah) in I Chronicles 9:37; אבי (Abi) in II Kings 18:2, from אב-יה (Abiyah) in II Chronicles 29:1.

Names With Other Symbolic Meanings

- Names with prophetic meaning. Such names often express a known thought or wish. Almost all such names in the Bible come from the books of the prophets:
  - עמנואל (Imanuel, or God is with us) in Isaiah 7:14
  - ידידיה (Yedidyah/Amedei/Bogomil/Teophil/Gottlieb, the last being the name given to Solomon by the prophet Nathan) in II Samuel 12:24-25
  - יזרעאל (Yizre-el, or God will plant) in Hosea 1:4

- לֹא־רֻחָמָה (Lo-Ruchama, or unforgiven) in Hosea 1:6
- לֹא־עַמִּי (Lo-ami, or not my people) in Hosea 1:9
- Names with emblematic symbolism related to animals. The giving of names related to animals is one of the most ancient of customs common to all prehistoric peoples. Interestingly, the choice of an animal as a symbol played no role in early societies; that is why we find in the Bible representatives of all species of animals as name sources, including those that are considered "unclean" by Jews. The existence of a wide variety of these names is clear from the following sample list of animals whose names served as sources of given names:
  - סוּס, סוּסִי (sus, susi), horse (Numbers 13:11)
  - חֲמוֹר (chamor), donkey (Genesis 44:14)
  - גַטֵּל־מַטְלִי (gamal), camel (Numbers 13:12)
  - חֲזִיר (chazir), pig (I Chronicles 24:15)
  - כֶּלֶב (kelev), dog (Numbers 13:6)
  - שָׁפָן (shafan), rabbit (Kings 12:12)
  - עַכְבָּר (akhbar), mouse (Kings 22:12)
  - רָחֵל (rachel), sheep (Genesis 29:17)
  - שׁוּעָל (shual), fox (Samuel 1:13)
  - דִּישׁוֹן (dishon), chamois (Samuel 1:38)
  - לִישׁ (lish), leopard (II Samuel 3:15)
  - צִפּוֹר (tsipor), male bird (Numbers 20:2)
  - צִפּוֹרָה (tsiporah), female bird (Exodus 2:21)
  - גְּדִי (gedi), kid (Numbers 13:11)
  - יוֹנָה (yonah), pigeon Jonah 1:1
  - דְּבוֹרָה (d'vorah), bee (Judges 4:4)
  - נָחָשׁ (nachash), serpent (Genesis 49:17)
- Some names were associated with either subjects or abstract concepts:
  - נַעֲרָה (na'arah), maiden (I Chronicles 4:5)
  - עֶבֶד (eved), servant (I Chronicles 8:22)
  - אֱנוֹשׁ (enosh), man (Genesis 5:6)
  - צֶמַח (tsemach), plant (Zachariya 3:8)
  - צוּף (tsuf), copper (Samuel 1:1)
  - וְשׁוֹשַׁנָה (shoshan, shoshanah), lily (Chronicles 2:31)
  - תָּמָר (tamar), palm (Genesis, 26:13)
  - אַלּוֹן (alon), oak (I Chronicles 4:37)
  - כֵּיפָא (kifa), cliff[5] (I Chronicles 8:30)
  - גֶּשֶׁם (geshem), rain (Nechemiya 2:19)
  - בָּרָק (barak), lightning (I Chronicles 8:35)
  - אוֹר (or), light (I Chronicles 11:35)
  - תִּקְוָה (tikvah), hope (Ezra 10:15)
  - נַחַת (nachat), comfort (Genesis 36:13)

---

[5] A synonym of the word כֵּיפָא (kifa) is used in the New Testament; it was translated into the Greek as Peter (feminine, Petra), meaning cliff.

- שָׁלוֹן (*shalom*), peace (II Kings 15:10)
- מָנוֹחַ (*manoakh*), calm (Judges 13:2)
- זִמָה (*zamah*), abomination (I Chronicles 6:5)
- פָּסֵחַ (*paseakh*), limping (Ezra 2:49)
- יָמִין (*yamin*), right-handed (I Chronicles 2:27)
- חֹרֶף (*choref*), winter (Nechemiya 7:24)

• Names associated with the conversational languages of the Jews in biblical times, either Aramaic or Greek. The neo-Hebrew (Mishnaic Hebrew)—which was a mixture of Hebrew and Aramaic and augmented by Latin, Greek and Persian words and formations—served literary purposes. It was a source of a number of names such as:
- אמונה (Emunah), belief
- חכמה (Khokhmah), wisdom
- תקוה (Tikvah), hope
- פנינה (Peninah) and מרנלית (Margalit) pearl, a Hebrew variant of the Greek name Margarit
- שָׁלוֹן (Shalom), peace

Some names contain both a translation and a paraphrase:
- צדוק (Tsadok), just
- יחזקאל (Yechezkel) and יחזקיה (Yechezkiah), God reinforced (support, reinforce)
- שושנה (Shoshanah), lily
- מֶלֶךְ (Melekh), king
- קנאה (Kinah), zeal or fervency
- כיפא-כיף (Kifa-Kiyaf), cliff
- משיח (Mashiach), the Lord's anointed
- טוביה (Tuvyah), kind
- ברוך (Barukh), blessed

Although it is often possible to preserve with precision the etymology of an original name, the etymology of a name was not always considered when names were translated. For example, ידידיה (Yedidiyah, or friend of God) corresponds in Russian to Feofil (from the Greek Theophyl), but it is more often translated as Bogomil (beloved of God), which is etymologically close to אלדוד (Eldod) and אלדד (Eldad). However, these subtleties were seldom followed, and the names were used interchangeably.

Babylonian Exile: First Use of Foreign Names (586–537 B.C.E.)

The Jewish pattern of life based on the concept of monotheism developed over a number of centuries. Monotheism was conceived in the dim aspirations of Abraham, was reinforced during the Egyptian captivity, became the primary element of national self-consciousness in the time of Moses, and was laid down as the foundation of the national life of the Jews. Belief in one God slowly became an attribute of the people who had lived for eight centuries in the land of Canaan and culminated during the Babylonian exile. The half-century-long Babylonian exile (586-537 B.C.E.) was a true purgatory of the people's spirit, similar to that of their earlier Egyptian captivity. The demise of the Judean kingdom served to reinforce religious consciousness. Thanks to the Levites and the prophets, the spirits of the Jewish prisoners did not waver; they acquired instead new trust in their teachers' prophecies. Although wealthy Jewish families gradually fell under the influence of pagan religion and morality, and some even adopted the Babylonian cult, the younger generation raised the Jewish religion and morals to new high levels. Twenty-five centuries in the past, Babylonian exile may seem today a mere footnote in the history of the Jewish people. It had, however, the most profound effect on many generations of Jews—on Jewish culture as a whole and on Jewish names in particular. During both the exile and the post-exile period, a trend toward name changes and the use of foreign names in general became noticeable. Thus, Hadassa became Esther, after the Babylonian goddess Ishtar (see Nehemiya, Babylonian Talmud and Megilat Esther); the name Mordechai came from the Babylonian god Bel-Marduka, which was especially revered by Nebuchadnezzar.[6] The book of Daniel gives several more examples of name changes, all new names of Chaldean origin: "The chief officer gave them new names; he named Daniel, Belteshazzar; Hananiah, Shadrach; Mishael, Meshaech; and Azariah, Abed-nego" (Daniel 1:7).

Generally speaking, the custom of a defeated people changing their personal names was common in the ancient world. Assimilation by Jews who had reconciled themselves with Babylonian customs led to their wider adoption of non-Jewish names common in Babylon. Even Jewish names acquired a slightly Chaldean character, although a sharp difference is not noticeable due to the close relationship between the two languages.[7] Even after having been granted permission to return to their own land, many Jews remained in Babylon. The close connection between the Jews who stayed and those who returned to Jerusalem led to a continuing influence of the Chaldean-Babylonian culture on Jewish life during the subsequent Persian period (537–332 B.C.E.). One dominant cross-cultural force during that period was the Chaldean-Aramaic language which also influenced name formation.

Along with old names, new names—evidence of the recent Babylonian exile—appeared, for example, זרובבל (Zerubabel, or dispersion in Babylonia) and עלם (Elam, or Iran). The list of names of that period also includes חריה (Charaia, or God's ire), פדיה (Pedaia, or redemption), חסדיה (Hasadia, or healing), נחמיה (Nechemiya, or consolation), הודיה (Hodaya, or gratitude for mercifulness). It is important to remember that Hebrew was rarely spoken in everyday life; people used the Chaldean language. Moreover, when they settled in various new localities, Jews also used the Persian, Arabic, Greek and Latin languages of their hosts. Invariably, new given names were adopted along with these new languages and often—but not always—translated into Hebrew. This was especially true in the case of the Aramaic language and for the names that began to replace both traditional Jewish names and the Hebrew language.

---

[6] Nebuchadnezzar (נבוכדנצר) was the Chaldean king of Babylon during the period 605-562 B.C.E.

[7] Chaldean is the name given to the Aramaic language as spoken in Babylon, where Chaldeans gained power.

The following are examples of the Aramaic influence on given names:
- Names with the suffix *ai*: Bebai, Altai, Zakkai, Hai, Shamai
- Names formed from Aramaic roots: Neemia Meshezabel, from the root Shezab; Esra Sherebia, from the root Shereb; Zebina, from the root Zeban; and Neemia Shabek, from the root Shebok. A number of Aramaic names replaced old Jewish names: Gibbor, Ezra, Abda, Melicha, Yaddua, Yehchua, Yeschu and Yesu—the last three used in place of Yehoshua.
- Names derived from the Arabic. These names include Shamsherai, from the verb *samser* (to be wise), and Shiza, from the verb *shiz* (to love).
- Names adopted from the Babylonians and the Persians. Examples are Mordechai, Belchasar (from Baltasar) and Sheshbazar (from Shenazar). A number of names were used by both Jews and pagans. Pagan names adopted by the Jews of that period are witness to swings in the national consciousness of the Jewish people. These include Nebo, from Mercury; Lebana, from moon; Shabshai, from Saturn; Tamuz, from Adonis; and Cherub, from mushroom.

The first known example of translation of a foreign name into Hebrew also took place in the post-exile period. The Arabic name Kharif became יסרה (Yoreh, or autumn rain). It is clear that the era of Babylonian exile and the Persian period that followed werre fertile times in the history of name formation and adoption of foreign names among the Jewish people. For the first time, names emerged that were to be used for a long time to come. The traditional Hebrew names were far from popular during that period.

Name Development During the Hellenistic Period (323–330 B.C.E.)

When Alexander the Great subjugated Persia in 332 B.C.E., Judea fell under his power and remained so until 323 B.C.E. Alexander gained the support of his conquered peoples by his religious tolerance, which he considered an important element in his plan to Hellenize[8] the East. After Alexander's death, however, his kingdom disintegrated. Judea fell to the Egyptian Ptolemies, who treated the Jews with benevolence. The dominant Greek culture met with the growing resistance of many post-Babylonian exile Jews who wished to preserve their religion. The turning point in the internal struggle between the pro- and anti-Hellenists culminated during the reign of King Antiochus, who attempted to substitute pagan worship for Jewish worship. This led to an explosion of patriotism and the revolt of the Maccabees in 168 B.C.E. During this period, Jews came in contact with many peoples and cultures that had been Hellenized to varying degrees, with the notable exception of the Aramaic culture of Syria and Upper Mesopotamia. The latter was still influencing Judaism because of ties with the Jews of these lands and gradually became accepted by the nationalistic portion of Jewry. It is clear that the interaction with and influence of the Aramaic culture played an important role in the character of Jewish names. First, Aramaization of old traditional Jewish names took place, for example,

---

[8] The word Hellenism, coined in the seventeenth century, refers to idolization of Greek thought, language and culture.

Admon, Gedidim, Jechechonem, Jechonia, Jevija, Jose (short for Joseph), Onia (instead of Nechonia), Poira, Prachja, Schetach. Other names with clearly Aramaic phonetics were Boba, Buta, Chabuba, Chaschmonai, Gadai, Gamba (Erastos in Greek), Ischai, Jannai, Magbai, Mahbai, Makbai, Menai, Nithal, Tabai and Siva.

A yearning for traditional names led to wider use of old biblical names and the creation of new Hebrew and Hebrew-Aramaic ones: Yakim, Yeshebal, Maon, Perachja, Phasael, Shamai, Ulla, and many others.

Greek names were a clear majority among those used in Eastern Asia, Greece, Italy, Palestine, Persia and Alexandria in Egypt. The most notable examples were Alexander (אלכסנדר), often used by the Hasmoneans; Hyrkanos (הורקנוס), high priest of the Hasmonean family; and Antigonus Ish Suko (איש סוכו אנטיגנוס), a teacher of Mishna. Some frequently used Greek names included Amyntas, Andronicus, Antiochus, Antipater, Appollonius, Aristobulus, Bachius, Bothus, Chärea, Diodorus, Dorotheus, Dositheus, Eupolemus, Jason, Kleodemus, Lisimachus, Menelaus, Numenius, Pitholaus, Pollio, Ptolemäus, Silas, Sosipater, Theodorus and Theodotus. Greek names represent a considerable portion of the names mentioned in the Talmud. Table 1 presents a compilation of Greek names used by the Jews of antiquity.

Table 1. Some Greek Names Used by the Jews of Antiquity

Agemon	Chares	Nikanor	Scholasticus
Alexander	Chrysippides	Nikodemon	Silanus
Alexas	Chabrias	Nikodemus	Simonides
Alphius	Dakes	Nikomachus	Sonicus
Andreas	Demetrius	Nomus	Sosa
Andromachus	Diogenus	Onasio	Sosigens
Antigonus	Dosa	Orion	Sosippus
Antipatros	Doso	Palation	Sosthenes
Antyllus	Epikurus	Pansanias	Soter
Apollo	Eucolus	Panther	Stephanus
Archagotus	Eudemais	Papias	Stration
Archelaus	Eugdemus	Papiscus	Stratonicus
Aristeas	Eumachus	Pappus	Symmachus
Aristeus	Euphranor	Patricus	Systratus
Aristius	Eutocmus	Patroclus	Theodosius
Ariston	Gerontius	Petrus	Thephilus
Arsamus	Hebdomos	Philippus	Theudas
Artemion	Helenus	Philo	Theudion
Asteion	Hygros	Philonides	Tryphon
Autokles	Hyrkanos	Pistus	Zemus
Autolaus	Kyrios	Polemo	Zeno
Buleutes	Leonteus	Poregorus	Zosimus
Bumias	Merton	Puncharius	Zygos
Bunus	Nanus	Pyxis	

One result of the Jews' duality of culture and the interaction of Jews with other peoples and cultures was the adoption of double names. The addition of a second name that was easier to understand phonetically by the foreign ear made interaction with non-Jews easier because the two names were independent of each other.[9] The first examples of double names borne by Jews appeared after the Babylonian exile: Beltschasar-Daniel and Ester-Hadassa. Beginning with the Seleucides period (fourth through second centuries B.C.E.), the following double names were widespread among Jews: Absaljon-Pollion, Acha-Ajmare, Ezra-Boethus, Herodes-Agrippa, Hilel-Iulus, Iojakim-Alkimos, Ioseph-Ise, Khayim-Zosimus, Mahalalel-Iehuda, Malich-Klodemos, Mathia-Levi, Mischel-Meschach, Salome-Alexander, Sara-Mirjam, Saul-Paulus, Simon-Petrus, Thaddai-Juda, Tobi-Ariston, Tzedek-Justus, Yedidya-Philo, Yochanan-Joseph, Yose-Jason, Yuda-Aristobulus and Yuda-Alfius.

The custom of naming a newborn after parents, relatives or benefactors, as well as the practice of naming a son after his grandfather, became common among Jews in this period. Names repeated often were Hyrkanos, Sutra, Simeon and Joseph.

It is worth noting that alien names—Greek names, especially—were adopted first by the higher classes of society and only then became widespread among commoners. This scenario was repeated again during the period of Roman rule.

Roman Rule (Second Century B.C.E.–Seventh Century C.E.)

The practice of Judaism was not a rarity in Roman society; a large Jewish community lived in Rome as early as the second century B.C.E. Moreover, as monotheism developed and spread among pagan peoples in the Mediterranean basin, Jews began to migrate to other lands and to start colonies there. Considerable credit for spreading Judaism went to the Jewish community of Alexandria, Egypt. As the Jewish scholars and writers of Alexandria familiarized themselves with the best examples of Greek and Roman literature and philosophy, they had the opportunity to share the concepts of Judaism with the pagan Romans, whose presence in Alexandria was well established at that time, and to plant the seeds of monotheism in the Roman minds. The success of Judaism led to a strong negative reaction throughout the Roman Empire by the pagan masses and their rulers. Thus, in 139 B.C.E., the pretor Hispanus issued a decree expelling all Jews who were not Roman citizens. Eventually, oppression by the Roman viceroys and attacks by pagan mobs, inspired by impunity, led to the destruction of the Temple in 70 C.E. and the fall of Judea.

The period of Roman domination left its mark on the formation of Jewish names as elements of Latin penetrated the Aramaic dialects. Thus, Jewish persons of that period often bore names such as Agrippa, Agrippinus, Aguila, Aliturus, Antonius, Apella, Capellus, Castor, Crispus, Dolesus, Domnus, Dortus, Drusus, Iulianus, Iulus, Iustinus, Iustus, Marcus, Marinus, Niger, Romanus, Rufur, Sisema, Tiberinus, Tiberius, Titus and Verus.

At the same time, one encounters a substantial number of Persian and

---

[9] The practice of giving double names was not uniquely Jewish. Early Christians often retained their pagan names together with their newly adopted Christian names.

Aramaic names adopted by the Jews of both Eastern and Western Asia. Some examples include Abaj, Abba, Acha, Ada, Ajo, Asche, Bagbag, Bali, Bisna, Chabiba, Guria (Gurion), Hanniba (a Phoenician name corresponding to the Jewish name Khanniel), Hinak, Hun, Huna, Iod, Mabug, Manna, Monobaz, Nanai, Papa, Sama and Samkai.

Non-Hebrew names carried equal importance; at the same time, many seemingly newly formed Hebrew names had an Aramaic flavor, for example, the Aramaic Abuja (instead of the proper Hebrew Abija), the Aramaic Chanin and Chanana (instead of the Hebrew Chanan and Chaninia), Yudan (instead of Yehuda), Lazar (instead of Eleasar), Lazaros (instead of Elasar), Mathia (instead of Matitia), Oschaja (or Hoschaja) (instead of Yesaja), Rafrem (instead of Rab Efraim), Tanchuma (instead of Tanchumet).

Names ending with *ai* were numerous, again with a distinct Aramaic flavor. Examples included Alfai/Alphäus or Chilfai (replacing Chalfi), Asai (replacing Elsi and Usa), Baribai (replacing Bar-Ibai), Bonai (replacing Banus, for example, in works of Josephus Flavius), Dinai, Ibai (instead of the commonly used Ibn), Milai (replacing Milalai) and Yochai (replacing Yocha).

Few biblical names were used in the Roman period, although many people bore them. They included Anan, Asaria, Binyamin, Chananya, Elasar, Elieser, Gamliel, Hillel, Isaak, Ismael, Levi, Mathia, Menachem, Nachum, Nathan, Nechemia, Pinchas, Samuel, Simeon, Ulla, Usiel, Yakob, Yeremiah, Yeschua, Yochanan, Yonathan, Yoseph, Yosia, Yosua, Yuda, Zacharia and Zadek.

Similarly few feminine biblical names were used. Of some fifty feminine names used in the post-Babylonian exile period, fewer than ten were biblical: Channa (Anna), Chogia, Elisabet (a synonym of Eliseba), Miriam (compare with Mariam, Greek Mariam, Maria, or Marianna in Josephus Flavius' works), Rachel, Selomit (Salome in Josephus Flavius' works), Yehosabet (instead of Yehoseba) and Yudit.

Some feminine Hebrew names that appearing later during the period of Roman rule were Donag, Ester, Hadassa, Kamchit, Yochana (Yohanna) and Zophnat.

Some feminine names in the Aramaic form include Imrata, Martha, Nehoral, Safira (שפיראם) and its masculine form Shir (שיר) and Tabitha; clearly Aramaic names included Beruria/Veluria and Osperta.

Names of the Roman period probably adopted from pagans included Choba, Ibu, Jaeta, Nefata, Nizebet, Papi, Stada (or Estha) and Tevi.

Greek and Roman names included Alexandra, Akkme, Berenice, Cölia, Doris, Drusilla and Priscilla.

It is understandable that a number of non-Jewish and foreign names were changed when they were being adopted by Jews. The main reason is that the alphabets of these languages that coexisted in the same time period differed so much that the phonetics of many names were impossible to transliterate.

Name Development in the First
Ten Centuries Of the Common Era

After the fall of Jerusalem in 70 C.E. and the rise of Christianity, the life of Jews became difficult. The Jewish spiritual center migrated to Babylonia, especially following the creation of the school in Yabna. It was there that the Babylonian Talmud was completed, and there the discipline was formed that enforced the spirit of the Jewish people that was to resist the unimaginable cataclysms of later history.

For several hundred years, until the ascendance of Islam in the seventh century C.E., Jews were the pawns of numerous rulers throughout the Middle East. Muslims, while passing many anti-Jewish and anti-Christian laws, tolerated Jews in everyday life. They later played a similarly salutary role in other countries of the Jewish Diaspora. For example, Jews were persecuted in Spain by West Gothic kings who had converted to Catholicism until the victory by Muslims in their war against Christians in the eighth century allowed some form of peaceful existence.

Muslim victories and the growth of their civilization in the eighth century coincided with a spiritual renaissance among the Jews. Spanish Jews, although they adhered strictly to their ethnicity and religion, drew near to the Muslims in many areas of civic and spiritual life. Arabic developed into the conversational and written language of the Jews, and Spain became the center of Jewish spiritual life. The importance of Babylon and the Babylonian *gaons* (learned men; literally, geniuses) diminished. In the tenth century, Jewish communities in Europe united and began independent cultural development.

This period was also marked by numerous political coups, persecutions of the Jews by Christians, and "ghettoization" of Jewish life. One area that was untouched by external restrictions, however, was the use of names by the Jews.

As in earlier periods, Jewish names were often paired with similar-sounding non-Jewish names. Examples are Abtallion-Pollion, Gilel-Yulus, Ioakim-Alkimof, Ioze-Yazon and Saul-Paul. Later, phonetic similarity became less important, for example, in names such as Buni-Nikodemon, Irodes-Agrippa, Yanai-Alexander, Yochanan-Girkan, Yuda-Aristovul, Yuda-Alfii, Simon-Peter and Salome-Alexandra. Historically, non-Jewish names were used by Jews only when they spoke a non-Jewish language or conversed with non-Jews. During the first century, these names were recorded in vital records.

Greek-speaking Jews translated Jewish root names into Greek. Examples include Yedida or Chabiba (dear, amiable) into Philon, Edidya (beloved of God) into Teophil, Matatiya (God's gift) into Theodor, Menachem (comforter) into Paregorus and Tobi (best) into Ariston.

Some of the most pious of Jews in this period bore pagan names: Agrippa (son of Elieser the Great), Antigon (first teacher of Mishna), Aristovul (high priest), Evridem (son of Rabbi Yose), Gyrkanus (son of the high priest Joseph ben Tobij), Julian (religious martyr), Justus (son of Josephus Flavius), Nikoden (member of the Sanhedrin), Papus (religious martyr), Teofil (high priest) and Zenon (synagogue employee).

From the middle of the fifth century through the tenth century, a number of Jewish names were formed from common Jewish words of both biblical and nonbiblical origin; these names had not been used for centuries in Europe: Abraham (father of a mighty nation), Amnon (faithful), Baruch (blessed), Chaim (life), David (beloved), Noah (rest, quiet, peace), Obadia (servant of God), Solomon (peace), Shemaria (protection of the Lord), Yatsliakh (let it be happy),

Yerocham (may he be compassionate), and Yom-Tov (good day). Ancient names ending with *el* began appearing, primarily in Italy: Chananel, Daniel, Iekutiel, Ioel, Itiel, Machael, Shealtiel and Uriel.

In addition to commonly used Persian and Chaldean names mentioned in the Talmud, a number of new names appeared between the seventh and tenth centuries: Bostani (seventh century), Gai (ninth century), Natronai (seventh century), Netira (tenth century), Chazib (ninth century) and Sherira (eighth century).

At about the same time, Jews living in the Muslim world started adopting Arabic names, for example, Abdala, Abuali, Abudevud, Abulgedshadsh, Bassar, Dunash (tenth century), Dzunavas, Kalifa, Kelab, Meshachala, Salakh and Temim. Later, the connection of some of these names to the original Arabic was lost, and these derived names took on lives of their own. Examples are Gassan and Dunash.

A number of non-Jewish European masculine names became common among Jews living in Christian countries: Asterius, Basilius, Gindiokus, Gosolas, Granelas, Gerbanos (Geraban), Jumnus, Julius, Justus, Kalonymus, Leon, Lupus, Megas, Priskus, Salpingus, Serenus, Sigerius, Teodorius and Vivatsius. Only a few non-Jewish European feminine names are known that were used by Jews: Justa, Memona, Sofia and Zeinab (similar to Zeinobiah (זינביה), who allegedly poisoned the prophet Mohammed).

Some foreign names initially were used only in tandem with a corresponding Hebrew name, for example, Bostani-Chaminai, Gassan-Yozea and Abulgedshesh-Yosef. Later, however, foreign names were used independently.

As early as the Talmudic period (third to fifth centuries C.E.), we find sons named after their father's father and, not as often, after their mother's father. Examples include Abba ben Khia ben Abba, Botnit ben Abba Shaul ben Botnit, Khalafta ben Yose ben Khalafta, Gurio grandson of Gurios, Yosef ben Rova ben Yosef, Menasse grandson of Menasse, Pedat ben Elassa Pedat and Prata ben Eliezer ben Prata.

In the tenth century, the main center of Jewish culture shifted from the Middle East to Western Europe, and it became possible for a Jewish community to continue to develop Jewish culture. Because of the low cultural level of the surrounding population and its religious intolerance, Jewish life was rather isolated, with the notable exception of Muslim Spain. Spanish Jews has gained leadership of the Jewish Diaspora and kept it for five centuries, with Spain and Portugal becoming its spiritual center. Biblical writing became the object of rationalistic, critical and grammatical studies; philosophy penetrated religion to a much greater extent. The religious philosophy started by Saadia Gaon (882–942) in Babylon found its best expression in the works of Maimonides (1135–1204). In sharp contrast to Spain, conditions in such Catholic states as France, Germany and Italy compared unfavorably. As the Catholic Council strengthened its grip, the situation of Jews in these countries worsened, plummeting towards the end of the eleventh century, during the Crusades.

Jewish Life and Name Development During the Middle Ages

Following the Crusades, which brought devastation to many European communities, Jewish life again reached a new low. During the thirteenth to the fifteenth centuries, the fanaticism of the Catholic Church was at its highest level; persecutions intensified, and the Holy Inquisition was established. Spanish Jewry resisted the deterioration of spirit longer than Jews in any other country, but there, too, freedom of thought died with the establishment of the Court of the Inquisition. The peak of religious intolerance was reached in 1492, when the Jews were expelled from Spain. Such was the end of the lustrous epoch of the Sephardim started by Saadia Gaon, author of the Arabic translation of the Bible.

Ironically, during the fifteenth and sixteenth centuries, following the expulsion from Spain, Jews became messengers of the Arabic culture to Christian Europe. Christian scholars who tried to access previously closed sources of Arabic science got the opportunity, thanks to the Jews.

With regard to personal names, the tradition of repeating names in the family that had started in the ninth and tenth centuries became more popular. Usually the eldest son was named after his paternal (or, rarely, his maternal) grandfather. For example, Maimonides' grandfather signed his name as Joseph ben Isaac ben Joseph ben Obadiah ben Shlomo ben Obadiah. Even more remarkable was the case of the Kalonymus family, which used only five names in fourteen generations: Meshullam ben Moses ben Itiel ben Moses ben Kalonymus ben Meshullam ben Kalonymus ben Moses ben Kalonymus ben Yekutiel ben Moses ben Meshullam ben Itiel ben Meshullam. One consequence of this tradition is that certain names became characteristic of certain geographical areas:

- Arabic and pseudo-Arabic names, such as Machir, Mubchar, Mukhtar, Machbub, Meborach and Seadel, were common in the West.
- Greek Jews and Karaites bore ancient biblical names such as Aucitai, Yafet, Kaleb, Schefatia, Schelachia, Ehud and Shet.
- Names common in Italy included Immanuel (brought from Greece), Daniel, Jechiel, Binyamin, Gad, Yair, Schabtai, Sheshet, Zidkia, Yoav (used almost exclusively in Rome), and Kalonymus and Theodorus (common in southern Italy).
- Among new names, Shemtob and Chefez were common in Arabic Spain; Jakar, Sinai and Nadi werer common in France; and Sinai and Pesach in Germany.
- Some ancient names became common in more than one country: Israel, Meir (until this period it was known from two sources only: Josephus Flavius and the Mishna), Moses, Salomo, Schelumiel and Shimson (the first known use was in the eleventh century).

The custom of giving boys two names at the time of circumcision was developed still further in the post-Talmudic period. One name was the religious or sacred name (*shem ha-kodesh*) used in the synagogue and in Hebrew documents. The other, a nickname (*kinnui*), was usually a secular name for everyday use, often borrowed or adopted from non-Jews. The sacred category included all biblical names, Talmudic names, old Aramaic names and the Jewish versions of Alexander, Kalonymus/Kolonimos and Theodorus.

Names used in everyday life, as opposed to synagogue (sacred) names, fell into several categories:

- Abbreviation or translation of the sacred name, for example, Dioffato from Asael, Leser from Elieser, Muel from Samuel, Schaja from Jesaja, Sender from Alexander, Tranquili from Manoach and Vita from Chaim
- Any name used in everyday life, such as Simcha from Simeon, Menachem from Immanuel, Joseph from Benet
- Hypocoristic, or pet, names such as Leibel from Löve/Loeb

If during a person's lifetime the original sacred name came into disuse[10] and the secular name was still used, the secular name could be augmented by a new sacred name that conformed to any of the following categories:

- Return to the source name: Eisak to Isaak, Ismail to Ismael, Koppel to Jacob, and Sanvel to Samuel
- Translations: Bär into Dov, Benet into Baruch, Bonet into Masoltob, Gottlieb into Yedidja, Hirz into Hirsch-Zevi, Masud into Mazliach and Phöbus into Uri. Later, some of these equivalent names became so common that they formed double names such as Dov-Bär and Ber-Dov, Naftali-Hirsch and Arie-Leib.
- Given names with a similar meaning: Gottschalk into Eliyakim (God will establish), instead of Obadia (servant of God), the original source of Gottschalk
- Homonyms: Kalman into Kalonymus, Bonam into Benyamen, Man into Menachem
- Symbolic relationships that link to the symbols of the twelve ancient tribes of Israel: Fishlein-Efraim, Hirz (Hirsch)-Naftali, Löve-Yehuda and Wolf-Benyamin

Another common practice during the Middle Ages was name changing. The name of a person who was dangerously ill would be changed in the hope that the Angel of Death, who summoned persons by name, would be confused. This custom, known as *meshanneh shem*, is noted in the Talmud and is mentioned by Judah Hasid (*Sefer Hasidim*, No. 245). It became customary among Ashkenazic Jews for a person to be given additional names early during his life. Some names were temporary—until marriage, for instance—while others were retained for life. Temporary names were usually bestowed without official ceremony and were limited mostly to the names Alter (old man) and Zeide (grandpa) for boys, and Alte (old woman) and Boba (grandma) for girls. Other names given to boys were Chaim, Joseph and Raphael. Strangely, these names were given more often to those children who were, for some reason, most favored by their parents and were used only until the wedding day of the children, when a new name, generally that of one of the Patriarchs, was given to them. Moreover, the real name of the children, that is, their official names entered in birth registers, were often hidden from the community and even from

---

[10] The examples in this series are from Kulisher's work. Unfortunately he did not indicate his source for this seemingly strange occurrence: for Jews to forget their sacred names.

the children themselves. In many cases these new names became principal names for life. Names such as Alter and Alta were usually given during a serious illness, and their bearers retained them for life, unless they were struck by a new illness [Pogorel'skij 1893:13]. It was also considered unlucky to call an only child by his right name.

Particular care was to be taken in the writing of names in legal documents, the slightest error in which would invalidate them. Hence there are a number of early monographs on names, both personal and geographical, the first of which, *Sefer Shmot*, published in 1657 in Venice, was written by Simcha ha-Kohen. The best known is that of Samuel ben Phoebus and Ephraim Zalman Margoliot entitled *Tuv Gittin* published in 1859 in Lemberg. The custom of using multiple names for one person survived until the twentieth century, fueling the problems between Jews and the governments of the countries in which they lived.

During the Middle Ages, it was thought that Jews with the same name should not live in the same town or permit their children to marry into each others' families. It was even urged that either one should not marry a woman with the same name as one's mother, or else the new wife should be required to change her name. (As late as the early twentieth century it was considered unlucky in Russia for a father-in-law to have the same name as the bridegroom.)

Although ignorance and barbarism on the part of Christians led to widespread persecution of Jews, no restrictions were imposed on name-giving by Jews during this time period. As mentioned above, Jews in the Middle Ages were inclined to adopt given names common in the countries in which they lived.

Before 1000 C.E., Jews called their children by any name they chose: Jewish, Aramaic, Persian, Arabic or European. Between 1000 and 1492, certain names were widely used by Jews. Table 2 lists common Arabic names used by Jews in the Middle Ages. German names used by Jews at that time are presented in Table 3. Table 4 lists other European names borne by Jews in the same period. The name lists were compiled from various sources by Kulisher.

Table 2. Arabic Names Used by Jews in the Middle Ages

Masculine Names

Abuget	Abulhassan	Chaiun	Mahomed	Mervan
Abuherum	Abulvalid	Faradsch	Maimun	Sadun
Abulgalib	Abunassar	Jachija	Makluf	Sahal
Abulgid	Barhun	Khalifa	Marsuk	Said

Feminine Names

Asisa	Guhar	Mumena	Nogema	Sahera
Gamila	Masuda	Muna	Saharum	Sethum

In Germany the tendency for Jews to adopt Christian names was perhaps most marked. Such names as Bernhard, Bero, Eberhard, Falk, Gumprecht, Knoblauch, Liebreich, Süsskind, Weiss and Wolf are among those evident in the

Table 3. German Names Used by Jews in the Middle Ages

Masculine Names

Aberlieb	Eberlein	Gottschalk	Leblang	Männchen
Aberlin	Ekschalko	Gumpa	Leblin	Mannekind
Abring	Enschin	Gumpchin	Leblin	Mannli
Achselrad	Ensel	Gumprecht	Lemmlein	Mannlieb
Anschel	Enslein	Gunelm	Lew	Mans
Anshelm	Ensli	Gutkind	Lewpolt	Manus
Bercht	Enslin	Hertze	Liebetraut	Mendel
Berchtold	Erlin	Himmeltraut	Liebreich	Menke
Bere	Falk	Hirz	Liutin	Mennlin
Bernhard	Fischlin	Ichel	Low	Menzel
Bero	Friedel	Isenlieb	Lowe	Menzelin
Bischof	Fritzel	Knoblauch	Löwe	Süsskind
Burlin	Fuchs	Kunold	Luz	Weiss
Dafflin	Gottlieb	Lebe	Mandel	Wolf
Eberhard	Göttsalk	Lebel		

Feminine Names

Agnia	Gudchen	Junta	Metzlen	Riklin/
Agnina	Guta	Juntlin	Min	Rachel/Rick
Bräunlein	Gutchen	Jutta	Minna/	Risle
Edelen	Guthilde	Kela	Minde(l)	Röske
Ell	Gutlein	Kele	Olinum	Röslin
Feinlin	Gutlin	Klar	Perla	Schöne
Gelein	Heile	Liebel	Perlin	Schönel
Genta	Himmeltrud	Maidel/Matel	Rechel	Schönfrauen
Gimchen	Hitzla	Maita	Reich,	Schönlin
Gnena	Hitzlin	Meiten	Reichza	Suetecota
Goldchen	Jachent/	Meitin	Reine	Tokel
Golde	Jachet	Methild	Richilde	Tröstel

early Middle Ages. The list of such names was extensive. Feminine names of German origin were used even more frequently, and they were often translated into Hebrew, for example, Margalit (מרגלית) and Nechama (נחמה).

In France the use of biblical names appears to have been equally as extensive as in Germany, judging by the long list in Gross's (1897) *Gallia Judaica*. The early Jews of England, who spoke French throughout their stay until the expulsion in 1290, also used biblical names; the most popular masculine name—in the twelfth century, at least—was Isaac, followed by Joseph. On both sides of the English Channel, there was a tendency to translate biblical names into French; thus Deulesalt for Isaiah, Serfdeu for Obadiah and Deudon for Elhanan. But ordinary popular names were adopted also, including Beleasez, Fleurdelis and Muriel by females, and Amiot, Bonevie, Bonenfaund and Bonfil by males.

Post-Spanish Expulsion Period (Sixteenth–Eighteenth Centuries)

When the persecutions of the fourteenth and fifteenth centuries subsided, and

Table 4: Other European Names Used by Jews in the Middle Ages

Masculine Names

Agimet	Bonami	Chetschel	Jaknit	Nicola
Aguet	Bonamic	Cok	Joseph	Pantaleon
Albert	Bonamicus	Conpaso	Jurnepln	Perigors
Alexander	Bonasctruc	Copin	Jurnin	Peter
Amiot	Bondua	Craueda	Kalonymus	Phöbus
Anguin	Bonenfaund	Delosaz	Leo	Prophat
Anthos	Bonet	Denys	Leon	Quintello
Astruc	Bonevie	Deudon	Leontin	Salvad
Banditon	Bonfant	Deulesalt	Lombard	Salvado
Belager	Bonfat	Dolan	Mali	Salves
Bellevigne	Bonfil	Dunin	Mamson	Sancto
Bendich	Bonfoi	Duran	Marcello	Santo
Bendit	Bongoa	Durant	Mareau	Serfdeu
Benedict	Bongoda	Falkon	Margeria	Serno
Benet	Bongodas	Fidel	Marinus	Solvet
Beneton	Bonias	Fisol	Martin	Sonet
Benoit	Bonifaz	Fleming	Massolet	Theodorus
Bertrand	Bonsenior	Hagin	Merlin	Ursello
Blasom	Brun	Herkules	Merote	Vidas
Bon	Callot	Iconet	Model	Vigal
Bonafus	Chakin	Issac	Motell	Vivas
Bonam	Chakinet			

Feminine Names

Bela	Brune	Speranza	Gracia	Pulcelina
Beladonna	Brunetta	Estelina	Jenny	Pulcelle
Beleasez	Bunchen	Estella	Justa	Redisch
Beleta	Bunla	Estrega	Ladisia	Regina
Belieta	Bunlin	Fiorina	Luna	Rodisch
Belk	Chera	Fleurdelis	Manon	Rosola
Bellona	Chiluca	Flora	Mignet	Selda
Belot	Dolza/Tolza	Floria	Muriel	Setbona
Belota	Donna	Galantina	Myrrha	Solka
Blanca	Duenna	Galina	Palomba	Teslowa
Blanda	Ephrosyne	Genonna	Phila	Ursula
Bonafilla	Esperanza/	Gentil	Präciosa	Veleda
Bonne	Sprinza/	Gentilis	Puercelle	Veslin
Bruna				

as Jews settled in new localities and founded new communities, new patterns of given name formation arose: German Jews preserved a mixture of English and French names; Polish Jews used some Swiss names; Italian names were Germanized; and some Germanic names changed under the Slavic influence and made a comeback in German-Jewish communities.

A number of words expressing beauty and positive feelings formed a sizable portion of the new given names [Zunz 1837]: Ahavah (love) אהבה; Berachah (blessed) ברכה; Chayim (life) חיים; Emuna (faith) אמונה; Mazaltov (lucky star) מזל-טוב; Menucha (rest) מנוחה; Nechama (comfort) נחמה; Rachamim (compassion) רחמים; Shemtov (good name) שם-טוב; Simcha (joy) שמחה; Sason (joy) ששון; Tsedakah (righteousness) צדקה.; Yomtov (good day) יום-טוב; and Yeshu'a (salvation) ישועה;

After the expulsions from Spain and Portugal, and the destruction of their respective Jewish cultural centers, the remnants of Sephardic Jewry found refuge in Italy and Turkey. Unfortunately, the spiritual center created by the Sephardim in Turkey was short lived and did not significantly affect the lives of Jews there. The arrival of the Sephardim in Italy fortuitously coincided with the spread of humanism in that locale and was more fruitful, but the Catholic's imposing of the Inquisition soon thereafter led to renewed persecutions and the decline of spiritual activities. An intellectual revival stimulated by marranos also took place in Holland, but only for a short time.

Ashkenazim, the Jews of German and Slavic lands, slowly came to the forefront of spiritual renaissance, Slavic Jews more so because of the continuing persecution of German Jews. Happiest of all, at least for a time, were the Jews of Poland. Toward the end of the fifteenth century, Poland became the center of Jewish cultural life, only to be damaged by the Catholic Church some fifty to sixty years later. The Ukrainian Cossack revolt and the subsequent Russian invasion, both lasting in the decade 1648–58, devastated Jewish life in much of Ukraine and Poland. According to various accounts (Dubnov 1916, 1:156), between 100,000 and 500,000 Jews were slaughtered. The next hundred years were marked by the Messianic movement of Sabbatai Zevi, the spiritual degeneration of Frankism, and birth of Hassidism. In the second half of the eighteenth century, a new cultural center for European Jews developed in Germany.

The gradual renaissance of Jewish culture and thought during this period was well reflected in naming practices. Three centuries of persecution and wandering had brought Jews face to face with many peoples who imposed on them observance of new customs. Jewish names shared the same fate. Toward the late eighteenth century, the Jewish vocabulary was augmented by many names borrowed from European peoples. Examples of the many new names adopted between 1492 and 1781 are listed in Table 5.

In addition to adopting new names, some Jews changed their originally Jewish names, either by adapting them to local tongues or by using local variants of old Jewish names. Examples of these names are listed in Table 6. Modifications of Arab, Latin, Germanic and Slavic names are evident in these examples.

Continued societal progress and the establishment of nation states during the eighteenth century affected many aspects of Jewish life, including name formation. This process was especially accelerated by those Jews who sensed and embraced the changes, and who were eager to adopt the customs and cultural ceremonies they found among the Christians. Adoption of the names of

Table 5. European Names Adopted by Jews 1492–1781

Masculine Names

Adolph	Brahim	Graziano	Itel	Pastor
Amadio	Cornelio	Gumpel	Jodocus	Rudolph
Amatus	Diodato	Gumpert	Kirschman	Selig
Anastas	Diofatto	Hartvig	Köllner	Selka
Angelo	Eslin	Hänle	Kusch	Selkelin
Ansilio	Fargum	Heinrich	Kusel	Stephangelin
Bali	Feist	Hendel	Liebkind	Trautlin
Bonan	Fernandes	Hirsch	Lippold	Ventura
Bonaventura	Geronim	Huzka	Marcus	Venturin
(Masoltob)	Gimpel	Joost	Marin	Victorin
Bonirak	Götz	Isman	Masud	Vivant
Bonper	Graziadio	Ismun	Nosson	Volklin

Feminine Names

Alsguta	Filadora	(Schöne)	Orduenna	Esmeralda
Bienvenida	Fiammetta	Kindel	Orebona	Sol
Blümchen	Fiore	Kressel	Ortensia	Sulpizia
Blume	Frommet	(Grace)	Paciencia	Süsschen
Camilla	Frummetla	Kusche	Reyna	Taube
Chryse	Gioja	Leonore	Rica	Traute
Clara	Glückel	Lubka	Rica-Minerva	Treindel
Gutrud	Graciosa	Malle (Amala)	Salva	Treine
Dalchen	Gretschel	Mamel	Sapphira	Treinle
Daila	Grete	(Mama)	Schwarze	Veilchen
Diana	Hünla	Muhmlin	Scissel	Violanta
Dobrisch	Hinda	Nechle	Seleta	Vogel
Ellenheid	Hindel	Nesel	Serena	Vögle
Estrella	Laura	Nesha	Sete	Vrümede
Eudokia	Julia	Näglin	Smeralda-	Zarte
Feige	Kale	Nüssel		

surrounding peoples—Persians, Syrians, Greeks, Romans, Arabs and Europeans—increased substantially. At the same time, a number of biblical names became more common and widespread: Aaron, Abraham, Amnon, Chajim, Chanoch, David, Gabriel, Israel, Jakar, Jesaja, Joab, Joel, Jomtob, Malachi, Meir, Mose, Nissim, Noa (Noah), Salomo, Schemtob, Simcha, Simson, Uriel and Zebi.

Historically, Christians did not object to the adoption by Jews of non-Jewish names, even in the darkest periods of the Middle Ages. The situation changed toward the late eighteenth century, however, when Jews encountered not only resistance on the part of the Christians, but also stringent restrictions imposed by new laws. For example, the Austrian decree of 1787 stipulated the use of family names by Jews, specifically limiting the choice of given names to biblical names. This law was abolished in Bohemia on August 11, 1836. Also in 1836, the Prussian government attempted to limit the choice of Jewish family names. This effort prompted the notable Jewish scholar Leopold Zunz (1837) to publish

Table 6. Jewish Names Changed to Adapt To Local Tongues and Customs (Fifteenth–Eighteenth Centuries)

Masculine names

Alcan (Elkana)	Jakew (combined	Judlein	Musi
Chakin	English-	Kobel (German	Muslin
Danël (Dan)	Yiddish)	abbr. of Jacob)	Said
Dävidel/Tewil	Jekelin	Kopelin	Saimin
Davud (David)	Jesel	Koppel (German	Salemas
Duvinet	Jäklin	abbr. of Jacob)	Salman
Gadel (Gad)	Joachim	Lase	Salmin
Hagin	Jocen	Lasen	Salmias
Henoch (Chanoch)	Jocet	Lazaro	Salmone
Höschel	Jochim	Leser	Samulet
Hosea (Josua)	Jokel	Leyser	Samvel
Lasen	Joklein	Manuel	Savel
Isaak	Josel	Masus	Scheftel
Ismail	Joselin	Matthis	Schelomo
Israel to Isserlin	Josep	Menecier	Schmelka
to Isser	Joseppel/Josbel	(Manasse)	Seklin
Izaak	Joske	Michel	Selmel
Jacob	Joslein	Masel	Simelin
Jahnklin	Jospin	Möschel	Solyman
Jäkel	Jude (Yehuda)	Moskin	Tewle
	Jüdel	Musa	Zak

Feminine names

Abigaya/Abigail	Hannele	Marye	Peierlein
Anneta	Hanke	Merya	Priwa
Bessel	Henne	Merli	Rachlin
Besselin	Hennelin	Merlin	Rachela
Besslin	Hänlin	Merlein	Reichel
Pesslin	Hännly	Merlen	Rachel
Pesslein	Hendlin	Merel	Sarlin/Zerline
Pessl	Hendel	Muriel	Särchen
Pessla	Chanlin	Merle	Saja
Pesschen	Chendlin	Mirusch	Seklin
Betschel	Channele	Michele	Zorlin/Zerline
Briva/Priva	Chaneta/	Pair	Zirle
Chanelle/Kaynne	Anneta	Pessel	
Deina/Dinah	Hewlein/Ewa	Pora	
Hanne	Juditha	(Zippora)	

Note: The masculine name Isaac warrants special attention as one of the most common and most changed names. The earliest variants included Chakin and Hagin; it was abbreviated as Zak and Cag, the latter leading to Rabicag; pronounced Eizak (spelled Isaac) in English; and abbreviated as Sekel and Seklin in German.

his monograph, *Die Namen der Juden* (Jewish names), which became a classic work of Jewish onomastics. Zunz cited numerous examples of Jews who were using biblical as well as local non-Jewish names freely, and exposed the absurdity of the Prussian law, which was subsequently revoked.

Partitions of Poland and Subjugation of the Jews by Russia (1772–1795)

The renaissance of the cultural and spiritual life enjoyed by Western European Jews bypassed the Jews of Russia. While the former were beginning to enjoy the fruits of education and enlightenment, the latter, in the words of Kulisher, had just started on a rough road covered with thorns. Until the late eighteenth century, Jews had never lived in Russia in large numbers. A small Jewish community had lived in ancient Kiev in the eighth to tenth centuries, but practically no Jews had resided in Russia during the Middle Ages. Since its inception eleven centuries earlier, the Russian Orthodox Church had been extremely hostile to the Jewish religion. Jews were declared the "enemies of Christ" and a number of decrees explicitly forbade them from entering Moscow Principality. The situation changed sharply with the partitions of Poland in 1772, 1792 and 1795, when massive numbers of Polish Jews became Russian subjects (about 200,000 people after the 1772 partition alone).[11]

Prior to the partitions, Jews had lived in Poland for centuries in relative freedom. They had enjoyed well-developed communal structures, interacted with the local non-Jewish population and generally adapted to local conditions. They contributed to the new empire an abundance of Polish names—a huge number that continued to swell as Jews embraced Polish culture, assimilated and, in some instances, converted to Catholicism. The Polish Kingdom that became part of Russia consisted of ten provinces called *privislyanske gubernii* (provinces of the Vistula River region). The ten provinces were Kalisz, Kielce, Łomża, Lublin, Piotrków, Płock, Radom, Siedlce, Suwalki and Warsaw.

---

[11] The number of Jews in Poland and Lithuania on the eve of the partitions amounted to 621,000 people, according to the Polish census of 1764–66 (Dubnov 1916, 1:187). Enumerator sheets for some areas have survived, and are currently preserved in the archives of Poland, Lithuania and Belarus.

Table 7. Jewish Names from the Ten Polish Provinces

Masculine Names

Abusia	Calko	Ferdinand	Henoch	Ippolit
Adam	Camshel'	Fiszek	Hercka	Ira
Aizyka	Cevi (used as	Fiszka	Herszek	Isaj
Ajzyk	religious;	Floryan	Herszk	Iser
Al'bert	translated as	Franciszek	Herszlik	Israel
Albert	Hirsch)	Franek	Heszka	Isroel'
Alfred	Cezar	Frantsisko	Heyman	Iteig
Alojze	Chaim	Fridel'	Hieronim	Itsyk
Amnon	Chanon	Frimet	Hilka	Iuda
Anastazij	Chemia	Froim	Hirsz	Iudel
Anatol	Chil	Fryderik	Iakob	Iudka
Anatol'	Chuna	Gabriel	Ian	Iulian
Anchel'	Cyne (from	Gadalya	Iankiel	Iustyn
Anselm	Synay)	Gavril'	Iarma	Izaja
Anton	Danel'	Gdal	Icyk	Izar
Antoni	Daniel	Gdaliya	Iedediya	Izayash
Antonij	Danil	Gedalij	Iegoshua	Izrael (from
Arie	Daurd	Gedaliya	Ieguda-Ariya	Iisral)
Ariya	Dodia	Gedalya	Iekel'	Kadysz
Arkadiush	Dodiya	Genol	Iekisyel	Kaiel
Arkadjusz	Donel'	Genrich-	Ierakhmyel	Kalma
Ascher	Dydya	Stanislaw	Ieremjasz	Kana (from
Assur	Edward	Genrig	Iermya	Elkana)
August	Efroim-Manos	Genrik	Ierz	Karl
Bajrakh	Eizyk (from	Genrikh-	Ierzy	Karol
Baruch	Ajzyk)	Stanislav	Ignatij	Karpel
Ben-David	Ejkhel'	Genrikh-	Iisrael	Kazimerz
Bendet	Ejzyk	Stanislav	Iisral	Kazimir
Benedykt	El'khuna	Gereig	Ioachim	Kellman
Benish	Elazer	Gerig	Ioel	Khajman
Benjamin	Eleazar	Geronim	Iokhen	Khamel'
Benzian	Eliezer	Gierszon	Iokhenen	Khanina
Ber (Dow)	Elimalakh	Gil'man	Iokhim	Khil'
Berek	Eljasz	Gilyarij	Iona	Khokhman
Bernard	Eremash	Gil'mar	Ionas	Kielman
Binekh	Esel'	Girariya	Ionasch	Kishel'
Bogumil	Evel'	Godel'	Ionash	Kisyel
Boleslaw	Ezechiel	Godfryd	Ionasz	Kiva
Bonawentura	Fabian	Goroz	Iosef	Klemens
Bonek	Fajbusia	Gotlib (transl.	Iosek	Konstant
Boris	Fajbusz	of Jedydja)	Iosel	Ksaverij
Brachia	Fajvel	Grojnem	Iosiya	Kuna
Brakhia	Fajvusz	Grzegorz	Iospa	Kushel'
Bronislav	Feibusz	Gustaw	Iozef	Lajb
Çadyk	Feivusz	Habusia	Iozel'	Lajbel
Çalel	Fejbus	Haskiel	Iozue	Lajbus
Çalka	Feodor	Heiman	Iozyasz	Lajzer (from

Eliezer)	Mates	Naum	Samson	Szylem
Lajzer	Mateusz	Navtal'	Samuel	Szymel
Leib	Matias	Nazariya	Sane	Szymen
Leibel	Matyas	Nedel'	Sanel'	Szymil
Leibus	Matys (from	Nehamiiz	Saul	Szymka
Leizer	Menachum)	Nehemia	Saweli	Szymsia
Leizor	Matysjoa	Nesanel	Schmul	Tadeush
Lejb	Mauritsy	Nevakh	Sebastian	Tana
Lejbe	Mauryc	Nikodem	Sejman	Tankha
Lejbel'	Mauryc	Nikolaj	Sergiush	Tankhim
Lejbka	Mavrikij	Noe	Sergiusz	Tanokh
Lejby	Mechislav	Nokhim	Severin	Tebel
Lemel	Mejlekh	Norbert	Shabsa	Tejvel'
Leo	Menash	Nosel'	Shapsa	Teodor
Leonard	Menassa	Novak	Shapsia	Teofil'
Levek	Menosza	Nusyn	Shender	Tobiasz
Levi	Michal	Orko	Shendor	Toefila
Lewie	Michel	Osser	Shetel'	Tomasz
Lewka	Mikhail	Ovshiya	Shimshya	Tsalel-Tobia
Lisza (from	Mikhal	Ovsiej	Shlyama	Tsudik
Elisza)	Mikhel	Owadia	Shmaya	Tsylka
Lizer	Mikhuel	Owadja	Shmerek	Uibus
Lozarus	Miklos	Owsiej	Shoel'	Ure
Ludvik	Mikolaj	Paul'	Shulim	Urele
Ludwik	Miron	Pavel	Siabusia	Uri
Luzer (from	Mniel'	Pejsak	Sigismund	Uriya
Elazer)	Mojlekh	Pelter	Sokhor	Ursy
Lyajzer	Mojsej	Peter	Solkina	Urysh
Lyudvig	Mojzeesz	Pineo	Solomon	Urysz
Lyutsion	Mordka	Pinkas	Srol'	Uunica
Lyuzer	Mordko	Pinkus	Srul	Valerij
Machola	Mordochaj	Piotr	Srul'	Vasilij
Maer	Mordukh	Puss	Stanislav	Vell
Majer	Mores	Rachmil	Stefan	Vell'
Majlekh	Moriceri	Rafael	Sucher (from	Vikentij
Majorek	Mortsenij	Rafail	Issachar)	Villyam
Maksim	Moryc	Rafal	Sumer (from	Vladislav
Maksimylian	Mosiek	Rafol	Isumer)	Vyacheslav
Manasse	Moszeh	Riel	Sumer	Wadja (from
Manel'	Moszek	Robert	Symcho	Owadja)
Manheim	Movsha	Roman	Syne	Walenty
Manil'	Mowsza	Romuald	Szaul	Waleriusz
Marcin	Nachum	Ruben	Szeloma	Wanca
Mardochaj	Naftala	Rubin	Szlam	Wancia
Marian	Naftali	Rudol'f	Szlama	Wencyan
Mark	Naftol'	Ruzha	Szlema	Wilhelm
Markelij	Najlich	Ryven	Szmul	William
Maskel'	Nakhemia	Sale (from	Szya	Wincent
Masur	Napoleon	Zale)	Szyie	Wladislaw
Matel	Natan	Salomej	Szykie	Wolf

Wowe	Yurga	Zelman (from	Zyel	Zysha
Yakov	Yurij	Szeloma)	Zygmunt	Zysla
Yakub	Yuzef-Al'bin	Zendel'	Zyl	Zyslya
Yan	Zachariasz	Zenoch	Zylka	Zysman
Yanash	Zakhariash	Zew (form	Zylko (from	Zysya
Yarmush	Zale	Wolf)	Szymen)	Zysz
Yazon	Zdislaw	Zigmunt	Zyndel	Zysza
Yudka	Zdislov	Zoruch	Zyndel	
Yulius	Zdzislov	Zuchen	Zysa	
Yuliyan	Zelich	Zundel (from	Zysh	
Yuliyus	Zelicz	Zyndel)	Zysh'	

Feminine Names

Adelaida	Berte	Felia	Glika	Itka
Adelina	Bina	Felicye	Gnesha	Iudes
Adelya	Blima	Feliksa (from	Gnessa	Iudyta
Adli	Bluma	Glika)	Godfrida	Iukl
Ajdla	Brandla	Felitsiya	Godla	Iuli
Ajdlya	Bronislava	Felka	Golda	Iulia
Ajdyl	Brygida	Ferka	Golya	Iuliana
Alicya	Cecylie	Filippina	Gudel'	Iulii
Alitsia	Chara	Flora	Gudes	Iustina
Alojza	Chasza	Frajdla	Gustava	Iustyna
Amalja	Cyna	Frajna	Hadesa	Izabella
Amelia-Amalja	Cynka	Frajndla	Hajdy	Janetta
(from Mala)	Cypera	Frammet	Hajzura	Janina
Anna	Cypryanna	Franciszka	Hana	Judifa
Anne	Cyreta	Frantsiska	Hanna	Kajla
Annelya	Cyrla	Franya	Helena	Kajlya
Anneta	Debora	Frejma	Hendla	Kamiliya
Antonina	Didiya	Frendli	Henka	Karolina
Asna	Dorota	Frimeta	Henrieta	Karolya
Asta	Elena	Fryderika	Henryka	Katarzyna
Astna	Eleonora	Fryderyka	Hersega	Katerina
Atara	Elisaveta	Fryneit	Hinka	Katlya
Atatia	Elisheva	Fryneta	Hojka	Ketla
Augusta-	Eliza	Fula	Iacheta	Khinda
Emilya	Elzbieta	Gabryela	Iadwiga	Khudessa
Aurelia (from	Emilia	Gandli	Ianna	Khuma
Golda)	Emiliya	Gebora	Ida	Klavdiya
Aurelja	Emma	Gelena	Idalia	Klementina
Babetly	Ernestina	Gena	Ietta	Konstantsia
Bajla	Estera	Gendlya	Ioanna	Krangla
Bajny	Etka	Genrieta	Iocha	Krendle
Balbina	Etla	(Jetta)	Iochad	Kunegunda
Barbara	Evzel'	Genya	Iofa	Laina
Basa	Ewelina	Gertruda	Iokhvet	Lata
Basiya	Faiga	Geruna	Iosavet	Laya
Beata	Fale	Gety	Iosefa	Lea
Bela	Falya	Ginedla	Ioweta	Ledka
Benlaki	Fanny	Gitla	Ita (Judifa)	Lejcha

Leoniya	Mirka	Regina (from	Slawa	Tsertlya
Leontina	Mirlya	Malka)	Sofiya	Tsesya
Lidka	Miryam	Rela	Soja	Tsetsiliya
Lifcha	Muncha	Rifka	Sola	Tsluva-Laya
Lina	Nadzieja	Roche	Soniya	Tsutlya
Linka	Nakha-Khaya	Roiza	Sora	Tsyl'ka
Lote	Nata	Rojla	Sosa	Tysa
Luba	Natalia	Rojza	Srai	Tyslawa
Lucyia	Nechma	Rojzja	Stefania	Udel'
Ludwika	Nekhana	Rojzla	Suchna	Udessa
Lyaska-Bajla	Nena	Rojzli	Sulamita	Udlia
Lyuba	Nesha	Rokhil'	Syna	Ullia
Maja	Netta	Rokhlya-	Szarlotta	Viktoria
Mala	Nikha	Mariya	Szejba	Vitlya
Malka	Noma	Rosa	Szendlia	Wanda
Malwina	Nucha (from	Rosalia	Szojna	Wilhelmina
Manucha	Manucha)	Ruchla	Szosza (from	Yadviga
Mar'yana	Olga	Ruchlja	Sora)	Yakhet
Mar'yanka	Paulina	Rudyscha	Szyfka	Yanina
Maresa	Pelka	Rysha	Taia	Yerka (from
Margubiosa	Pelyana	Rywka	Tatiana	Yura)
Mariem	Pera	Sabina	Tekla	Yuliya
Marta	Perka	Salamanda	Temna	Yura
Marya	Perlya	Salomea	Teodora	Yustina
Maryanna	Pesi	Sal'ka	Teofila	Zabella
Marye	Pesse	Sara	Teofilia	Zanda
Masia	Pulcherja	Sary	Teresa	Zanetta
Masza	Rachel	Scharlotte	Tertsa	Zhana
Matel'da	Rachele	Schendla	Tona	Zofia
Matylda	Rajla	Scyvy	Towa	Zylka
Merka	Rakhelya	Selima	Traindlya	Zysla
Michaila	Raschka	Sendla	Tranya	Zyslya
Michala	Ratsya	Serafina	Tsalk	Zyzanna
Mieta	Rebeka	Shejna	Tserk-Laya	
Miranda	Rega	Shvartsa	Tserlya	

Note: Many names are cited in both the Polish spelling and their transliteration into the Cyrillic (Russian) alphabet and then back into the Latin alphabet.

The second partition of Poland (in 1792) added to the Russian Empire the provinces of Volhyn and Podolia, a large part of which was incorporated into Kiev province. Names common among Jews in these provinces (see Table 8) differed in many cases from names used in Lithuania and Poland. Different Yiddish dialects used by the Litvaks (Lithuanians) and the Galitsianers (Galicians), and history, lifestyle and different relations with the surrounding non-Jewish population often led to unique local name formations.

Table 8. Jewish Names Typical in the Southwestern Russian Empire (Volhyn and Podolia Provinces)

Masculine Names

Aba	Berka	Evsej	Iojzyp-Osip	Lejbysh
Abel'	Berko	Ezkhea	Iokhiel'	Lejvij
Abil'	Betsalel'	Fajbish	Iosh-Khaim	Lejvy
Abish	Bina	Fajvish	Ioshua	Lemko
Abram	Binim	Falik	Ioshuva	Leontij
Abramko	Birakh	Fishel'	Iosya	Leopart
Abus	Bogdan	Fraden'	Iovel'	Lev
Abus'	Boris	Fridel'	Iriya	Lipman
Adol'f	Borokh	Froim	Irma	Lipush
Ajzyk	Boyaz	Frojka	Isaj	Lytman
Akhiezer	Burakh	Frojko	Iser	Maiorka
Akiva	Burukh	Frojm	Ishia	Mal'
Aleksandr	Buva	Fushel'	Isidor	Man'
Alkon	Chaskiel	Gavriel'	Isrul'	Manes
Alkuna	Daniil	Gavriil	Its'ka	Manus
Alter	Danil	Gavril	Itse	Marius
Amuniel'	Danil'	Gejlikh	Itskhol	Mark
Ananiya	David	Gejnakh	Itsko	Markus
Anshel'	Eber	Gel'man	Itskol	Masej-Moisej
Antsel'	Efim	Gendzel'	Itsya	Matus
Arel'	Efroim	Genrikh	Iuda	Meer
Arkadij	Ejber	Georgij	Izamil	Mejlakh
Arol'	Ejlik	Gershko	Izrail	Mejlekh
Avna	Ejna	Gershon	Kadysh	Mekhul'
Avner	Ejnakh	Gershun	Kal'man	Men'
Avodiya	Ejsha	Gesel'	Kaskel' (from	Menakhim
Avramchik	Ejzik	Gil'	Yechezkiel)	Menashe
Avrum	Ekef	Giler	Kejfman	Mevsha-
Avrumchik	Ekhel'	Ginakh	Kel'man	Mevshe
Avtulij	Ekheskel'	Godel'	Kesil'	Mikhail
Azril'	Ekhiel'	Goshiya	Khaim	Mikhel'
Bajnim	Ekhil'	Govshiya	Khanon	Mikhuel'
Bal'	El'	Grigorij	Khil	Mikhuil
Beez	Elio	Iber	Khil'	Mikhyl'
Bejaz	Elkona	Iekhiel'	Khuna	Miron
Bejrish	El'ya	Ieshiel'	Kisel'	Moisej
Ben'yamin	Elya	Iezekiel'	Kisiel'	Moisej-Mojsej
Ben'yu	Elyu	Iko-Itskhok	Kisil'	Monash
Bena	Emilie	Il'ya	Kiva	Monashko
Bendet	Eremia	Ioail'	Kofman	Mordkhaj
Beniamin	Erma	Ioakhim	Kojftsya	Mordko
Benio	Esiya	Ioann	Kosril'	Mordokh
Beniomin	Evad'ya	Iodka	Ksiel'	Mordukh
Bentsio	Evad'yo	Ioel'	Kusha	Mordukhaj
Benya	Evadij	Iojkel'	Lejbel'	Moshe
Benyumen	Evadiya	Iojkhin	Lejbish	Moshij
Benyumin	Evel'	Iojzip-Iojzik	Lejbko	Mot'

Mot'ko	Ovsej	Shabshel'	Simon	Vol'ko
Mote	Ovshej	Shakhne	Sivan	Vul'f
Motel'	Ovshij	Shamshel'	Skhariya	Vyl'f
Movsha	Pajsha	Shamshon	Smulik	Wolwisz
Munish	Pejsha	Shamson	Sobol'	Yakef
Naftula	Pejsya	Shapshel'	Sokher	Yaker
Nakhshon	Pin'yu	Shaya	Soskher	Yakhod
Natan	Pinkus-Pinkas	Shejl'	Srol'	Yude
Naum	Rafail	Shejlik	Sukher	Yudko
Nekhemiya	Rafuel'	Shejlon	Sumer	Yukel'
Nesanel'	Raful'	Shejvakh	Szie	Yurdko
Nevakh	Rakhaiel'	Shilim	Tankhim	Yurij
Nikolj	Rakhail	Shimel'	Tav'ya	Yurkovich
Nisel'	Rakhmil'	Shimen	Tev'ya	Yusif (Iosif)
Noj	Refael'	Shimon	Tevya	Zajmvel'
Nokhim	Refoel'	Shimshon	Todris	Zamvel'
Nosel'	Refuel'	Shlema	Todya	Zedel'
Noyakh	Rivom	Shmerka	Tovij	Zejdel'
Nus'	Rovel'	Shmil'ko	Tovit	Zejlik
Nusen	Ruven	Shmorak	Toviya	Zel'man
Nusin	Ruven'	Shmul'	Tsal'	Zhurakh
Nusya	Ruvil'	Shmulik	Tsodik	Zigbor
Nut'	Ruvin	Shmun'	Tsudik	Zis'
Nuta	Samooil	Shmunya	Tsudya	Ziskel'
Nys'	Saul	Shmur	Urim	Zisya
Nysel'	Saul'	Shoel'	Uron	Zkhariya
Ojvish	Sema	Sholom	Urym	Zorokh
Olev	Semen	Shomon	Usher	Zurakh
Osha	Semion	Shopel'	Ven'yamin	Zus'
Osher	Sergij	Shukher	Viktor	Zusel'
Osip	Shaba	Shulim'	Vladimir	Zusya
Ovadiya	Shabsel'	Simkha		

Feminine Names

Adelaida	Bashiva	Brendlya	Donya	Elina
Adelya	Bastsion	Brokha	Dora	Elisa (Esta)
Agata	Bastsiya	Bryukha	Drejzya	Elisheva
Aleksandra	Basya	Budina	Drobna	Elizaveta
Alta	Bejla	Bukha	Dvejra	Emma
Ama	Belkha	Buntsya	Dvera	Endya
Amaliya	Bella	Bunya	Dvesya	Eniga
Ameliya	Berta	Chesa	Dynya	Enta
Anastasiya	Besya	Chizha	Dyshlya	Entlya
Aneta	Bilya	Debora	Edel'	Erish
Anna	Bina	Dejra	Ejda	Erka
Asna	Bine	Dinya-Dina	Ejdya	Ernestina
Aster	Bintsya	Dobar	Ejzhl'	Esfir
Badyana	Binya	Dobrish	Ekaterina	Esfir'
Base	Bogdana	Dobrusya	El'ka	Esya
Basheva	Brandlya	Donka	Elena	Etis

Etlya	Grina	Liaba	Nesa	Rulya
Evel' (from Eva)	Grukha	Lidiya	Nesya	Rykel
Evgeniya	Gudes (Adalya)	Lipka	Nina	Ryl'tsya
Fane	Gulya	Lishiva	Nisya	Rynya
Fanya	Gunya	Lista	Nokhama	Ryvka
Felya	Gusta	Lizbeta	Ol'ga	Sabka
Fenya	Gutlya	Luiza	Pajsya	Sara
Finklya	Idessa	Lushcha	Pasha	Saro
Fishel'	Idesso	Lyba	Paulina	Sarra
Fradsya	Ido	Lyuba	Perel'	Serafima
Fradya	Iokhvet	Lyubov	Peril'	Serlya
Frekha	Ior-Khaya	Lyubov'	Perlya	Shejndle
Frenda	Ira	Makhlya	Pinya	Shejndlya
Fridya	Itel'	Mal'tsya	Pisya	Shejva
Frima	Itkis	Malka	Prima	Shenva
Frima-Itsel'	Jrejnya	Manis	Pylya	Shiva
Frimet	Kha	Mar'em	Racha	Shnerra
Frum	Khada	Mar'im	Raisa	Shul'ka
Gadya	Khana	Mar'm	Rajcha	Shura
Galya	Khanna	Mar'ya	Rajkhil'	Shurtsya
Gannya	Khanya	Mar'yam	Rakhel'	Silviya
Gantsya	Khasha	Mar'yasha	Rakhil'	Simka
Gejdya	Khava	Marasha	Rakhlya	Simkha
Genda	Khay	Marem	Ranya	Slova
Gesya	Khekha	Mariim	Rashel	Sluva
Geta	Khin'ka	Marim	Rasheli	Soblya
Gides	Khina	Mariya	Rassel'	Sobol'
Gil'tsya	Khinda	Masha	Rasya	Sofiya
Gilya	Khine	Matlya	Regszoina	Soflya
Gindlya	Khiner-Khaya	Matula	Rehklya	Sonya
Ginenda	Khintsa	Mejna	Rejzlya	Sora
Ginenden	Khinya	Melya	Rekhuma	Sorka
Ginendlya	Khisya	Menikha	Renzel'	Sorlya
Ginesya	Khlata	Mentsya	Reveka	Sprintsya
Ginya	Khnitsya	Merim	Rez'ka	Sruva
Giriya	Khova	Merlya	Riklya	Stysya
Gisha	Khristina	Mervyasya	Riska	Sura
Gissya	Khuva	Mina	Rislya	Svitlya
Gitel'	Klyara	Mirel'	Rivlya	Symka
Gitlya	Krenya	Mirka	Rodya	Tel'tsya
Glika	Krislya	Mirlya	Roiza	Teofilya
Gliklya	Krisya	Motya	Rojza	Tovba
Godil	Kryanya	Muntsya	Rokhlya	Tsejtlya
Godlya	Lejya	Musya	Rosha	Tsejtya
Gol'da	Leonora	Mylka	Roza	Tsesya
Golda	Lesha	Nadezhda	Rozaliya	Tsetsiliya
Golde	Leslya	Nakha	Rualya	Tsif'ya
Gosya	Lesya	Nakhama	Rudlya	Tsipejra
Gotlya	Leya	Nekhama	Rudya	Tsipera
		Nekhuma	Rukhlya	Tsirel'

Tsirle	Tsyne	Udele	Yakhed	Zinaida
Tsirlya	Tsytsal'	Udlya	Yares	Zindel'
Tsisya	Tsyupa	Udya	Yudashka	Zisel'
Tsita	Tsyv'ya	Varvara	Yudes	Ziskel'
Tsitlya	Tsyviya	Vena	Yudif'	Zislya
Tsitra	Tyl'tsya	Vera	Zaftya	Zisya
Tsiv'ya	Tylya	Vitlya	Zefir	Zizel'
Tsiva	Tysya	Vykhnyu	Zel'da	Zlat'
Tsuftelya	Tortsya	Yakhada	Zhenya	

The third partition of Poland in 1795 added Vilna and Grodno Provinces to the Russian Empire, thus completing the formation of the so-called Pale of Settlement, the largest Jewish ghetto in the world, which existed for more than a century. Lithuanian Jews, who became Russian subjects, also contributed to the pool of names.[12] Table 9 lists names common in Lithuania and the four northwestern provinces of the Russian Empire—Vilna, Kovno, Grodno and Minsk.

Table 9. Jewish Names Typical of Lithuania and the Northwest (Vilna, Kovno, Grodno and Minsk Provinces)

Masculine Names

Aaron	Arnold	Benyamin	Eisig	Ephraim	Fajvush
Aba	Aron	Benzion	Ejkhen	Erakhmiejl	Feb
Abel'	Aryash	Berachie	Ejzep	Ermash	Fendel'
Abo	Ascher	Berl	Ejzer	Ernest-	Frederic
Abragam	Asher	Bernard	Ejzyk	Ernst	Fridel'
Abulfaragii	Asir	Berthold	Ekalets	Ernst	Frishka
Abusia	Auzer	Berush	El'ij	Erukhim	Froim
Aemilian	Avner	Bibenschitz	El'ya	Erzhij	Gabriel'
Afrash	Avraam	Bina	El'yash	Eshij	Ganko
Afroim	Avram	Bogdan	Elchanan-	Eska	(Ianko)
Agron	Avrelij	Bunya	Elchanon	Esko	Gavriel'
Aizika	Azon	Calvin	Elia	Eslo	Gdal'yash
Al'bert	Baer	Chanko	Elias	Eugen	Gdalyash
Albrecht	Baruch	Conrad	Eliaser	Eugenio	Gejshel'
Alesana	Batko	Danel'	Eliash	Eusebio	Gemas
Alexander	(Karaite	David	Eliazar	Evnos	Gemash
Alfred	name)	Dionizij	Elicha	Evsej	Gerson
Alter	Bejnash	Edidiya	Elie	Ezekiel'	Gertsyk
Amsel'	Bejnes	Edidiyash	Eliokum	Ezekiil	Gesel'
Ar'ya	Ben'yamin	Edmund	Elisej	Ezel'	Getsko-
Ariya	Ben'yash	Eduard	Elyakum	Ezif	Gets'ko
Ariyash	Bena	Edvard	Eman	Fabius	Gidel'
Arje	Benes	Efraim	Emanuel	Fajba	Gil'ko
Arka	Bentsel'	Efroim	Emil	Fajva	Girsha
Armand	Benya	Egoshia	Enoch	Fajvish	Glebko

---

[12] For a detailed linguistic analysis of Lithuanian Jewish given names, see Alexander Beider, "Jewish Given Names in the Grand Duchy of Lithuania," *Avotaynu* (Summer 1996).

Gonko	Iosko	Krivonya	Mejrik	Noan	Rubin
Gorko	Iosl	Ksiel	Menachem	Noj	Rudolph
Goshko	Iosna	Kusel'	Menakhim	Nokhum	Ruvel'
Gosko	Iovna	Kushel'	Mendka	Nosel'	Ruvim
Govsej	Isaak	Kushko	Mendl	Nosko	Ruvin
Gozhko	Isachko	Kusiel'	Menkhen	Noson	Safronij
Grigorij	Isidor	Kusko	Menko	Notel'	Sakhno
Gutel'	Isroel'	Laska	Merkel'	Notka	Salemon
Heiman	Isser	Latsko	Meshulem	Notki	Sal'nikovich
Heinrich	Isuchor	Lazar'	Michael	Nuchem	Samson
Henryk	Itskhak	Leb	Mikhal	Nuchim	Samuel
Herschel	Itskhanko	Leib	Mikhel'	Okhron	Samuil
Herz	Itskhon'ko	Leo	Mikhne	Onesimus	Sarka
Hila	Itsko	Levi	Minko	Orchik	Saul
Hilary	Iuda	Levko	Miron	Orel	Schmarie
Hirsch	Iulius	Levon	Mishko	Osias	Selig
Hugo	Ivan	Levush	Moisej-	Otto	Semen
Iair	Izaash	Liebman	Mojsej	Ovel'	Sender
Iakhel'	Izrael'	Löb	Mojzhesh	Ovotya	Shabse
Iakov	Izral'	Longinos	Mojzysh	Ovsej	Shalom
Idel'	Izroel'	Lorenz	Mones	Ovshiya	Shaulko
Iechiel	Kal'man	Löw	Mordish	Ovzer	Shaul'
Iechil	Kal'men	Lucian	Mordkhaj	Pantelej	Shchensnyj
Ieremyash	Kappel'	Ludwig	Mordkhel'	Paul	Shebsel'
Iesaia	Karl	Lyatsko	Mordukh	Pejlet	Shenka
Iesua	Karpel'	Lyuba	Morkha	Pejshka	Shimel'
Igudka	Kaspar	Maior	Mortkhaj	Pekhturets	Shimontso
Ikhel'	Kasriel'	Mair	Mosej	Peliutko	Shimshon
Ikhudko	Kasyel	Majer	Moses	Perko	Shinka
Il'ya	Kel'man	Majko	Mosha	Pesakh	Shlema
Iliyash	Kershon	Malko	Moshej	Pesnyj	Shlioma
Ilyash	Khachkel'	Man	Moshka	Peter	(Godajl')
Ioel	Khachko	Mana	Moshko	Pierre	Shmechko
Ioil'	Khaim	Mane	Mosko	Pina	Shmil'
Iojzhe	Khaim-Ioda	Manke	Mota	Pinel'	Shmojlo
Iokhan	Khasko	Marcus	Motka	Pinkhus	Shmonko
Iokhel'	Khatsko	Mardus	Movsha	Pinkus	Shmuel'
Iokhezkiel'	Khichko	Marechko	Muemin	Pinya	Shmujlo
Iokhim	Khil'	Marek	Nachimias	Rabej	Shmulo
Iona	Khochko	Mark	Nakham	Rafael'-Ber	Shoel'
Ionas	Khona	Marko	Nakhim	Rafel'	Shokhne
Ionash	Khonakh	Mates	Nakhman	Rakhmel'	Sholeme
Ionathan	Khatskil'	Mathias	Nashka	Rakhoviya	Sholomets
Iorosej	Kishlak	Matys	Naum	Rechejka	Sigismund
Ios'	Kisyel	Max	Neftel'	Reuben	Simen
Ioscha	Kivel'	Meer	Nekhemiash	Richard	Simon
Iosef	Kofman	Meier	Nevakh	Robertson	Simyan
Ioseph	Kokhman	Meilech	Nisel'	Rokhval	Smarko
Iosephi	Konyuk	Mejchik	Nisen	Rubach	Smokhno
Iosif	Krivon	Mejkhen	Nisko	Ruben	Smonko

Smujl'	Tobyash	Ureil'	Vol'chko	Yakush	Zejlik
Solomon	Tovij	Urel'	Volchek	Yanush	Zel'man
Srol'	Toviya	Uriyash	Volf	Yuda	Zenon
Srul'	Tsalel'	Urka	Vul'f	Yudel'	Zhurakh
Strozhan	Tsaliko	Uryash	Widal	Yudka	Zilik
Sumshin	Tsalko	Ur'yash	Williams	Yukhno	Zis'ka
Tal'ko	Tsoduk	Vel'vel'	Yaker	Yusko	Zkhariyash
Tankhel'	Tsodyk	Velya	Yakhim	Yuzheva	Zorakh
Tankhum	Tubiash	Ven'yamin	Yakim	Zakhar	Zorokh
Tevel'	Tubyash	Venyamin	Yakob	Zakhariya	Zrael'
Theodor	Tuviya	Vigfora	Yakov	Zalel	Zsigmond
Tobias	Tuv'ya	Vitalij	Yakub	Zarakh	Zuska
Tobiash	Ura	Vitoshin			

Feminine Names

Agata	Eshka	Grunya	Marianna	Raisa	Shejne-
Basheva	Estera	Gutlya	Mar'enka	Rajna	Rajtsa
Bejlya-Zisa	Estera-Yudis	Ida	Mar'ya	Rashel'	Shima
Bella	Etta	Iokheved-	Mar'yana	Rashka	Shimka
Bogdana	Eugenie	Iokhved	Matil'da	Raska	Shul'ka
Brenya	Evva	Ita-Krojna	Meri	Rauza	Shera
Bunka	Fanni	Iudasa	Merka	Rebeka	Simka
Bunya	Fanya	Jetta	Meryam	Regina	Sofiya
Clara	Fejga	Johanna	Minda	Rejza	Sojtsa
Corolina	Fejge	Judith	Mirka	Rejzlya	Sonya
Dariya	Feofiliya	Kasena	Musha	Ressa	Sora
Dashka	Frume	Khasha	Mushe	Rivka	Sorka
Debora	Galya	Khaska	Muska	Roda	Stekhna
Dina	Gana	Khay-	Musya	Rojkha	Stirka
Dishka	Geldjana	Shimkha	Nakhema	Rojza	Sulya
Dissa	Gena	Khena	Nataliya	Rokhl'	Taube
Dobka	Genya	Khiena	Nekhama	Rokhma	Tel'tsa
Dobrusa	Gesa	Khvolesa	Nekhe	Roza	Tirua
Domanya	Geska	Kostsina	Nena	Rozaliya	Tserna
Drejzel'	Gesya	Lesya	Nesha	Ruda (may	Tsetsiliya
Drezlya	Gis'e	Leya	Nikha	also be	Tsiviya
Drobna	Gitel'	Liba	Nojma	masculine)	Vikhna
Dvejra	Gitta	Likhanka	Nojmi	Ruf'	Vitka
Dvora	Glika	Liya	Nokhida	Ruth	Yakha
Ejdlya	Gnendel'	Liza	Paya	Ruzha	Yudes
Elisaveta	Goda	Lyuba	Pera	Ryfka	Yudif'
Elisheva	Grune-	Marasha	Perlya	Sara	Zhiv'nitsa
Emma	Tsirlya	Margolis	Peska	Sejna	Zlata
Enta					

Since the Jews of the Baltic lands (modern Latvia and Estonia) for generations lived among the Germans, it is no surprise that the German cultural influence affected the lives of many Jews and that German names were in widespread use among them. Table 10 lists Jewish given names from the Baltic privinces of Estlyand, Courland and Lyfland.

Table 10. Jewish Names from the Baltic Provinces
(Estland, Courland and Lyfland)

Masculine Names

Ahron	Fajvel	Kadish	Naftolij	Shamson
Al'fred	Fewl	Kal'man	Neemiya	Shimon
Anatolij	Gabriel'	Kal'men	Neus	Shliema
Antsel'	Garri	Khananij	Nikolaj (Nison)	Shmuel'
Aria	Gejman	Khlouno	Nokhum	Simen
Arie	Gejnrikh	Khonel'	Noson	Simon
Arkadiya	Gel'man	Khonon	Nota	Simson
Arngol'd	Genakh	Kidejr	Notel	Smuel'
Arnol'd	Genrikh	Kiviya	Notel'	Sneer
Artur	Gerasim	Konstantin	Nover	Sussman
Ar'e	German	Kron	Orel	Tev'e
Avodiya	Gessel'	Kusheil'	Oser	Thevder
Avraam	Getsel'	Kusiel	Osiya	(Todrus)
Avragam	Govsej	Lazar	Otto	Tubias
Avrakam	Grigorij	Lazer	Paul (Ioel/Yoel)	Tuvie
Avrogom	Gubert	Lejman	Paul' (Ioel/	Tuviya
Avsej	Gugo	Lemekh	Yoel)	Urel'
Azur	Gutel	Leongard	Peisak	Urij
Bär	Gutel'	Levan	Pertsi	Urin
Bejnes	Heinrich	Levik	Prejdel'	Vel've
Bejnus	Hosias	Litman	Rafail	Ven'yamin
Benno	Iakob	Lui	Rimon	Victor
Bension	Ierukhem	Majrim	Robert (Ruvin)	Vil'gel'm
Bentsa	Il'ya	Maksim	Rubik	Vinyamin
Bentse	Iokhel'	Maksimilian	Rudol'f	Vladimir
Bentsel'	Ionas	Man	Ruvel'	Wulf
Bentsen	Ionat	Mane	Ruven	Yakob
Berel'	Iosef	Mathis	Säelig	Yerukhem
Berngard	Iosel'	Matvej	Salmon	Yeshua
Bertgol'd	Iosip	Mejna	Samariya	Yokhel'
Bruno	Iovnin	Menas	Samuil	Yonas
Eliash	Isaiya	Mir	Sana	Yonat
El'kon	Isaj	Modkhil'	Sanel'	Yulius
El'yash	Ishaj	Monas	Santel'	Zaduk
Enakh	Israel	Mordkhel'	Sanvel	Zael'
Eorg (Getsel')	Itsyk	Moris	Saul	Zamuel'
Eremiya	Iuda	Mortkhel'	Savelij	Zhanno
Erikh	Izaak	Movsha	Sergej	Zirsh
Evgenij	Izekiil'	Mozes	Shabsel'	Ziska
Ezekiil'	Jeckel'	Mrits	Shalmon	Zusel'
Fabian	Joseph	Muzes		

Feminine Names

Ada-Ado	Alisa	Antoniya	Bash-Sheva	Berta
Adelina	Al'ma (Ama)	Asna	Basse	Beti
Agata	Anna	Asne	Beatrisa	Betti
Aleksandra	Anneta	Avgusta	Bella	Betty

Bodane	Fejge	Kenda	Muslya	Shira (Dina)
Brajne	Felitsiya	Kende	Nadezhda	Shlovo
Bronka	Fenya	Kenge	Neschka	Sima
Bunya	Feya	Khana	Nesha	Slova
Chesna	Frade	Kisha	Nessa	Sofiya
Chiesse	Freda	Kuna	Nochame	Solomea
Chirlo	Freude	Kunya	Nora	Sonya
Daube	Friderika	Leontina	Ol'ga	Stira
Dina	Frome	Lesha	Oremiya	Stirkel'
Dobre	Gada	Lideya	Paulina	Styrlya
Dora	Gajla	Lidiya	Pera	Sulamit
Dorotea	Ganna (Anna)	Liebe	Pere	Susana
Drejza	Gedviga	Lilli	Rachel	Tat'yana
Dvejra	Genna	Lina	Rachel'	Taube (Teka)
Dvora	Genrieta	Lyuba	Raisa	Tekla
(Deborah)	Gesha\	Magda	Rajtse	Tserna
Ede	Gindel'	Makhla	Rebbeka	Tsetsiliya
Edit	Gisha	Manna	Reize	Tsira
Ejde	Gisse	Manya	Rejkha	Tsiviya
Ejga	Gitte	Marietta	Rejse	Valentina
Elena	Glike	Mariya	Rejza	Vera
Eliza	Grunya	Maryam	Renata	Vil'gel'mina
Elke	Gusta (Ita)	Mar'yana	Reshne	Yakha
Ella	Guta	Masha	Rokha	Yeta
Ellinor	Hanne (Ganna)	Mashe	Rokhe	Yozefina
Ellya	Iesse	Melke	Rozaliya	Yuliana
El'frida	Ieta	Mere	Ruckle	Zabina
El'za	Ioganna	Meri	Samma	Zhanneta
Emalie (Emme)	Iozefina	Mina	Sara	Zhenni
Emiliya	Ira	Minna	Sarah	Zhorzheta
Emma	Irina	Mirjam	Sare	Zigrid
Erna	Irma	Mir'yam	Schejse	Zil'viya
Ernestina	Isabela	Mishelina	Schime	Zina
Esfir'	Izabella	Molli	Schöne	Zinaida
Essel'	Jache	Musha	Sharlotta	Zippe
Eta	Janne	Mushka	Shchera	Ziso
Ette	Judeth (Yudis)	Mushla	Sherl'	Zlata
Evgeniya	Karolina	Mushle	Sheshano	Zusa
Fanni				

Nineteenth-Century Russian Legislation
Regarding Jewish Given Names

The development of Jewish given names in Russia was influenced significant-ly by a steady stream of anti-Jewish laws and regulations. As early as 1791, an imperial decree specifically stated that "Jews have no right to enroll in merchant corporations in the inner Russian cities or ports of entry, and are permitted to enjoy only the rights of townsmen and burghers of White Russia" (Dubnov 1916:316). In the early years following the acquisition of Poland, the

Russian government made a number of half-hearted attempts to address the issue of the Jewish population within the imperial borders. It passed numerous decrees that restricted Jewish movement, trade, and land and property ownership. Use of the Russian language, which became mandatory in the newly acquired territories, had limited effect on the formation of Jewish names until the late 1820s. Compulsory integration aimed at assimilation went hand-in-hand with increased oppression. The most infamous of the decrees of Czar Nicholas I was the *ukaze* (edict) of 1827, which imposed military service upon the Jews. Particularly cruel were the so-called cantonist schools in which Jewish boys of eight to ten years of age were forced to enroll. It was the start of military service that could last upwards of twenty-five years, if the individual survived the hardships that long. A large number of Russian names penetrated into Jewish life because of the many Jewish boys drafted into the army and given Russian names there. However, many of the boys were forcibly baptized and were thus lost to the Jewish people; some committed suicide; and others remained as Jews, but were never left alone and, under constant pressure, gradually assimilated.

Increased exposure of Russian Jews to Russian culture and the beginning of Jews' general acceptance into Russian society took place during the reign of Alexander II, who also liberated the Russian serfs and approved a number of relatively liberal laws. The level of assimilation among Jews grew steadily until the assassination in March 1881 of Alexander II by Russian revolutionaries. Jews were blamed for the assassination, and a wave of bloody pogroms followed, which precipitated mass emigrations, mainly to America.

For those who remained in Russia, the 1880s was another dark period of reaction, rising anti-Semitism,[13] expulsions from large cities and many other general restrictions. German anti-Semitism, promulgated in the international press, filled local Jew-haters with renewed energy, thus further aggravating the situation. The Russian government of that period made a concerted effort to impose various new restrictions upon its Jewish population and passed a number of anti-Jewish laws, several of which pertained to Jewish names.

According to the decrees, a Jew was required at all times to use the name given to him or her at birth. The Russian Senate emphasized the right of Jews to take any name, be it Jewish, Christian, or Muslim. However, when the Defense Ministry, which administered the Surgical Academy, in 1871 at the State Council, raised the question of allowing Jewish university graduates to replace their Jewish given names on their diplomas with corresponding Christian names, because the original names in vital records often were diminutives, the State Council refused to consider the case. It referred the question instead to the Interior Ministry, whose Commission on Organizing Everyday Jewish Life stated in its preliminary ruling that it was mandatory for Jews "to keep the same names that had been entered in the vital records." To

---

[13] The term "anti-Semitism" was coined in 1879 in Germany to define vicious anti-Jewish campaigns underway at that time.

avoid the use of distorted names in the future, the commission assigned to St. Petersburg University Professor Kossovich and the baptized Jew and anti-Semite Yakov Brafman the task of compiling a list of "correct" Jewish given names. Their work was found to be incomplete and imprecise, and the question of what were proper Jewish names remained unanswered.

Because the problem remained unresolved, many Jews petitioned the government with requests to replace with proper Russian names their often senseless and derogatory nicknames entered in the official documents. Most petitions were initiated by Jewish merchants who resided outside the Pale of Settlement and who maintained daily contact with Russian merchants.

Another commission, Palen's Ministerial Commission, which conducted its work from 1883–88, made one of the most serious attempts to study the problem of Jews using Christian names. It properly observed:

> According to Jewish religious laws, Jews are not forbidden, following their wishes, to give their children any names, including Christian names, and the rabbis, therefore, do not consider it to be in their power to restrict either the choice of names or the registration of such names in the vital record books.

As a result of the activities of these commissions, the law passed on April 23, 1893 required that:

- Jews were to be called only by the names as written in the vital records. With the exception of correcting a clerk's error, as stated in article 1082, no corrections of the vital record books were allowed.
- Every Jewish head of household was to be informed of the name and family name by which he was entered in the vital record books, family lists, indexes, passports and other documents.
- Jews found guilty of appropriating names that were not theirs would be punished according to article 1416 of the Criminal Code (up to 200 rubles for the first offense).

The last provision was a clear threat to prosecute those Jews "who, in their private life, call themselves by names differing in form from those recorded in the official registers." The practice of many educated Jews to Russianize their names, such as Gregory instead of Hirsch, Vladimir instead of Volf, etc., could now land the culprits in prison. In several cities the police brought actions against Jews for having adopted Christian names in newspaper advertisements, on business cards or on door signs (Dubnov 1916, 2:427).

Apparently the practice of giving newborns Russian-looking and -sounding names became more widespread, because the Russian Senate issued a decree ten years later stating that if a rabbi refused to register a newborn under a Christian name, a complaint could be filed to the special Rabbinical Council via the Ministry of Interior.Despite an appearance of lawfulness, problems with Jewish names continued.[14] Jews were still assailed for using not just single

---

[14] Dubnov, in his *History of the Jews in Russia and Poland* (1916–20, 2:397–98), relates: The governor of St. Petersburg, Gresser, made a regular sport of taunting the Jews. One ordinance of his [issued on December 17, 1890] prescribed that the signs of

names, but whole categories of names, and their right to use these names was contested. One of the most popular notions that persisted, despite rejection by the Palen's Commission, was that Jews could use only biblical names. Such an approach, however, was completely impractical. During any given period in Jewish history, only some biblical names were in use, while others were used little or not at all. Moreover, Jews have always used non-Jewish names, many of them having become inseparable from Jewish history and Jewish suffering. The subject of inherently Jewish names versus inherently non-Jewish names requires a closer look at how names migrated between peoples as it helps to understand the conflict between the Russian Jews and the government. According to Zunz (1837), throughout history, Jews have adopted names from other peoples. See Table 11 for some examples.

Table 11. Non-Jewish Names Adopted by Jews Throughout History

Masculine Names

Adolph	Cornelio	Hercules	Lysimachus	Romanus
Albert	Crispin	Himmeltraut	Marcello	Rudolph
Alexander	Demetrius	Immanuel	Marcus	Rufus
Anastas	Denys	Isenlieb	Marinus	Santo
Andreas	Diogenes	Itel	Masud	Scholasticus
Angelo	Dorotheus	Joachim	Micheltraut	Silanus
Anshelm	Drusus	Julian	Morin	Stefangelin
Antoninus	Euphranor	Julius	Motell	Symmachus
Antonius	Fernandes	Kalonymus	Nikodemus	Theodorus
Ausilio	Flaminio	Kleanth	Nikomachus	Theophilus
Basilius	Gasparo	Kleonymos	Orion	Tiberius
Berchthold	Gottlieb	Kunold	Pappus	Ventura
Bero	Gottschalk	Leo	Pastor	Vidal
Bischof	Götz	Leontin	Peter	Vit
Bonet	Graman	Leopold	Petrus	Zeno
Bonfil	Gunelm	Liebetraut	Phöbus	Zosimus
Callot	Heinrich	Luz	Quintello	

---

the stores and workshops belonging to Jews should indicate not only the family names of their owners but also their full first names as well as their fathers' names, exactly as they spelled in their passports. . . . The object of this ordinance was to enable the Christian public to boycott the Jewish stores and, in addition, to poke fun at the names of the owners, which, as a rule, were mutilated in the Russian registers and passports to the point of ridiculousness by semi-illiterate clerks. . . . The Jewish storekeepers, who realized the malicious intent of the new edict, tried to minimize the damage resulting from it by having their names painted in small letters so as not to catch the eye of the Russian anti-Semites. Thereupon, Gresser directed the police officials (in March 1891) to see to it that the Jewish names on the store signs should be indicated clearly and in a conspicuous place, in accordance with the prescribed drawings and to report immediately any attempt to violate the law.

Feminine names

Alexandra	Doris	Gutrud	Mary	Rosa
Anneta	Drusilla	Helena	Mathild	Salva
Bella	Elli	Himmeltrud	Mina	Serena
Blanca	Estrella	Jenny	Minne	Sol
Blanda	Eudokia	Julia	Myrrha	Sophia
Brunetta	Flora	Justa	Paciencia	Speranza
Camilla	Florentina	Kale	Phila	Sulpicia
Clara	Formosa	Kutta	Präciosa	Sultana
Coelia	Gracia	Laura	Pulcelle	Ursula
Diana	Graciosa	Ledisia	Regina	Veleda
Dolce	Guta	Leonore	Rica	Violante
Donna	Guthilde	Manon	Richza	Zerline

Since names were always undergoing evolution—not only among Jews, but also among Christians—many names that originally had been used by Christians were dropped by them at different times and later used by Jews (see Table 12).

Table 12. Non-Jewish Names Adopted by Jews No Longer Used by Christians at the Turn of the Twentieth Century

Masculine names

Aberle	Boppelman	Hänel	Liebkind	Seligman
Aberlin	Dafflin (from	Helman	Liebman,	Sender
Abrink	Daffo)	Henlin	Lipman	(English-
(Abraam's son)	Eberlin	Hiinel	Lippoman	Alexander)
Achselrad	Egschalk	Hirsch	Maimon	Sonami
Alexander	Ensi	Hirschmann	Man	Sulbo
Amsel	Enslin	Hirz	Mans	Sundel
Anseman	Erlin	Jäklin	Maselin	Sunila
Astig	Falk	Jekel	Meinster	Sunlin
Benedit	Feist	Jocelyn (Old	Menco	Sussman
Benjamin	Fischlin	French)	Mendicho	Tudrus (from
Ber	Friedeman	Josse	Menlin	Theodorus)
Berlin	Gimpel	Jud	Mennelin	Ulman
Berman	Godesol	Kalman	Mocke	Veit
Bero	Gozolo	Kasman	Oberlin	Vicelin
Boldeman	Graman	Koplin	Salkind	Vitlin
Bon	Gumbert	Koppel	Salman	Völklin
Bonaguidus	Gumpel	Kosman	Sander	Wibelin (fem.
Bonami	Gumpold	Kusel	(English-	Wibelina)
Bonet	Gumprecht	Lembelin	Alexander)	Wibelo
Bonin	Gutkind	Lemlin	Schmelka	Wolf
Boninfanti	(Cuotchind)	Lewin	Schönman	
Bonsenior	Hagin	Lieberman	Selig	

Feminine names

Bele	Frawelin	Hizlin	(English-	Risheza (Pol -
Bess	Gela	Liebel	Mawd)	ish)
Blume	Gentile	Liuba	Mesa	Rylen
Edele	Gunta	Liubila	Meza	Simlin
Ella	Guta	Maidel (Eng-	Nesa	Traute
Elli	Gutlin	lish-Mawd)	Richila	Viola
Frali	Gutrud	Mathilde	Richza	

In the early twentieth century, a number of names once considered both Jewish and non-Jewish were used only by Christians. These names are presented in Table 13.

Table 13. Names No Longer Used by Jews
By the Early Twentieth Century

Abel	Bartimaios	Joachim	Matthäus	Susanna
Adam	(also	Johanna	Nikodemus	Thaddäus
Alphäus	Timäus)	Johannes	Paulus	Thersa
Andreas	Elisabeth	Lazarus	Petrus	Thomas
Anna	Emanuel	Lebbäus	Philipp	Tobia
Baltazar	Ewa	Magdalena	Sapphira	Zachäus
Barabba	Hanna	Maria	Sella	Zebedäus
Bartholomäus	Jesus	Martha	Stephanus	

The greatest conflict initiated by both Russian nationalists and anti-Semites was the movement to prohibit the use by Jews of "purely Christian" names that appear in the New Testament. This argument was baseless; nearly all New Testament names originally were Jewish (biblical) or passed on by pagan forefathers of the Christians. One look at the beginning of a list of saints of the Russian Orthodox Church (Bulgakov 1900, 654–71) reveals the Jewish origins of their names: Havakuk (הבקוק), Avdiyah (עבדיה), Avdon (עבדון), Aviv (אביב), Avraham (אברהם), Chagav (חגב), Chagay (חגי), Adam (אדם), Azariya (עזריה), Amos (עמוס), Hananiyah (חנניה).

Of the 691 names on Bulgakov's list of saints, one finds 80 masculine names of Arabic origin, 82 Jewish, 89 Roman, 311 Greek, 4 Syrian, 1 Indian, 4 Slavic and 4 of Russian origin. Among the feminine saints there are 120 Greek names, 16 Roman, 10 Jewish, 3 Slavic, 1 Russian and 1 Persian. It is easy to see that Jews had more right to the "holy" Christian names than the Christians themselves—the Jews were first to use them. Certainly no sin was committed when a Jew was called Isaac, Natan or Moses, instead of Itsko, Notka or Moshko. Jewish names were often distorted by Christians as they tried to ease their pronunciation of phonetically foreign sounds. This approach, influenced in large part by their strong dislike of Jews, produced many diminutive, supposedly Jewish, names. On the other hand, when Jews adopted non-Jewish names, they, too, transliterated the names phonetically, often distorting them.

Taking into account that many names adopted by Jews in everyday life were Christian versions of Jewish biblical names, while others were diminutive, hypocoristic or conversational versions of "holy" Christian names, a maze of Jewish names was created in Russia by the mid-nineteenth century. All variations and distortions were duly recorded in the vital records, with more errors created in the process of recording them. The confusion was multiplied due to the fact that many rabbis did not know the Russian language, and, most importantly, no standard phonetics were shared by Polish, Lithuanian and Russian Jews. In real life, many of these distortions and versions replaced the original, proper names.

Such confusion of Jewish names could occur only in the absence of a guide similar to Bugakov's list of Russian Orthodox saints. The Christians would have had the same problems had parents been given the same freedom as the Jews in choosing names for their children, and had also dealt with semi-literate vital record clerks. Ferdinand Kuhl (1891) gives an excellent illustration of this point in *Zur Muhrüng des Verständnises Unserer Heimischen Votnamin*:

> Quite often, peasants used parts of their own names to create a name for their child, so a daughter of Theodulf and Erkatbertha was named Theotbertha; a son of Adambod and Ingilda was named Ingobod, etc.

Kuhl further asserts that since freedom to create derived names was limited by a relatively small number of German roots, names were also created by mixing syllables in reverse order, for example, Baldulf from Wulfblad, Baltfried from Freidbald, Haderich from Richard, etc. It is easier to follow the well-documented and well-studied evolution of German names and to extrapolate the findings into similar processes in the evolution of Jewish names. Suffice it to say that original or root names often underwent many transformations and eventually became totally unrecognizable. In the absence of a reference document listing traditional Jewish names, the result was total confusion.

A traditional Russian naming convention that affected Russian-Jewish name formation was influenced significantly by the Russian custom of using extremely diminutive name forms when relating to the government and its officials. The most common way to diminish someone's image was to add to his or her name the suffix *ka* or *ko*, as in Van'ka, Vas'ka, Moshka, etc. The suffix, which is derogatory in Russian when it refers to an adult, migrated into Jewish naming practices, as in the creation of names such as Moshko, Abramka, Berko, Ios'ka and many others. As Jews became more familiar with the nuances of Russian culture, many became dissatisfied with the belittling names that had been dispensed to them. The well-known (at the time) Jewish writer Osip Rabinovich published an article in a 1858 Odessa newspaper titled "On Moshkas and Ioskas," in which he ridiculed the use of the diminutive name forms.

Formation of Russian-Jewish Patronymics

The evolution of patronymics in Russian-Jewish name formation was a reflection of the evolution of the society and its people. In the beginning, patronymics indicated membership in a tribe; later, they signified connection with a family. Gradually patronymics became individualized. This evolution did not occur for all cultures on the same level and at the same time. While Jews still maintained their 3000-year-old tradition of stating the father's name after the name of the child (for example, Yehuda ben Yitzhak or Miriam bat Zeev), other cultures abandoned this form and used only the given name followed by the family name, for example, Richard Wagner, George Washington. Patronymics among the Russian people, on the other hand, evolved into an attribute of respect.

Unlike given names, patronymics in Russia were regulated neither by a guide nor by government decree; rather they evolved according to local customs and traditions. The evolutionary process led to many forms of patronymics that derived from the same name. For example, the Russian name Pavel led to the patronymics Pavlov, Pavlovich and Pavlych. People of various social strata preferred some forms of patronymics to others. For example, peasants and merchants almost exclusively used patronymic forms ending in *ov* or *ev*, for example, Andrei Ivanov (Ivan's son), Peter Yakovlev (Yakov's son).

This relatively homogenous practice changed sharply toward the end of the eighteenth century. Ethnic Poles, Germans[15] and Jews who became Russian subjects at that time brought with them totally new and different customs, national characters and names. All were obliged to accept and use totally strange and unnatural forms of Russian patronymics whenever they entered into official dealings with the Russian government; the first such contact often concerned a birth, marriage or death record. In the absence of written guides or regulations, government clerks created patronymics literally on the fly. Thus Karl, son of Berngardt Schoenberg, became Karl Berngardov and Berngartovich Shenberg in defferent Russian documents; Sigizmund, son of Boleslaw Grabowski, became Sigizmund Boleslavov and Boleslavlevich Grabovskij; Moisha ben Itzhak Finkelson became Moisha Itskov and Itskovich/Itskevich Finkelzon. (The situation repeated itself 150 years later when the Soviet Union annexed Bessarabia, western Ukraine and the Baltic States after World War II. There, Jonas, son of Kazys Malevichius, was entered in Soviet official papers as Yonas Kazisovich and Kazevich Malyavichius.)

Government clerks, acting autonomously and without guidance, often created patronymics that did not conform to either the conventional Russian language or phonetics. The clerk's ignorance or whim often led to creation for Jews of patronymics whose form was analogous to those common in their particular region. Thus Itzchok ben Moshe became Isak Moshkovich in Podolia, Isaak Moshkov in Central Russia and Isaak Moishev in Lithuania. Even within the same region, clerks were not inclined to be consistent or to create documents consistent with those previously created for a person. In a case of a hypothetical Avram ben Khatzkel Rabinovich:
- Family list could read: Khatskel Rabinovich, his son Avram, etc.
- Government school (gymnasia) diploma could read: Avram Khatskelev Rabinovich
- Draft papers could read: Avram Khatskelevich Rabinovich
- Military identification could read Avram Khatskilovich Rabinovich

Examples of these multiple naming patterns were numerous and created many hardships for Jews, leading at times to the accusation of criminal forgery. When the government began to enforce regulations regarding the identical spelling of names (in the 1890s to the early 1900s), a large number of violators were discovered—all non-Russians and mostly Jews.

As described above, attempts to rectify the problem by reconciling different versions of a name proved too laborious for both the petitioners and the

---

[15] A large number of ethnic Germans, invited by Catherine the Great, also settled in Russia beginning in the mid-eighteenth century.

government officials involved.[16] Even worse, the root of the problem was not addressed. In the absence of unified standards and regulations for forming given names and patronymics, the question remained of how to construct a patronymic for a name such as Man. The answers were too plentiful: Manev, Manov, Manevich, Manyev, Man'yovich, etc. The rules of Russian grammar are simple and logical for the formation of Russian patronymics. For names ending with *a*, patronymics end with the suffix *ich* or *ych*, for example, Foma/Fomich, Sila/Silych; for names ending with a consonant, patronymics end with *ovich* or *evich*, for example, Ivan/Ivanovich, Andrej/Andreevich. The non-Russian population suffered because of the imagination of half-literate clerks. Recording the name Gershko, instead of Girsh, forced creation of patronymics such as Gershkov and Gershkovich instead of the correct Girshov and Girshovich.

In some cases, a patronymic bore no resemblance to the name from which it was derived. In practical terms it meant that in a record for, say, Berko Nokhimov, Berko's father's name could be Nokhim (root: Nakhim), but it could also be Amsel' (root: Asher).[17] Table 14 illustrates atypical patronymics in terms of Russian grammar and the localities in which they were formed.

Table 14. Patronymics That Were Exceptions To Russian Rules of Grammar

Name	Patronymic	Location
Abus	Abusiovich	Volhyn, Podolia
Afrash	Rakhmaelovich	Lithuania
Alesana	Zrollevich	Lithuania
Amsel'	Nokhimov	Lithuania
Ariyash	Iokhelev	Lithuania
Arka	Fajvelevich	Lithuania
Avrum	Zejmisovich	Volhyn, Podolia
Benyamin	Godolovich	Lithuania
Benyamin	Lejba-Shebselev	Lithuania
Bogdan	Igudich	Lithuania
Bogdan	Byshkovich	Volhyn, Podolia
Daniil	Danielevich	Volhyn, Podolia
Edidiya	Meer-Bejnakhov	Lithuania
Elyakum	Lipmanovich	Lithuania
Evsej	Erovich	Volhyn, Podolia
Gemas	Mikhajlovich	Lithuania
Gonko	Goloshevich	Lithuania
Gosko	Sabsaevich	Lithuania
Ieremyash	Nakhemyashev	Lithuania
Ioil'	Geretsov	Lithuania

---

[16] See ChaeRan Y. Freeze, "To Register or Not to Register: The Administrative Dimension of the Jewish Question in Czarist Russia," *Avotaynu* (Spring 1997).

[17] All examples in this section are Kulisher's. It is assumed that he extracted the names from Russian-Jewish vital records, comparing Russian and Hebrew entries.

Ionas	Tishkovich	Lithuania
Iosh-Khaim	Iomva-Khaim	Volhyn, Podolia
Itskhak	Khats'kelovich	Lithuania
Izral'	Kaplanovich	Lithuania
Khachko	Lazarovich	Lithuania
Khaim	Smir'evich	Volhyn, Podolia
Konyuk	Mosheevich	Lithuania
Lazar'	Izaakovich	Lithuania
Levi	Ioseliovich	Lithuania
Lyuba	Izabelevich	Lithuania
Mark	Zimon-Lipkovich	Lithuania
Mark	Zavil'-Zelikov	Lithuania
Mark	Eskovich	Lithuania
Mejkhen	Abramovich	Lithuania
Men'	Maneliovich	Volhyn, Podolia
Miron	Evdokimov-Kadeshov	Lithuania
Mordukh	Shlomich	Lithuania
Moshej	Mordoshevich	Lithuania
Moshko	Sankovich	Lithuania
Movsha	Majrimov	Baltics
Okhron	Ekhudich	Lithuania
Pejlet	Simok	Lithuania
Pekhturets	Shmojlovich	Lithuania
Pesakh	Mordashevich	Lithuania
Rafael'-Ber	Gilelev	Lithuania
Rakhmel'	Shebselev	Lithuania
Rechejka	Klimovich	Lithuania
Rubin	Ievnov	Lithuania
Rubin	Izraelev	Lithuania
Shenka	Sakharovich	Lithuania
Shmojlo	Mojrevich	Lithuania
Simkha	Ejkhorovich	Volhyn, Podolia
Tal'ko	Naftalovich	Lithuania
Urel'	Fajvushov	Lithuania
Uryash	Mikhaelev	Lithuania
Vitalij	Markusov	Lithuania
Yakim	Gejmelovich	Lithuania
Yakim	Shimonovich	Lithuania
Yakov	Geshelev	Lithuania
Yakub	Iskhakovich	Lithuania
Yakush	Evlevich	Lithuania
Yakush	Martishevich	Lithuania
Yakush	Sakovich	Lithuania
Yakush	Feliksovich	Lithuania
Zakhar	Yaskovich	Lithuania
Zarakh	Doktorovich	Lithuania
Zhurakh	Khoroskovich	Lithuania

The problems of patronymic creation were aggravated by two additional factors: improper patronymic spelling and the existence of various versions of a father's name in different documents. Both situations were the result of the abnormal life inside the Pale of Settlement and local administrators oblivious to problems in the lives of ordinary Jews. An example of the misspelling of two the common names, Abram and Moishe, shows how combinations of the two grow exponentially:

	Abramov	Avramov	Abramovich	Avramovich
Moisha	Moisha Abramov	Moisha Avramov	Moisha Abramovich	Moisha Avramovich
Movsha	Movsha Abramov	Movsha Avramov	Movsha Abramovich	Movsha Avramovich
Moisei	Moisei Abramov	Moisei Avramov	Moisei Abramovich	Moisei Avramovich
Moshko	Moshko Abramov	Moshko Avramov	Moshko Abramovich	Moshko Avramovich
Moshka	Moshka Abramov	Moshka Avramov	Moshka Abramovich	Moshka Avramovich

While these twenty name combinations are similar, they differ in their spellings, thus allowing the government to treat poor Moshe ben Abram as different persons in different circumstances. Here lay the beginning of numerous horror stories related to charges of draft evasion, refusal of residential permits, expulsion from universities, etc. As if that were not enough, Russian Jews had a custom of using double names, for example, Avrum Zelman. Russian documents are filled with entries such as Avrum Zelman Movshov, with no hint as to whether the person is Avrum Zelman ben Moshe or Avrum ben Zelman Moshe.

The absence of standards for the official recording of Jewish names was a direct consequence of a generally ignorant and hostile attitude towards Jews on the part of the Russian government. Its contemporary result, as recently opened archival records show, is the difficult puzzle that challenges many a researcher today who ventures to study the relationship between Jews and the Russian government, and to understand better their lives and times.

The principal product of Iser Kulisher's detailed work is a list of Jewish names used in Russia that was the most comprehensive of his time and that remains today one of the best references on Russian-Jewish onomastics.

Jewish Names Used in Russia, Including Their Known Derivations, Abbreviations and Distortions

Dictionaries of given names usually are divided into feminine and masculine sections. This order has been followed in the current work.

Structure of Entries

Entries are structured as follows:

> **Root name** \alternate name\ {source} Abbreviations: *list of abbreviations*
> Kinnuim: *list of kinnuim* Variants: *list of variants*

- *Root name*: The base name from which are derived all abbreviations, *kinnuim* and variants. The root names are transliterated from Cyrillic into the Roman alphabet based on a Russian translation of the Old Testament published in Wien (Vienna) in 1887.
- *Alternate name*. Enclosed in back slashes \ \. The root name transliterated from Ashkenazic Hebrew. This exists primarily for root names of biblical origin.
- *Source*. Enclosed in braces {}, Origin of the name. In the case of biblical origins, the book, chapter, verse of the *Tanakh* is given. Other sources are cited in the "Bibliography" section of this book. Three sources are cited by an abbreviation of the author's name: {O.R.}—O.A. Rabinovich; {Pg.}—M. Pogorel'skij; and {Zh.R.}—K.S. Zhurakovskij and E.S. Rabinovich. Most given names that do not have a source are non-Jewish names used by Jews.
- *Abbreviations*. Abbreviated and diminutive versions of the root name.
- *Kinnuim*. Folk variants (nicknames) of the root name. Their creation and use were not regulated by any religious doctrine or tradition. *Kinnuim* sources cited by I. Kulisher were primarily Jewish scholarly books listed as the "Name Sources" in the bibliography section of his book.
- *Variants*. Variations of the root name due to migrations and local pronunciation and spelling.

An important difference between *kinnuim* and variants or abbreviations is that a *kinnui* can be any name known historically as related to a particular root name while both variant and abbreviation contain a root syllable of the root name (compare Zelik-Asir vs. Osir-Asir)

Letters in brackets [ ] after a given name show the region(s) of the Russian Empire where, according to Kulisher, the name appeared. The codes are: [B]-Baltic area, present-day Latvia. [L]-Lithuania, present-day Lithuania and northern Belarus. [P]-Poland, the ten Polish provinces of the Russian Empire, also known as the Kingdom of Poland. [V]-Volhyn, present day Zhitomir, Rovno, Luts'k and Volyn regions.

Example:

> **Iezekiil** \Ekhezkejl\ {Ezekiel 1:3} Abbreviations: *Khaskel', Khatse, Khazkl.* Kinnuim: *Fajvish, Fajvl, Ges, Geshl, Gesikis, Gisikis, Kgizel', Khatskel', Vajvish, Vajvl.* Variants: *Ekhezkel, Ezekhil* [L]*, Ezekiel'* [P]*, Gaskiel'* [P]*, Iekhezkel', Iekhezkiel'* [P]*, Iezekhil, Iezekiel'* [B, L, V]*, Iezekiil, Iokhezkiel'* [L]*, Khaskiel'* [P]

The example above describes the name Ezekiel, whose root name in Russian is Iezekiil. The pronunciation by Ashkenazic Jews is Ekhezkejl. The source of the name is the *Tanakh*, specifically Ezekiel, Chapter 1, Verse 3. Russian abbreviations of the root name are Khaskel', Khatse, Khazkl. *Kinnuim* are Fajvish, Fajvl, Ges, Geshl, Gesikis, Gisikis, Kgizel', Khatskel', Vajvish, Vajvl. Variants are: Ekhezkel, Ezekhil [common in Lithuania], Ezekiel' [common in Poland], Gaskiel' [common in Poland], Iekhezkel', Iekhezkiel' [common in Poland], Iezekhil, Iezekiel' [common in the Baltic, Lithuania, Volyhn], Iezekiil, Iokhezkiel' [common in Lithuania], Khaskiel' [common in Poland].

Transliteration Scheme

Russian names were transliterated from the Cyrillic alphabet into the Roman alphabet, according to the scheme developed by Alexander Beider (1993 xxi) with some exceptions. The transliteration pattern is described in Table 15.

Table 15. Cyrillic to Roman Alphabet Transliteration Scheme

Cyrillic	Roman	Notes
А, а	A, a	
Б, б	B, b	
В, в	V, v	
Г, г	G, g	(in Russian, pronounced as *g*; in Ukrainian and Belorussian, pronounced as *h*)
Д, д	D, d	
Е, е	E, e	(pronounced as *ye* or *e*)
Ё, ё	E, e	(pronounced as *yo*; in Russian spelling, this letter is rarely used; it is regularly substituted for by E, e)
Ж, ж	Zh, zh	(pronounced as in "pleasure," equivalent to French *j*)
З, з	Z, z	
И, и	I, i	(in Russian words); Y, y (in Ukrainian words; close to Russian ы)
Й, й	J, j	(pronounced as *y* when placed after vowels)
К, к	K, k	
Л, л	L, l	
М, м	M, m	
Н, н	N, n	
О, о	O, o	
П, п	P, p	
Р, р	R, r	
С, с	S, s	
Т, т	T, t	
У, у	U, u	(pronounced as *oo*)
Ф, ф	F, f	
Х, х	Kh, kh	(pronounced as *ch* in loch)
Ц, ц	Ts, ts	
Ч, ч	Ch, ch	
Ш, ш	Sh, sh	
Щ, щ	Shch, shch	
ъ	"	(the sign designating the hardness of the preceding consonant)
ы	y	(back *i*)
ь	'	(the sign designating the softness of the preceding consonant)
Э, э	È, è	(pronounced as *e*)
Ю, ю	Yu, yu	
Я, я	Ya, ya	

Based on Alexander Beider, *A Dictionary of Jewish Surnames from the Russian Empire* (Teaneck, N.J.: Avotaynu, 1993) xxi.

In this book, as compared to Beider's work, the English combination *ts* represents only the Russian letter ц (no Russian combination тс was observed); the Russian letter э is transliterated as *E*, instead of *È*; the English letter *I* represents both the old Russian *I* (used before other vowels, as in Iona) and и (used before consonants as in Isaak).

When transliterating names back into Cyrillic, one must remember that the Russian language requires that all letters be pronounced the same way in all cases. There are no open versus closed syllable pronunciations variants and there are no silent *E*s in the end of a word. As Beider explained, to arrive at the original name in the Cyrillic alphabet, one must first transliterate combinations of the English letters into the appropriate Russian characters (e.g. *shch* into щ, *sh* into ш, *ya* into я). Ambiguous combinations such as *tsh*, as in Amgutsha, should be transliterated as тш, because the English letter *h* does not have a Russian equivalent. Once combination letters are translated, the remaining letters of the Roman alphabet are transliterated into Russian.

Feminine Names

Ada \Udo\ {Genesis 4:19} [B] Variant: *Odo*

Adaliya [V] Variant of Adeliya

Adina {I Chronicles 11:42}

Afidra {Kneset Hagedolah}

Afidupula {Kneset Hagedolah}

Afinda {Bet Shmu'el}

Afru {Bet Shmu'el}

Agaf'ya {Pg.}

Agar' \Gugor\ {Genesis 16:1} Kinnuim: *Gugorkhen, Gugorl*. Variants: *Gagara* [P], *Gogor*

Agata [V, B, P]

Aiola {O.R.} Variant: *Iola*

Ajda \Ajdya\ *Adeliya, Adelya*

Akhinoama \Akhinoajm\ {I Samuel 14:50} *Akhinoam*

Akhrudupla {Bet Shmu'el}

Akhsa \Akhso\ {Judges 1:12} Variant: *Askhan'*

Aleksandra {Zh.R.} Kinnui: *Senda*

Alfdina {Bet Shmu'el}

Algugr \Algugra\ {Bet Shmu'el} Long form of Gugr (Sh. Gam.)

Aligra \Aligria\ {Bet Shmu'el}

Alisa [B]

Alitsiya [P] From Polish: Alicia

Alojzu [P]

Alta \Alte\ {Ohalei Shem}

Altaduna {Ohalei Shem}

Altaruna {Ezrat Nashim}

Aluna {Kneset Hagedolah} Abbreviation: *Luna*

Ama [V]

Amado {Bet Shmu'el} Variant: *Amato*

Amata \Alaoda\ {Be'er Yitzchak}

Ameliya \Amaliya\ [V, P] From Polish: Amalia

Amgutsha {Bet Shmu'el}

Amira {Kav Nuki} Kinnui: *Mira*. Variant: *Amiro*

Amna {Ezrat Nashim}

Anashta {Ezrat Nashim}

Anastasiya [V] Abbreviation: *Anastasi*

Andza [P]

Angila {Shulkhan Gama'arekhet}

Anna \Khano\ {I Samuel 1:2} Kinnuim: *Anelya, Anelya* [P], *Aneta* [B, P, V], *Anneta, Anyuta* [B, V], *Gane, Ganele, Ganka, Ganku, Ganla, Gantsya* [V], *Ganuna, Gena, Genka, Ginka, Ginka* [P], *Khajenko, Khajke, Khajnke, Khakhnashik, Khancha, Khanele, Khanie, Khaninashum, Khanka, Khankhin, Khanne, Khantsi, Khanula, Khanuna, Khanush, Khanusha, Khas'ka* [L], *Khasa, Khase, Khasha* [L, V], *Khasya, Khejna, Khena, Khenke, Khiena, Khina* [V], *Khine* [V], *Khinka, Khinkhe, Khintsa* [V], *Khintsya* [V], *Khinya* [V], *Khisse* [B], *Khisya* [V], *Khona* [B], *Khunke, Khusha* [P], *Khusya, Pela*. Variants: *Anne* [B, P], *Annelya, Ganna* [B], *Gannya* [V], *Khana* [V], *Khanna* [V, P], *Khanne, Khanya* [V]

Ansta {Kneset Hagedolah}

Antonina [P]

Antoniya [B]

Antsha {Bet Shmu'el}

Arandra \Arandria\ {Bet Shmu'el} A Greek name.

Araviana {Bet Shmu'el}

Arduinaja {Ohalei Shem}

Arginti {Bet Shmu'el}

Arkhudu {Ohalei Shem}

Arkhundu {Bet Shmu'el}

Ashruga {Ezrat Nashim} Variants: *Ishruga, Ishtruga*

Ashtapla {Bet Shmu'el}

Asila {Bet Shmu'el} Variant: *Esli*

Asnefa \Osnas\ {Genesis 41:45} Variants: *Asma* [P], *Asenat, Asna* [B, V], *Asnat, Astna* [L, P], *Osnat*

Astru {Kneset Hagedolah} Abbreviations: *Stru*

Ataduna {Bet Shmu'el}

Ataliya [P]

Atara \Atoro\ {I Chronicles 2:26} Kinnuim: *Krajndlya, Krejndel', Krejne, Krouna*

Aureliya [P]

Avgusta [B, P] Variant: *Avgusti*

Avigeya {I Samuel 25:3} Kinnuim: *Avgali, Aviga*. Variants: *Avigail, Abigail*

Avisaga \Avishag\ {I Kings 1:3}

Avitala {II Samuel 3:4} Variants: *Avital', Khavitol'*

Azibuina \Izbuina\ {Bet Shmu'el}

Aziza {Bet Shmu'el}

Baba {Ohalei Shem} Kinnui: *Babtsi.* Variant: *Babe*

Babetli [P]

Babuk {Bet Shmu'el}

Badana [L]

Badyana [V]

Bajn \Vnida\ {Kav Nuki}

Bal'bina [P]

Balita {Kneset Hagedolah}

Balshojn {Bet Shmu'el}

Barojna {Ezrat Nashim}

Bas-Sheva {II Samuel 11:3} Variant: *Betshil*

Bastsion [V] Feminine of Bentsion.

Baza [P]

Beatrisa [B]

Bebagani {Bet Shmu'el}

Beilaki [P]

Belkha [V]

Bentsya {Be'er Yitzchak}

Berakha \Brukho\ {I Chronicles 12:3} Variants: *Berakha, Brokha* [V], *Brukha, Brukhche* [P], *Bryukha* [V]

Berin {Bet Shmu'el}

Berta [V, B, P] Variant: *Berte*

Bess {O.R.} This name was also used by Christians in the Middle Ages (O.R.).

Betti \Betil\ {Kav Nuki} [B]

Bif'ya \Bis'e\ {I Chronicles 4:18} Kinnuim: *Bashke, Bastsiya* [V]. Variants: *Bas'e, Base* [B, V], *Basi, Basio, Basiya, Basya* [V], *Besya* [V], *Bezya* [V], *Bisio*

Bilajda {Ezrat Nashim}

Bilkovo {Bet Shmu'el}

Bingi {Bet Shmu'el}

Blanka {Zhur.Rab.}

Bluma \Blyuma\ {Bet Shmu'el} Variants: *Blima, Blimche, Blimkhen, Bliml, Blimla, Bliomo, Blumlin*

Bogodna {Bet Shmu'el} Variants: *Bagdana, Bogdana* [B, P, V], *Boigdana*

Bontsie {Tuv Gittin} Variants: *Bajni* [P] *Bine* [V], *Bintsya, Binya* [V] *See* Devora, Buina, Bujna, Bun'ka [L],

Buna, Bunanv, Bunila, Bunkhin, Bunla, Bunlajn, Bunlin, Buntsya,[1] *Bunya.* Bontsie is derived from Ben-Tsion.

Bootsie {Tuv Gittin} Variant: *Buelan*

Brana {Be'er Yitzchak} Kinnuim: *Brajndel', Brajndla* [P], *Brajntsya, Brandl, Brandlya* [V], *Brendlin, Brendlya* [V], *Brenya* [L], *Brojneta, Brojnlajn, Brojnlin, Broniya* [P], *Bronka* [B], *Bruna, Brunilin, Brunlin, Tsherna, Vruna.* Variants: *Brajna, Brajne*

Brigida \Brigitta\ [P]

Brikha \Prikha\ {Kneset Hagedolah}

Brina \Brojna\ [V]

Briva {Bet Shmu'el} Variant: *Priva*

Brojnita {Bet Shmu'el}

Bronislava [P] From Polish: Bronislawa

Bru {Bet Shmu'el}

Bshajtsa {Bet Shmu'el}

Budina [V]

Bukha [V] Etymology is unclear; may be a misspelled Brukha.

Bula {Bet Shmu'el} Variant: *Bulu*

Bulada {Bet Shmu'el}

Bulisa {Bet Shmu'el} Kinnui: *Bulitsa*

Bulta {Bet Shmu'el}

Bungada {Bet Shmu'el}

Bunguo {Bet Shmu'el}

Bunuza {Bet Shmu'el}

Charna \Charne\ {Kav Nuki} Variants: *Cherna* [L, V], *Tsarne* [P], *Tsarnil'* [P], *Tserna* [L, V] Formed from the Russian *chornaya* or black; replaced Schwartze (O.R.).

Chesa \Chesna\ [B, V]

Chinya \Tshina\ {Ohalei Shem}

Chisha *Chicha, Chizha*

Dagavaj {Ezrat Nashim} Means *gold-plated* in Arabic.

Dajamanti {Bet Shmu'el} Variant: *Dimanti*

Dajkha {Bet Shmu'el} Abbreviation: *Dakha*

Dajla {Bet Shmu'el}

Dajna {Nakhlat Shiv'ah}

Dana Variant: *Danya*

Dariya [L] Kinnuim: *Dar'cha* [P], *Dashka* [L], *Dishka* [L]

Darna {Bet Shmu'el}

Devora \Dvojra\ {Genesis 35:8}
Kinnuim: *Doba, Dobrish* [V]. Also see
Buntse (O.R.), *Dobrush, Dobrusha,
Dobrusya* [V], *Dovsa, Dveril'-Bina.*
Derived from the German translation
of Devora (Bee), *Dvesya* [V], *Dvorka,
Dvorsha, Dvosha, Dvosya.*
Abbreviation of Debosya. Variants:
Debora [B, L, V], *Debosya* [P], *Dejra*
[V], *Dvejra* [B, P, V], *Dvera* [V], *Dvora*
[B, L]

Didiya [P]

Dilikada {Bet Shmu'el}

Dina \Dino\ {Genesis 30:21} Kinnuim:
Din'che [P], *Din'ka, Donka* [V],
Duntsya [P, V]. Variants: *Denya* [V],
Dine, Dinya [L, V], *Dunya.* Also pet
name for Evdokiya (Pg.)

Dishiada \Duziada\ {Bet Shmu'el}

Dissa [L]

Doba {Kav Nuki} Variants: *Daube* [B],
Dobche [P], *Dobka* [L], *Dobtsi.* Also see
Devora.

Dobra. {Tuv Gittin} Kinnuim: *Alzgute
Dobrusha, Gitel', Gute, Gutel',
Gutrejd.* Variants: *Dobar* [V], *Dobre*
[B]. May have derived from the
Russian word *dobraya,* or kind (Zh.R.)

Dojkhana {Kneset Hagedolah}

Dojltsa {Ohalei Shem} Kinnui: *Toltse*

Domanya [L]

Dona {Be'er Yitzchak} Variants: *Danya,
Duna, Dunaj, Duni*

Dora [B, P, V]

Dorotea [B] Abbreviation: *Dorota* [P]

Doshe [P]

Drazna {Bet Shmu'el} Variants:
Drashna, Drasna, Drasne

Drezil {Bet Shmu'el} Variant: *Drejzel'*
[L]

Drezil' {Bet Shmu'el} Variants: *Drazil,
Drejza* [B], *Drejzya* [V], *Drezel'* [P],
Drezlya [L], *Drezya*

Drobna [L, V]

Duinaya {Ezrat Nashim}

Dul'sa {Tuv Gittin} Variants: *Dul'tsa,
Toltsa*

Duranta {Ohalei Shem}

Dushil' {Bet Shmu'el} Variant: *Dyshlya*
[V] Misspelled version of Dushl'.

Dushl' {Kav Nuki}

Dushna {Ohalei Shem} Kinnui: *Tushna*

Dutsl' {Kav Nuki}

Duziadu {Bet Shmu'el}

Edit [B]

Eizhel'

Ejda \Eidya\ {Kav Nuki} Variants:
Adeliya [P, V], *Adelya* [P, V], *Edel'*
[V], *Ejdl* [V], *Udliya* [P], *Udlua* [P].
Variants: *Ajdil* [P], *Ajdla* [P], *Ajdlya*
[P], *Ede* [B, P], *Edel', Edzha* [B, P],
Ejda, Ejde [B], *Ejdi* [B], *Ejdla* [L],
Ejdlya [L], *Gudl* [P, V], *Udel'* [P, V],
Udele [P, V], *Udil, Udl*

Ejdsha \Ejtsha\ {Ma'agalei Teshuvah}

Ejga {Ohalei Shem} Kinnuim: *Ejgila,
Ejgle*

Ejzhel' [V]

Ekaterina [V] Abbreviation: *Katerina*
[P]

Ekuta \Ekute\ {Bet Shmu'el}

El'frida [B]

El'za [B]

Ela {Bet Shmu'el} Variants: *Alika,
Ejlka, El'ka* [P, V]. This variant was
also used by Christians in the Middle
Ages (O.R.), *Elka* [P, V]. This name
was also used by Christians in the
Middle Ages (O.R.), *Elke* [B, P, V],
Elkla, Ella [B], *Ellya* [B]. This name
was also used by Christians in the
Middle Ages (O.R.)

Elena \Gelena\ [B, P, V] Abbreviation:
Gelya [P]

Eleonora \Leonora\ [L, P] *Eleinor* [B]

Elina [V]

Elisa \Gesta\ [V]

Elisaveta \Elisheva\ {Exodus 6:23}
Variants: *Elisheva* [V], *Elizaveta* [V],
Elzbieta [P], *Liz'beta* [V]

Elle {Zh.R.} Kinnui: *Elke*

Elta [P] Variant: *El'cha* [P]

Em-Barakha {Kav Nuki}

Em-Saad {Kav Nuki}

Emiliya \Emilya\ [L, P] Variant: *Emalie*
[B]

Emino \Emuno\ {Bet Shmu'el} Variant:
Amina

Emira {Be'er Yitzchak} Abbreviation:
Mira [V]

Emma [B, P, V] Kinnui: *Emme* [B]

Endya [V]

Eniga [V]

Enta {Bet Shmu'el} Variants: *Ente, Entil', Entl'* [V], *Entlin, Ionta, Yanta*

Erish [V]

Erl {Ohalei Shem}

Ernestina [B, P, V] Abbreviation: *Erna* [B, V]

Esfir' \Estejr\ {Esther 2:7} Kinnuim: *Estrula, Ete, Etl', Shal'va, Shterna.* Variants: *Aster* [V], *Ester, Gestera* [L, P]

Esperansa \Esperantsa\ [P] Variants: *Ashpiransha, Esperanza, Shprintsa* [V], *Shprintsl* [V], *Sperantsa* [P], *Sperantza* [P], *Sprintsya* [V]

Essel' [B]

Estusha [P] Possibly pet form of Esther.

Eta {Ohalei Shem} Variants: *Et'ka, Eti, Etil, Etis* [V], *Etka, Etki, Etl, Etlya* [V], *Ette* [B]

Eva \Khava\ {Genesis 3:20} Kinnuim: *Khaf'che* [P], *Khave, Khavka, Khavke, Kheva, Khiva, Khova* [V], *Khuva* [V]. Variants: *Eva* [L], *Evva* [P]

Evel' [V]

Evelina [P]

Evgenie [P] Variant of Evgeniya

Evgeniya [B, V] Abbreviation: *Zhenni* [B], *Zhenya* [V]

Evzel' [P]

Fajna {Be'er Yitzchak}

Fanni {Be'er Yitzchak} [L, P] *Fane* [L, V], *Fanya* [L, V], *Fenya* [B, V]

Fejcha {Ohalei Shem}

Fejga {Ohalei Shem} May have derived from the German Vöglein (O.R.). Variants: *Faga* [P], *Fajga* [P], *Fejge* [B, L], *Fejgi* [B, L], *Fejga, Fejgl, Fejgla, Fejgu, Fojgil, Fojgl, Fojgla.* Also kinnui from Tzipora (Zh. R.).

Feliksa [P] Kinnuim: *Fel'ka* [P], *Fil'ka* [P]. Variants: *Fale* [P, V], *Fela* [P, V], *Felitsie* [B, P], *Felitsiya* [B, P], *Feliya* [P, V], *Felya, Fula* [P, V]

Feofiliya \Feofilya\ [P]

Ferka [P]

Fiala \Fiyala\ {Bet Shmu'el}

Filipina [P]

Fimna \Timne\ Variant: *Temna* [P]

Finklya \Finkl\ [V]

Firmuza {Bet Shmu'el}

Fishel' [V] Also masculine name.

Flora [P]

Fluma {Bet Shmu'el} Variant: *Flumu*

Fradi {Ma'agalei Teshuvah} Variants: *Frade* [B, P], *Fradelya, Fradi, Fradka* [L, V], *Fradsya* [L, V], *Fradya* [B, P], *Frajdl* [P], *Frajdlya* [P], *Frejda, Frejdl'*

Frajna \Frejna\ [P] Variants: *Frajndlya* [P], *Frendlya* [P], *Frinejt* [P], *Frineta* [P], *Fronya* [P]

Frantsiska \Frantsishka\ From Polish: Franciska. Kinnuim: *Franka* [P], *Franya* [P]. Variant: *Fronishka* [P]

Frasha [P] From Polish: Frasza

Frekha [V]

Friderika [B, P] Abbreviation: *Freda* [B]

Frima \Fruma\ {Ma'agalei Teshuvah} Kinnuim: *Framet* [P], *Frimet* [P, V], *Frimeta* [P], *Frome* [B, L], *Frume* [B, L], *Frumt*

Gadassa {Esther 2:7} Abbreviations: *Dasya, Godes.* Kinnuim: *Getaskhen, Gudes, Gudesl* [P, V], *Gudi.* Variants: *Adasa, Gadase, Gadesa, Gudessa* [P]

Gajdi [P]

Gajl {Bet Shmu'el} Variant: *Gajlin*

Gal {Bet Shmu'el}

Gala {Bet Shmu'el}

Galaj {Bet Shmu'el}

Gali {Bet Shmu'el}

Galia {Ezrat Nashim}

Gamila {Bet Shmu'el}

Gandel' {Bet Shmu'el}

Gantil' {Ezrat Nashim} Variant: *Gintil'*

Garieta \Garriet\ [B]

Gavriela \Gabriela\ [P]

Gazila {Bet Shmu'el}

Gazla {Kav Nuki}

Gebora [P]

Gedviga [B]

Gejdya [V]

Gekhl {Kav Nuki}

Gela {Bet Shmu'el} Variants: *Gaila, Gajla* [B], *Gale* [P], *Galya* [V], *Gejela, Gela, Geli* [P], *Gil'tsya* [V], *Glaj, Golya* [P]

Gelkhi {Bet Shmu'el}

Gena \Genya\ {Nakhlat Shiv'ah} Kinnuim: *Geidel'khin, Gendl', Gendlya* [P], *Gene, Geni.* Variants:

Gendla [P], *Gendli* [P], *Geniya* [P]
Genrieta [B]
Genrika [P] From Polish: Henryka
Gerta [B]
Gertruda [P]
Gertsega [P] From Polish: Hercega
Gesa \Gessa\ {Ohalei Shem} Kinnuim:
Gesha, Geshka [L], *Gesn, Gesya* [L, V],
Gisa, Giska, Giska, Gisse, Gissya
Geta [V]
Geti [P]
Gilo {Bet Shmu'el} *Gilya* [V]
Gima \Guma\ {Kav Nuki} Kinnuim:
Gimel'trojt, Giml, Gimla
Gina {Nakhlat Shiv'ah} Variant: *Ginya*
[V]
Ginandl {Bet Shmu'el} Variants:
Ginedla [P], *Ginenda* [V], *Ginenden*
[V], *Ginendil, Ginendlya* [V], *Gnedl,*
Gnejdil, Gnendl, Gnendel' [L],
Gnondel' [P]
Ginda {Bet Shmu'el} Variants: *Genda*
[V], *Gendil, Gindale* [P], *Ginde,*
Gindel' [B], *Gindl, Gindlajgin,*
Gindlajkhin, Gindlajn, Gindlin,
Gindlya [V]
Ginesa \Ginesya\
Girana \Kirana\ {Kneset Hagedolah}
Girasa \I'irasha\ {Kneset Hagedolah}
Variants: *Kajrasa, Tsirasha*
Girglaj {Bet Shmu'el}
Giri {Ohalei Shem} *Giriya* [V]
Girmuza \Firmuza\ {Bet Shmu'el}
Gisa \Gisya\ {Kav Nuki} Variants: *Gesha*
[B, V], *Gesha* [B], *Gesko* [L], *Gesya*
[V], *Gis'e* [L], *Gissa* [B], *Gisse* [B],
Gissya [V], *Gosiya.* May have been
derived from Golda (O.R.), *Gosya* [V],
Gusya
Gita Variant: *Gutlajn*
Glika \Glike\ [P, V, L] Kinnuim: *Glik,*
Glikel', Glikkhen, Glikkhin, Gliklya,
Glikman, Gluk
Gmul {Bet Shmu'el} *Gitsla*
Gnana {Bet Shmu'el}
Gnesa {Kav Nuki} *Ginesya* [V], *Gnese,*
Gnesha, Gnishe [P], *Gnoshe*
Gnese \Ginandl\ {Kav Nuki} *Gnendil*
Gofoliya \Asal'e\ {II Kings 11:1}
Kinnuim: *Asila, Saliya*
Goga [L]

Gojka [P]
Golda \Gol'da\ {Bet Shmu'el} Variants:
Gol'd'yana, Gojldkhen, Golde [V],
Gulda
Gomera \Gojmer\ {Hosea 1:3}
Gotfrida [P]
Grant {Bet Shmu'el} Variant: *Grunt*
Grasya {Bet Shmu'el} Variants: *Grasal,*
Grasil'za, Gresil
Gratsiya {Ezrat Nashim} Variants:
Grasayuza, Grasiuza, Gratsya
Grine [V]
Gritshl' {Bet Shmu'el}
Grukha [V]
Gruna {Bet Shmu'el} Variants: *Geruna*
[P], *Grone* [P], *Grune* [L], *Grunya* [B,
L]
Gudajkha {Ohalei Shem} Variant:
Gudajkhi
Gudl \Godl\ {Ohalei Shem} Variants:
Godil [V], *Godla* [P], *Godlya* [V],
Godya [V], *Gudel* [V], *Gudi, Gudlya*
[V], *Gudya* [V], *Gulda*
Guej {Kneset Hagedolah}
Gugara {Ezrat Nashim}
Gulin {Bet Shmu'el}
Guni \Gunya\ {Genesis 46:23}
Gurdikhen {Bet Shmu'el}
Gushta {Bet Shmu'el}
Gusiya \Gosiya\ Variants: *Gesha, Gesko,*
Gesya, Gis'e, Gissa, Gisse
Gustava [P] Abbreviation: *Gusta* [L]
Guta {Ohalei Shem} Kinnuim: *Alzguta ,*
Gitla [P], *Gitli, Gitlya* [V], *Gotlya* [V],
Gutil', Gutkhin, Gutlya [L, V].
Variants: *Gita, Gitl, Gitlin, Gitta* [L],
Gitte [B], *Gitul, Guti*
Gutliba {Bet Shmu'el}
Gutrid {Bet Shmu'el}
Guttsya \Gutsya\ {Ohalei Shem} Kinnui:
Gitslya. Variants: *Gisa, Gitsya, Kutsya*
Gyugo [L]
Gzala {Kneset Hagedolah}
Iaad [P]
Iegojsheva \Iegoshavat\ {II Kings 11:2}
Iegudifa \Iegudis\ {Genesis 26:34}
Variants: *Dakhe*,[2] *Ida* [B, L, P, V],
Idessa [V], *Idesso* [V], *Iegudit, Iidasi.*
Derived from Iudif' (O.R.), *Iides, Iita.*
Derived from Iudif' (O.R.), *Iudasa* [L],
Iudif' [L, V], *Iyudita* [P], *Yudashka*

[V], *Yudes* [L, P, V], *Yudsa* [V], *Yudsya* [V]

Iegudifya \Iegidis\ {Genesis 26:34} Variant: *Iudis*

Iekholiya \Iekhelche\ {II Kings 15:2} Kinnui: *Yakhle*

Ierka [P]

Ierusha \Erusha\ {II Kings 15:33} Kinnuim: *Ierl', Iore*. Variant: *Erusa*

Iese \Iesel'\ [B]

Iezavel' \Izevel'\ {I Kings 16:31} Kinnuim: *Bejla* - Pet form (Pg.), *Zabella*. Variants: *Iezabel, Iezabel', Isabela, Izabela*

Ioganna [B] Variants: *Ianna* [P], *Ioanna* [P], *Yanina* [P], *Zhanne* [B], *Zhanneta* [B]

Iokhaved \Iojkheved\ {Exodus 6:20} Kinnuim: *Donya* [V], *Dunya* [V],[3] *Ekhlin, Iojkha, Iojtlin, Iokha* [V], *Iokhla, Iokhlin, Khevcha, Kheved, Yakha* [L], *Yakhe* [B], *Yakhne, Yakuta*. Variants: *Iokhaveda, Iokhebed, Iokhved, Iokhvedunya* [V], *Iokhvet* [P, V], *Yakhvod*

Iokhl' {Ohalei Shem} Variants: *Iokhejl', Iokhil'*

Ior-Khaya [V]

Iora Derived from the masculine Iair.

Iosavef \Iegojshevas\ Variant: *Iegoshavas*. May also be a version of Elisaveta (Pg.).

Iosfa \Iosifa\ {Zh.R.}

Iospa [P] Variant: *Iozefa*

Ioveta [P]

Ira \Iro\ [V] Variant: *Irena* [P]

Iras {Tuv Gittin} Variant: *Yares* [V]

Ire [B]

Irina {Bet Shmu'el} Variant: *Irinaj*, Irena [P]

Irma [B]

Irmut {Tuv Gittin}

Ishklavuna {Ezrat Nashim}

Ishtnuna {Ohalei Shem}

Ishtrima {Bet Shmu'el}

Ishtruna {Bet Shmu'el}

Ismiralda {Ma'agalei Teshuvah}

Istajso {Ezrat Nashim}

Istamta {Kneset Hagedolah} Variant: *Stamta*

Istarupula {Ezrat Nashim} Variant: *Strupula*

Isterlaj {Kneset Hagedolah}

Istmu {Kneset Hagedolah}

Istrungila {Kneset Hagedolah} Variant: *Strungila*

Ita {Ohalei Shem} Variants: *Etta* [B, V], *Iita, Ita, Itale* [P], *Ite, Itel'* [V], *Iti, Itil, Itka, Itkis* [V], *Itkoshe* [P], *Itla* [P], *Itle, Yuta, Yute*

Iyudaliya [P] From Polish: Judalja

Iyura [P] From Polish: Jura

Izmirilada \Ismaralada\ {Ma'agalei Teshuvah}

Kachka {Tuv Gittin}

Kadina {Ma'agalei Teshuvah}

Kagana Can also be maculine.

Kalu {Ma'agalei Teshuvah} Variants: *Kalaj, Kali*

Kamarida \Kamar\ {Ezrat Nashim}

Kamiliya [P] From Polish: Kamilja

Kara {Bet Shmu'el}

Karna {Bet Shmu'el}

Karolina [L, P] Abbreviation: *Karolya* [P]

Kasena [L]

Kasha {Tuv Gittin}

Kashina {Bet Shmu'el}

Kashtu {Bet Shmu'el}

Katlya \Ketlya\ [P]

Kazina {Nakhlat Shiv'ah}

Kejla \Kela\ {Nakhlat Shiv'ah} [V] Variants: *Kaila* [P], *Kailya* [P], *Kajle, Kojla* [P]

Kenya {Tuv Gittin} Kinnuim: *Kendil', Kendl*. Variants: *Kenda, Kende* [B]

Ketsina {O.R.} Abbreviations: *Tsine, Tsinka*. Variants: *Rajkhe, Rajkhl, Rika*.

Kha [V]

Khada [V]

Khajmo *Khajma*

Khalu {Bet Shmu'el}

Khamama {Ezrat Nashim}

Khanuna {Get Pashut}

Khasida \Khasido\ {Bet Shmu'el}

Khasna {Shulkhan Gama'arekhet}

Khat {Bet Shmu'el}

Khava *See* Eva.

Khavuva \Khavivo\ {Ezrat Nashim}

Khavu {Bet Shmu'el}

Khaya \Khae\ Kinnuim: *Khajcha*,

Khajka, Khajtsya, Khasha, Khiese.
Not a Biblical name, but very popular
among Russian Jews who often gave it
to female babies who were sick
because of its association with the
Hebrew word for "life." According to
Pogorel'skij, it was possibly used to
translate the non-Jewish names Vitta
or Vittalia.

Khekha [V]

Khekhomo *Khuma* [V]

Khela \Khel'o\ {I Chronicles 4:5} Kinnui:
Gele.[4] Variant: *Khalvo*

Khimula {Bet Shmu'el}

Khinda [P, V] *See* Ginda.

Khiner \Knine\ [V]

Khirana {Kneset Hagedolah}

Khlata [V]

Khogla \Khoglo\ {Numbers 26:33} *Egla*

Khojmo {Bet Shmu'el} Variant: *Khajma*

Khojvo {Bet Shmu'el}

Khristina [V]

Khudesa *See* Gudesa.

Khudi {Bet Shmu'el}

Khumutal' \Khamtal'\ {II Kings 23:31}
Variants: *Amitala, Khamutala*

Khundi {Bet Shmu'el}

Khunya {Mekor Barukh}

Khurshea \Khurshna\ {Bet Shmu'el}

Khursi {Bet Shmu'el}

Khvalet \Khvali\ {Bet Shmu'el} Variant:
Khvolesa

Kina {Ohalei Shem}

Kiratsa {Ma'agalei Teshuvah}

Kirna \Krejna\ {Kav Nuki} Kinnui:
Krajnchale. Variants: *Krajndl* [P],
Krajne [P], *Krandlya* [P], *Krejndel'*
[P], *Krejndel'khen, Krejnkhen,
Krejnlan, Krejntsa, Krejntsya, Krendl,
Krojn, Krojna* [L], *Krojnlin*

Kirtsu {Ma'agalei Teshuvah}

Klara {Bet Shmu'el} Kinnuim: *Klera,
Kleril, Klerkhen, Klerl.* Variants:
Klarisa, Klarisi, Klura, Klyara [V]

Klavdiya [P] From Polish: Klawdija

Klementina \Klimentina\ Abbreviation:
Klementa

Klumira \Kalumira\ {Bet Shmu'el}

Klutivi {Ma'agalei Teshuvah}

Knina {Bet Shmu'el}

Kojna {Bet Shmu'el}

Konstantsiya [P] From Polish: Kostacja

Kostsina [L] From Polish: Koscina

Krasha \Krashi\ {Ohalei Shem} *Krasna*

Kresel' {Ohalei Shem} Kinnui: *Kreslajn.*
Variants: *Krejse, Krejsl, Kreschiya,
Kresil', Kreskiya, Kreslya*

Krida {Bet Shmu'el}

Krisa \Krislya\ [V]

Krishpulya {Ma'agalei Teshuvah}

Kritsu {Ma'agalei Teshuvah}

Kudojn {Get Pashut}

Kukina {Get Pashut}

Kunigunda \Kunegunda\ [P]
Abbreviation: *Kina, Kuna, Kunitsa,
Kuntse, Kunya*

Kupa \Kupya\ [B]

Kurshidmu {Bet Shmu'el}

Kushi {Bet Shmu'el} Variants: *Kisha*
[B], *Kusha, Kushya*

Kutsa \Kutsya\ {Tuv Gittin} Kinnui:
Gutsya

Kuza {Kav Nuki}

Lata [P]

Lea *See* Liya.

Ledka [P]

Lejbel {Bet Shmu'el} *Lejbla*

Leni {Kav Nuki} Kinnuim: *Lvie, Lvio*

Leonniya [P] Kinnui: *Leonche* [P].
Variant: *Leontina* [B, L]. Formed from
the masculine Leon, a Greek name.

Leonora [V]

Lesha [B]

Leslya \Lesya\ [V]

Levi [P]

Liba {Bet Shmu'el} Kinnuim: *Libche,
Libisha, Libsha, Libshe, Libshits,
Libtsa, Libtsi, Libusha, Libushe,
Lif'cha* [P], *Lifsha, Lifshits, Livsha,
Lyubka.* Variant: *Libe* [B]. This name
was also used by Christians in the
Middle Ages (O.R.)., *Libka* [V], *Libke*
[P], *Liyaba* [V], *Lyuba* [B, P, V],
Lyubka [V], *Lyubov'* [V], *Lyupka* [V]

Lidisiya {Bet Shmu'el}

Lidiya [P] *Lideya*[5] [B, V]

Likhanka [L]

Lilli [B]

Limuta {Bet Shmu'el} Variant: *Limut*

Lina [B] Kinnui: *Linka* [P]

Lipa {Bet Shmu'el}

Lishiva [V]

Lisru {Bet Shmu'el}

Lista [V]

Liya \Lejo\ {Genesis 29:17} Kinnuim: *Elize, Lana* [B]. May also be a variant of Leonora (O.R.), *Lajcha* [P], *Lane* [B], *Lejka, Lejche* [P], *Lejke, Lejku, Lejol'ka, Lejole, Lejshka, Lejtsa, Lejtsi, Lejtsil'* [P], *Leol, Lojtsa, Luishka, Luishku.* Variants: *Eliza* [B, P], *Laja* [P], *Laya* [P], *Lejya* [V], *Leya* [V], *Liz* [V], *Liza* [L, P, V], *Luiza* [V]

Lolya [P]

Lota *See* Sharlotta.

Ludka [P]

Luna \Aluna\ {Kav Nuki} Kinnui: *Buga*

Lushcha [V]

Lyaska [P]

Lyudvika [P]

Maakha {II Samuel 3:3}

Madzha [P]

Magda [B, P]

Maja [P]

Majmlin {Bet Shmu'el}

Majnka \Manka\ {Ohalei Shem}

Majta {Ohalei Shem} Kinnuim: *Majt'e, Majti, Majti, Majtin, Majtl', Majtlin, Mata, Mate, Matil, Matl, Matla* [L], *Matlya* [V], *Matya, Mejta, Mejte, Mejtel, Mejtl, Mitil', Mojdl', Motlya* [P], *Motya* [V], *Mutil'*

Makhluf {Kav Nuki}

Mal'vina [P]

Malka {Bet Shmu'el} Kinnuim: *Mal'e, Mele.* Variants: *Malikhe, Maliya* [P], *Malle* [P]. Malka is a feminine form of מֶלֶךְ (*melekh*, or king).

Mamel {Ezrat Nashim} Variants: *Mamla, Mamli*

Mamtsi {Kav Nuki}

Mamush {Tuv Gittin}

Manis [V]

Margolis {O.R.} Kinnuim: *Margala, Margola, Margoli, Margolisa, Margolish, Margule, Peril, Perl, Perla.* Variant: *Margalit*

Margozhata [P] From Polish: Margosza Abbreviation: *Margosha* [P]

Mariam' \Mar'em\ {Exodus 15:20} Abbreviation: *Man'cha, Man'tsi, Mani, Manka, Manna* [B], *Manya* [B, P, V], *Masha* [V], *Mere, Meri* [B, L], *Merka* [L, P], *Min'cha, Min'chi, Min'chla, Min'tsi, Mintsla, Mirel', Mirka* [L, P, V], *Monna, Muse* [V] , *Musya* [L, V]. Kinnuim: *Khanuko, Marl.* May have also derived from Myrrha (O.R.), *Marlin, Masa, Masi, Masya, Mazi, Mazya, Mesa, Mesha, Messe, Mesya, Mezi, Mezya, Mira* - See also Mida, *Mirel'* [V], *Mirlin, Mirlya* [P, V], *Mirsh, Mirukhna, Mirush, Mirusha, Mirushka, Miza, Mizya, Muzula, Muzya.* Variants: *Mar'em* [P, V], *Mar'm* [V], *Mar'ya* [L, P], *Mar'yam, Mar'yanka* [L], *Mar'yasya* [L], *Marasha* [L, V], *Marem* [V], *Maresa* [P], *Mariam, Mariamma* [P], *Marianka* [L], *Marianna* [P], *Mariasha, Mariasha, Marie* [P], *Mariem* [P, V], *Marietta* [B], *Mariim* [V], *Marim* [V], *Mariom, Mariya* [L, P], *Mariyasya* [L], *Merim* [V], *Mervyasya* [V], *Meryam* [L], *Mir'yam* [P], *Miriam* [P]

Marta [P]

Mashe \Masha\ {Kav Nuki} Variants: *Musha* [B, L], *Mushe* [B, L], *Mushka* [B], *Mushla* [B], *Mushle* [B], *Muslya* [B]. This feminine name is derived from masculine Mojshe (Kav Nuki); Masha is also a pet name of the Russian feminine Mariya.

Masuda {Bet Shmu'el}

Matil'da [L, P]

Matsa {Bet Shmu'el}

Matula [V]

Matvel'da [P]

Mayur {Bet Shmu'el}

Mechislava [P] From Polish: Meczyslawa

Mejna [V]

Mejshulemes {Zh.R.} Variant: *Messolam*

Mel'che [P]

Melkhola \Mikhal\ {I Samuel 14:49} Variants: *Makhla, Makhlya, Mejkhush, Mekhli* [P], *Mekhlya, Mikhala* [P], *Mikhl', Mikhla, Mikhlajn, Mikhlin, Mikhlya, Mina, Minka*

Mema {Ohalei Shem} Variant: *Memil*

Menukha \Mnikha\ {Bet Shmu'el} Kinnuim: *Meni, Nekha, Nekhil', Nikha*

[P], *Nukha, Nukhl.* Variants: *Menikha* [V], *Mnukha*

Meojros {Bet Shmu'el}

Merova \Mejrav\ {I Samuel 18:19}

Meshullemee \Mshilemes\ {II Kings 21:19}

Mida {Bet Shmu'el} Variants: *Midlajn, Midlin*

Mieta [P]

Mikhalina [P]. Variant of non-Jewish name. Same as Mishelina.

Mikri {Bet Shmu'el}

Milka {Genesis 11:29}

Mindil' {Bet Shmu'el} Kinnui: *Minlin.* Variants: *Mentsya* [V], *Mincha, Minda* [L], *Mindi, Mindl.* May have also derived from Vilhelmine/Minne (O.R.), *Mindlin, Mindlya* [P, V], *Mindya* [L], *Mindzha, Mini, Minka, Minsa, Mintla, Mintsa, Mintsla, Mintsya, Minya, Mitshya, Muntsya* [V], *Muntsha*

Mingit \Mingut\ {Bet Shmu'el}

Minklin {Bet Shmu'el}

Miranda [P]

Miras {Kneset Hagedolah} Kinnui: *Mirule*

Mishelina [B]. Variant of non-Jewish name. Same as Mikhalina.

Mitsya {Kav Nuki}

Miva {Bet Shmu'el}

Mnojro {Bet Shmu'el}

Model {Kav Nuki} Variant: *Mojdl.* This name was also used by Christians in the Middle Ages (O.R.).

Molli [B]

Muda {Kav Nuki}

Mulhajra {Bet Shmu'el}

Mulina {Bet Shmu'el}

Mulom {Bet Shmu'el}

Munkha [P]

Murina {Kav Nuki}

Mushkru {Bet Shmu'el}

Mushkut {Bet Shmu'el} Variant: *Mishket*

Naama \Naamo\ {Genesis 4:22}

Naara \Naaro\ {I Chronicles 4:5}

Nadezhda [B, V]

Nadzieja [P] Polish form of Nadezhda; see also Shprintsa.

Nagama {Bet Shmu'el}

Nataliya [P] Abbreviations: *Nata, Netta*

Nekhomo Abbreviation: *Khuma* [P]. Kinnuim: *Nakha* [V], *Nakhe, Nekha, Nekhamka, Nekhe* [L], *Nekhil, Nekhla, Nekhlajn, Nekhlin, Nishka.* Variants: *Nakhama* [L, V], *Nakhema* [P], *Nekhama* [L, V], *Nekhana* [P], *Nekhma* [P], *Nekhuma* [V], *Nokhama* [V], *Nokhame* [B]

Nekhushta \Nekhushto\ {II Kings 24:8} Kinnui: *Tile*

Nena {I Samuel 1:2} Kinnuim: *Nan'cha* [P], *Nenash, Nendl, Nendla, Neni, Nenkhin, Nenla, Nenlin*

Nesa \Nesya\ [V] Kinnui: *Neshka* [B]. Variants: *Nesha* [B, P], *Nessa* [B]

Netl' {Tuv Gittin}

Nina [V] May also be a pet form of Anne, a Russian translation of Hannah.

Nisli {Bet Shmu'el} Variants: *Nisil', Nislya, Nisya* [V], *Nusil'*

Noemin \Noomi\ {Ruth 1:2} Variants: *Nojemi, Nojma* [L], *Nojmi* [L], *Noma* [P], *Nomka* [L]

Nokhnyu [P]

Nora [B]

Nukha {Bet Shmu'el} Possibly abbreviated from Mnukha (Bet Shm.).

Ofeliya [B]

Ogusha \Ogush\ {Tuv Gittin}

Ol'ga [B, P, V] Abbreviation: *Olya.* Olya has also been used as a Russianized version of Elka.

Palkuna {Shulkhan Gama'arekhet}

Paluma {Kneset Hagedolah} Variants: *Palumba, Palunba*

Palya \Peyana\ [P]

Papusa {Bet Shmu'el}

Pasha [V]

Pasna {Bet Shmu'el}

Patsha \Patshi\ {Kav Nuki}

Paulina [B, P]

Paya \Paje\ {Kav Nuki} [L]

Pazi \Paza\ {Bet Shmu'el} Variants: *Pizi Pozi, Pujza, Puza, Puzi*

Pel'ka [P]

Pepa \Pepi\ {Kav Nuki} [P]

Pera Kinnui: *Perka* [L, V]

Perl \Pirla\ {Bet Shmu'el} Variants: *Peral* [P], *Peril, Perlajn, Perle, Perlo, Perlya* [L, P, V]. *See* Margolis.

Pesa {Bet Shmu'el} Variants: *Bessa,*[6] *Pajsya* [V], *Peshka* [P], *Pesil' Pesile, Peska* [L], *Peskhen, Pesl, Peslajn, Peslin, Pesse* [P], *Pessi, Pesya, Pisla, Pisya* [V].

Peshu {Shemot Gittin}

Peurlkhin {Ohalei Shem}

Pilya [V]

Pinsha \Pinsa\ {Bet Shmu'el} Variants: *Pinshkha, Punsha, Punshikha*

Pintsa {Nakhlat Shiv'ah} Variants: *Pintsi, Pintska, Puntska*

Pinya [V]

Pirna {Bet Shmu'el}

Pojri \Pojra\ {Bet Shmu'el} Variants: *Porelo, Poriya, Pur'ya*

Pojza {Kav Nuki}

Prashtura {Bet Shmu'el}

Prikha \Brikha\ {Kneset Hagedolah}

Puerlan \Puerlajn\ {Bet Shmu'el}

Pul'kheriya [P]

Puna {Kav Nuki} Variant: *Puni*

Puza {Ohalei Shem}

Rada Variant: *Rida*

Rajna {Bet Shmu'el} Kinnuim: *Rajnula, Rinusha, Ron'ya*

Rajtsa {Bet Shmu'el} Variants: *Rajts, Rejtsa*

Rajtse {Bet Shmu'el} [B] Variants: *Rajcha* [V], *Rajtsl'*. May be a kinnui from Rajtsa (Zh.R.), *Rajtslin, Rajtsva, Ratsya* [P, V], *Rejtslan, Rejtsva*. May have derived from Reiz.

Rakhil' \Rukhejl\ {Genesis 29:16} Kinnuim: *Rajkha* [L], *Rashka, Rashki, Rejkha* [B], *Rekhlajn, Rokha* [B, L, P], *Rokhcha, Rokhchya* [V], *Rokhe, Rokhtsya* [V], *Rosa, Rosya* [V], *Taklin, Tiklin, Tokl, Tukil', Tukl, Tuklajn, Tuklan*. Variants: *Rajkhil'* [V], *Rajkhl, Rakhel'* [B, P, V], *Rakhelya* [P], *Rakhenya* [P], *Rakhil, Rakhlya* [V], *Rakhyl* [P], *Rashel'* [B, P, V], *Rasheli* [B, P, V], *Rekhil, Rekhlya* [V], *Rokhil'*[P], *Rokhl'* [L], *Rokhliya* [P, V], *Rokhlya* [P, V], *Rukhla* [P, V], *Rukhlya* [P, V]

Rakhna {Bet Shmu'el}

Rala {Tuv Gittin} Variants: *Rajla* [P], *Rejla* [P], *Rela, Relya, Rudlya* [V], *Rulya* [V]

Rale {Tuv Gittin} Variant: *Rela* [P]

Reitsa \Reitsya\ {Ohalei Shem} Kinnuim: *Ruzha* [P, V], *Ruzya* [P, V]

Rejna {Ohalei Shem} Variant: *Rejnusha*

Rejza \Rejzya\ {Ohalei Shem} Kinnuim: *Rajzel, Rajzla* [P], *Rajzli* [P], *Rajzol* [P], *Rajzya, Rejse* [B], *Rejzha, Rejzkhen, Rejzl, Rejzlin, Rejzlya, Rejzlya* [P, V], *Rez'ka* [V], *Rojza, Rojzel* [P], *Rojzla, Rojzula, Rojzya* [P], *Rouza* [L], *Roza* [B, P, V], *Rozaliya* [B, P, V], *Roze* [B, P, V], *Rozlya, Ruzha* [P, V], *Ruzya* [P, V]. Variants: *Rejze, Rejzl, Rojza*

Renata [B]

Reshna [P]

Reuma \Reumo\ {Genesis 22:24}

Revekka \Rivko\ {Genesis 24:15} Kinnuim: *Rajvtsa, Rika, Rikl, Rise, Riva, Rivele, Rivkele, Rivlya* [V], *Rivshe, Rivtsa, Rivtse, Rivtsi, Rivtsya*. Variants: *Rebeka* [L], *Rebekka* [L], *Reveka* [B, P, V], *Rifka* [P, V], *Ryfka* [P, V]

Revr {Bet Shmu'el}

Rikhila {O.R.} This name was also used by Christians in the Middle Ages (O.R.)

Rikl {Mekor Barukh} Variants: *Rikel'* [V], *Riklajn, Riklin, Riklya* [P, V], *Rukl'* [V]. Rukl' may also be a kinnui from Revekka (Zh.R.).

Risa \Risha\ {Kav Nuki}

Ritsh {Bet Shmu'el} Variants: *Ritshel', Ritshil'*

Roda {Bet Shmu'el} Kinnuim: *Radesh, Radish, Radl, Redl, Rida, Rodi, Rodya* [V], *Ruda, Rude* [P], *Rudisha, Rudlya* [V], *Rudya* [V]

Rojzvan {Bet Shmu'el}

Rokhmo \Rukhomo\ {Kav Nuki} *Diminutive: Rekhe.* Kinnuim: *Rekhana, Rokhma.* Variants: *Rekhama, Rekhuma* [V], *Rkhama, Rokhama*

Rona {Ohalei Shem} Variants: *Rajna* [L], *Ranya* [V], *Ronya, Rynya* [V]

Rosa \Rosya\ {Ohalei Shem} Variants: *Raisa* [B, L, V], *Rasel'* [V], *Rasha, Rashel'* [B, P, V], *Rasheli* [B, P, V], *Rashka, Rashke, Rashya, Raska* [L,

V], *Ressa* [L], *Risha* [P, V], *Riska* [L,
V], *Rislya* [V], *Ros'e*, *Rosha*, *Roshe* [P,
V], *Roshya*, *Rosi*, *Rusa*, *Rusha*,
Rushka, *Rushya*, *Rusya*, *Rysha* [P, V]

Ruf' \Ris\ {Ruth 1:4} Variants: *Rufa*,
Rut

Rulya Derived from the masculine
Roguil (Pg.).

Ryl'tsya [V]

Sabdki \Sabtki\ {Bet Shmu'el} Variant:
Sabtka

Sabina \Zabina\ [B, P] Variant: *Savina*

Sabol' {Bet Shmu'el} Variants: *Sobe*,
Soblya [V], *Sojbl*

Safira {Kav Nuki}

Sakhna \Sakhne\ {Bet Shmu'el} *Sukhna*
[P]

Sala [P]

Salamanda [P]

Salma [B]

Saltana {Ohalei Shem} *See* Shultana.

Salva {Bet Shmu'el} From Latin *savia*,
or healthy.

Sarra \Suro\ {Genesis 17:15} Kinnuim:
Sara, *Seril'*, *Serka*, *Serke* [V], *Serkhen*,
Serkhin, *Serl*, *Sertsa*, *Sheril'*, *Sherke*
[V], *Sherlin*, *Shorke*, *Shosa*, *Shosha*
[P], *Shosya*, *Sirka*, *Soje*, *Soniya* [P],
Sonya [P], *Sos'e*, *Sosl*, *Sosha*, *Soshka*,
Soshya, *Sosya*, *Tsirl*. Variants: *Saro*
[V], *Serlya* [V], *Shera* [L], *Shora*,
Shura [L, V], *Sorka* [P], *Sorke* [P],
Sorlya [V], *Sos'ki*, *Sura* [L, V], *Sure*

Saruiya \Tsruio\ {II Samuel 2:13}
Kinnuim: *Tsrit* , *Tsuril'*

Sas {Ohalei Shem}

Sasalbanas {Bet Shmu'el}

Sejsej {Bet Shmu'el}

Selima [P]

Semakh {Zh.R.} *See* Tsemakh.

Sepfora \Tsipojro\ {Exodus 2:21}
Kinnuim: *Chipa*, *Paje*, *Pajvis'*, *Pavis'*,
Pavsh, *Pojer*, *Pojerl*, *Pojra*, *Priva*,
Tsajpa, *Tsapa*, *Tsile*, *Tsipa* [V], *Tsipe*
[B], *Tsipera*, *Tsyupa* [V]. Variants:
Tsipejra [V], *Tsipora* [P, V], *Tsipoura*.
See also Fejga

Serafima \Serafina\ [V] Abbreviation:
Sima. Feminine formation of שרפם
(Serafim).

Shabsiya {Bet Shmu'el}

Shabsu {Bet Shmu'el}

Shabsule {Ezrat Nashim}

Shaj [P] From Polish: Szaj

Shakhna \Sakhna\ {Be'er Yitzchak}
Kinnui: *Sukhna*. Variants: *Sokhna*,
Sakhne.

Shakra {Ma'agalei Teshuvah} Kinnui:
Rusha. Derived from the masculine
name Ashkar.

Shalvo {Bet Shmu'el}

Sharlotta [B, P] Abbreviation: *Lotta* [P],
Lotte [P]

Shatl' {Kav Nuki} Variants: *Shitl*,
Tshitl

Shchera [B] May be a variant of Shira.

Shejka {Ohalei Shem} Variants:
Shenka, *Shunka*, *Shenkhl*

Shejna {Bet Shmu'el} Variants: *Sejna*
[P], *Sendla* [P], *Shajna* [P], *Shajna*
[P], *Shandlya* [V], *Shejndil'*, *Shejndl*,
Shejndlin, *Shejndle* [V], *Shejne* [B, L,
P, V], *Shejnla* [P], *Shejnlin*,
Shejntsha, *Shejntsya*, *Shendl*,
Shendla, *Shendlin*, *Shene* [B, L, P, V],
Shojnlin, *Shundlajn*, *Shundlin*,
Tsejntsya

Shejniurula {Kneset Hagedolah}

Shejze [B]

Shimeafa \Shim'os\ {II Kings 12:22}
Semeafa

Shenkha {Be'er Yitzchak} Variants:
Shenka, *Shenkhl*

Shenva [V]

Sheva {II Samuel 11:27} Variants:
Sheiva [P, V], *Shiva* [P, V]

Shidana {Ma'agalei Teshuvah}

Shifra {Exodus 1:15} [V] Kinnui: *Shifka*

Shimo {Kav Nuki} Variants: *Shima* [B,
L], *Shime* [B, L], *Shimka* [B, L]

Shimrifa \Shimris\ {II Chronicles 24:26}
Variant: *Samarifa*

Shinajrula {Shemot Gittin}

Shira [B]

Shishvojna {Kneset Hagedolah}

Shlima \Shlimu\ {Bet Shmu'el}

Shnerra \Shner\ [V]

Shrentsa {Ohalei Shem}

Shretsa {Kav Nuki}

Shtamta {Shulkhan Gama'arekhet}

Shtera \Shterna\ {Kav Nuki} Kinnui:
Stirka. Variants: *Shterne*, *Sterne*

Shtersi {Kav Nuki}

Shtila {Bet Shmu'el}

Shul' {Bet Shmu'el} Variants: *Shul'ka* [L, V], *Sul'* [V], *Sul'ka* [L, V]

Shultana \Sultana\ {Bet Shmu'el} Variant: *Saltana*

Shunlin \Shunlajn\ {Bet Shmu'el}

Shunya \Shunka\ {Ohalei Shem}

Shuya \Shuo\ {I Chronicles 7:32} Variant: *Sula*

Shvartsa [P] From Polish: Szwarca

Sil'viya \Zil'viya\ [B, V]

Simkha {Bet Shmu'el} Kinnuim: *Frejda, Frejdal', Sima, Simme* [P], *Tsima, Tsimpa, Vrejde.* Variant: *Shimkha* [L]. Both feminine and masculine name.

Sinaj {Bet Shmu'el} Kinnuim: *Tsina, Tsini.* Variant: *Sina*

Sireta [P]

Sirpianna [P]

Slatka {Bet Shmu'el} Possibly misspelled Zlatka (Zlata).

Slava {Kav Nuki} Kinnuim: *Sal'va, Shal'va, Tislava* [P]. Variants: *Shlova* [B, V], *Slova* [B, V], *Slova, Slove* [V], *Tslava* [V], *Tsluva* [V]

Sofiya \Zofiya\ [P] *Soflya* [V]

Soja [P] Possibly misspelled Zoja.

Solomoniya {Zh.R.}

Srejba [P]

Sruva [V]

Stashek [P] Also masculine pet form, both from Russian-Polish Stanislav/Stanislaw.

Stefaniya [P] Greek name.

Stekhna [L]

Sterluba \Sterul'ba\ {Ohalei Shem}

Stira[B] Variants: *Stirka* [L], *Stirlya* [B], *Styrkel'* [B], *Styrlya* [B]. Derived from Shtera.

Stru \Struchila\ {Kneset Hagedolah}

Strupula Derived from Sarra (Pg.).

Stusya \Shtusya\ {Kav Nuki}

Sul' {Shulkhan Gama'arekhet} Kinnuim: *Sal'ka* [P], *Sil'ka, Silka, Sul'ka, Sul'ke, Sul'ko, Zilka, Zul'ka*

Sulamita \Sulamis\ {Song of Songs 7:1} Variants: *Salomeya [B, P], Shalomif, Shelomif, Shlojmis, Shloumis, Solomif, Solomif', Sulamit* [B, L]

Susanna \Shojshano\ Kinnui: *Syuzanna*

[B, P]. Syuzanna is used as an epithet for Shulamith in the Song of Songs. It is translated as rose ("I am a rose of Sharon, a lily of the valley" {Song of Songs 2:1} and has given rise to the name Rose and its numerous variants.)

Svitlya [V]

Tafaf \Tofas\ {I Kings 4:11} Variant: *Tefas*

Tajya [P]

Tana {Bet Shmu'el} Kinnuim: *Tejejna, Tejna.* Variants: *Tani, Tenya, Tona, Tone*

Tanina [P]

Taranta \Tarantu\ {Kneset Hagedolah}

Tatiyana \Tat'yana\ [P] Kinnui: *Tanya* [P, V]

Tauns {Bet Shmu'el}

Tejno \Tajne\ {Bet Shmu'el}

Tekea \Teka\ [B, P]

Tekhterlajn {Bet Shmu'el}

Tekla \Teklya\ [B, P]

Tela {Kav Nuki} Variants: *Tel'tsya* [V], *Teltsil', Teltsl, Tila* [V], *Tile* [B], *Tilya* [V], *Tyl'tsya* [V]

Tema {Ohalei Shem} Abbreviation: *Temchlin, Temtsa, Temtsi*

Tena [P]

Teni {Ma'agalei Teshuvah}

Teodora [P] Feminine version of Theodor.

Teofiliya \Feofiliya\ Variants: *Feofila* [P, V], *Teofila* [P, V], *Teofilya* [P]

Tereza \Teresa\ [B, P, V]

Tetsdzina \Chidzina\ {Ohalei Shem} [B, P, V]

Thamar \Tumor\ {Genesis 38:6} Kinnuim: *Tamaril', Temeril', Temerl, Temerlin, Temirl, Temril, Tumoril, Tumorl.* Variants: *Tamara, Tomor*

Tikva \Fikva\ {II Kings 22:14} Kinnui: *Fekuev.* Used as masculine name in the Bible.

Tirtsa \Tertsa\ {Numbers 26:33} Variants: *Fersa, Tircha, Tirtsi, Tortsya* [V]

Tirua [L]

Tisa \Tishl'\ {Bet Shmu'el} [P] Variants: *Stisya* [V], *Tis'ya* [V], *Tislaba, Tislojba, Tisluba*

Tishpe [P]

Tojba {Bet Shmu'el} Variants:
Taberlajn, Tabl [P], *Tabul* [P],
*Taburla, Tajbelin, Tajbl, Tajblain,
Tajblin, Tauba* [L], *Taube* [L], *Toba,
Tojbelin, Tojvo* [V], *Tovba* [V], *Tuba*

Tol'tsa \Tol'sa\ {Ohalei Shem} Variants:
Doltse, Tel'tsa [L], *Tol'tsi* [B], *Tol'tsya,
Toltse, Tul'tsa* [B]

Trajna \Trajne\ [P] Variants: *Trajndlya*
[P], *Trajnuna, Trana* [P], *Trandlya,
Tranu, Tranuna, Tranya* [P]

Trushel' {Bet Shmu'el}

Tsalka [P] Variants: *Tsilka* [P], *Tsilke*
[P] Possibly feminine version of
Tzalel, an abbreviation of Betzalel.

Tsarka [P] Variants: *Tserka* [L]

Tsarkhil' {Ohalei Shem}

Tsarne *See* Charna.

Tsarnil' *See* Charna.

Tsart {Bet Shmu'el} Variants: *Tsarit,
Tsartil, Tsartl, Tsertlya, Tsurtlya*

Tsejtlya \Tsejtya\ [V] Kinnui: *Tsejtl.*
Yiddish form of Tzipora.

Tsemakh {Zakhariah 3:8} Kinnuim:
Tsima, Tsiml', Tsimlya. Also used as a
maculine name.

Tsena {Kav Nuki}

Tserka \Tserna\ [L, P]

Tserta \Serta\ {Zh.R.} Kinnui: *Tsertlya.*
Yiddish form of Tzipora.

Tsesya \Tsisya\ [V] *Tsesha* [P]

Tsetsiliya \Teitsiliya\ [L, P, V]

Tshitsha {Ohalei Shem} Variant:
Tshitel'

Tshiza \Chiza\ {Ohalei Shem}

Tsil'te {Pg.} Feminine form of Tziltai {I
Chronicles 8:20}.

Tsilla \Tsila\ {Genesis 4:19} *Chillo, Sella*

Tsimel' {Zh.R.}

Tsimpkha {Bet Shmu'el}

Tsina {Bet Shmu'el} Kinnui: *Tsinka* [P].
May have also derived from Ketsina.
Variants: *Tsine* [V], *Tsini* [V]

Tsipora {Exodus 2:21} Kinnuim: Tsipa,
Tsipe

Tsipra {Kav Nuki} *See* Tsipora.

Tsirasha {Kneset Hagedolah}

Tsiril {Ohalei Shem} Variants: *Sirla,
Sirle, Tserlya* [V], *Tsirel'* [V], *Tsirl,
Tsuril', Tsurli, Tsurlin*

Tsisha {Bet Shmu'el} Variants:
Chidzana [P], *Chicha, Chiza, Chizha,
Tatsdzina* [L], *Tsatdzina* [L], *Tsiza,
Tsizani* [P], *Tsizi, Tsizya*

Tsitsya \Tsitsal'\ {Kav Nuki} [V]

Tsita \Tsitlya\ [V]

Tsitra [V]

Tsruio Variant: *Tsrit*

Tsuftlya [V]

Tsumpa {Bet Shmu'el}

Tsvetl' \Tsvetlya\ {Tuv Gittin} [P]

Tsvio {Bet Shmu'el} Kinnui: *Tsvia.*
Variants: *Saviya, Tseviya, Tsif'ya* [V],
Tsiv'che, Tsiv'e, Tsiv'ya, Tsiva [V],
Tsvie

Turkaya {Get Pashut}

Tushna \Dushna\ {Ohalei Shem}

Udlya [V]

Umgustu {Bet Shmu'el}

Umrufya \Umurufya\ {Bet Shmu'el}

Umya [P]

Ura \Uru\ {Bet Shmu'el}

Urarusho {Bet Shmu'el}

Urdunanina {Bet Shmu'el}

Urulajdu {Bet Shmu'el}

Urusul {Bet Shmu'el}

Uziala {Kneset Hagedolah}

Valentina [B] A feminine version of
Valentin.

Vali {Nakhlat Shiv'ah}

Valla \Bilho\ {Genesis 29:29} Kinnui:
Bal'cha [P], *Bejlka, Belta, Bilta, Baya*
[V]. Variants: *Bajla* [P], *Bajlya* [P],
Bejla, Bejlaj, Bejle, Bejli, Bejlo [V],
Bejltsi, Bele. This name was also used
by Christians in the Middle Ages
(O.R.), *Bella* [V], *Bilkhya, Billya* [V],

Vanda Variant: *Vnida* [P]

Varda {Shem Yosef}

Varvara [P]

Vejlka \Velika\ {Tuv Gittin} *Velkova,
Velkova*

Veli {Kav Nuki}

Vena [V]

Vera [B, V] *See* Emino.

Vif'ya \Bis'e\ Variant: *Vefiya*

Vikhna {Bet Shmu'el}

Viktoriya [P]

Vilajda {Bet Shmu'el}

Vilgelmina [B, P]

Vilnu {Kav Nuki}

Vintura {Ohalei Shem}

Virsaviya \Bas-Sheva\ {II Samuel 11:3}
Abbreviation: *Balgusha, Bas'e, Bas'ka,
Basha, Betshil, Betshl*. Kinnuim:
Bash-Sheva [B], *Basheva* [L, V],
Bashiva [V], *Bassheva, Batsheva*

Virtuaza {Ohalei Shem}

Vita \Vida\ {Ohalei Shem} Variants:
Bitsha, Vitil, Vitka [L], *Vitl, Vitla* [P],
Vitlya [P, V], *Vitsha, Vitul, Vitush,
Vitya* [V]

Vrajda {Bet Shmu'el} Variants: *Frajdl,
Frejda* [V], *Vrajdel'khen, Vrajdkhen,
Vrajdl, Vrejda* [V], *Vrejdkhen*

Vravda {Kav Nuki}

Vrimt {Shulchan Arukh} Variants:
Vrumit, Vrumut

Vrojda {Kav Nuki}

Vruna \Bruna\ {Ohalei Shem}

Yadviga [P] From Polish: Jadwiga

Yakhat \Yakhad\ Variants: *Yakhada* [P,
V], *Yakhet* [P, V], *Yakhit, Yakhud*

Yakhnat {Ohalei Shem}

Yalsa \Yalse\ {Be'er Yitzchak}

Yudsa {Ma'agalei Teshuvah} A variant
form of Yehudith.

Yukl' [P]

Yuliya \Yuliana\ [B, P] Abbreviation:
Yuli

Yustina [P]

Zafira \Safira\ {Bet Shmu'el} *Zefir* [V]

Zaftya [V]

Zagra \Zakhara\ {Tuv Gittin}
Abbreviation: *Zara* [L]

Zajna From Arabic for pretty.

Zakhra {Kav Nuki}

Zanda [P]

Zel'da {O.R.} Variant: *Zel'cha* [P]
Yiddish form of Old German name
Selata.

Zel'ma {Bet Shmu'el} Misspelled Zemla
(Tuv Gittin).

Zelfa \Zilpo\ {Genesis 29:24}

Zempl' {Kav Nuki}

Zenftil' {Tuv Gittin}

Zgovis {Bet Shmu'el}

Zharzheta [B]

Zhivnitsa [L] Slavic form of the Hebrew
Khaya {Beider}.

Zhvi {Zh.R.} Mispronounced Russian
zhivi (live); equivalent to the Russian
feminine Zoya.

Zigfrid [B]

Zinaida [B, V] *Abbreviation: Zina* [B]

Zindel' [V]

Zlata {Bet Shmu'el} Variants: *Slatka,
Zlat'* [V], *Zlatka*

Zmojrida {Ezrat Nashim}

Zoza [P]

Zusa {Bet Shmu'el} Kinnuim: *Zashka*
[P], *Ziskel'* [V]. Variants: *Zisa* [B, L],
Zisel, Zisel' [V], *Zisla* [P], *Zislya* [P,
V], *Zisya* [V], *Zusl, Zusla, Zuslin,
Zusya* [B]

Zushta {Bet Shmu'el}

Masculine Names

Aaron \Agrojn\ {Exodus 4:14}
Abbreviations: *Agrele, Aral* [V], *Are, Arel* [V], *Arele, Arke, Arko, Arnojn, Arojn, Aru, Orel* [B, L], *Orelo, Orko* [P], *Orule, Uron* [V]. Kinnuim: *Agrojnko, Ajzik, Ajzyk [P], Arche, Arkadij* [V], *Arkadiush* [B, P], *Arkadiya* [B], *Arngol'd* [B], *Arnol'd* [B, P], *Arnun, Aro, Aron, Artsi, Gemerlin, Gimmerlin, Orlik, Oro, Ortchik, Orun, Shikar, Zelig, Zeligman, Zelik, Zelikin, Zelikman.* Variants: *Agarojn, Agaron, Agron* [L], *Arn, Ogron* [L], *Okhron* [L]

Abada {Shulkhan Gama'arekhet}

Abadalkrim {Shulkhan Gama'arekhet}

Abadalshalom {Shulkhan Gama'arekhet}

Abadrakhman {Kav Nuki}

Abaej {Shulkhan Gama'arekhet}

Abdalrakhum {Shulkhan Gama'arekhet}

Abduelelem {Shulkhan Gama'arekhet}

Abdula {Shulkhan Gama'arekhet}

Abo {Shulkhan Gama'arekhet}
Kinnuim: *Aba,*[7] *Abali, Abbo, Abel'* [B, L, V], *Abele, Abesh, Abil'* [V], *Abish* [V], *Abus* [V]. Variants: *Aba, Abbo, Avva*

Abo Shoul \Abu Shuil\ {Kav Nuki}

Abomori \Abumuri\ {Ezrat Nashim}

Abualkhir {Ezrat Nashim}

Abulfaragu [L]

Abulkhasin {Shulkhan Gama'arekhet}

Abusaad {Shulkhan Gama'arekhet}

Adam \Udom\ {Genesis 2:7} Used by Christians in nineteenth century Russia. Jews normally did not use Adam as a given name but instead used it as the word for "man;" however, they widely used the German version Mann and its many derivatives (Pg.).

Addon \Udojn\ {Nehemiah 7:61}

Adnaj {Bet Shmu'el}

Ado {Bet Shmu'el}

Adonim \Adojnim\ {Ohalei Shem}

Adoniya \Adojnio\ {II Samuel 3:4}

Afida {Shulkhan Gama'arekhet}

Afinda {Shulkhan Gama'arekhet}

Agavo {Shulkhan Gama'arekhet}

Age \Ugej\ {II Samuel 23:11}

Aggej \Khagi\ {Haggai 1:1} Variants: *Aggej, Aggij.* The prophet's name was not used by Russian Jews in the nineteenth century.

Agiman {Shulkhan Gama'arekhet}

Aguvio \Agiv'e\ {Bet Shmu'el} Kinnuim: *Gitlin, Gotlib, Gotlip, Gutlib, Gutlif, Gutlifo.* Variant: *Aguvij*

Ajid {Ezrat Nashim}

Akasriel' \Akasrijl'\ {Nakhlat Shiv'ah}

Akavio {Ohalei Shem}

Akhiezer {Numbers 1:12} Variant: *Akhiyazer* [V]

Akhinoam \Akhinojam\ {I Samuel 4:13} *Akhinaam, Akhinoam*

Akhiya \Akhio\ {I Samuel 14:3}

Akho {Nakhlat Shiv'ah}

Akhso \Akhso\ Variant: *Askhan'*

Akiva {Bet Shmu'el} Variants: *Kiva* [L, P, V], *Kive, Kivel'* [L], *Kiviya* [B]

Aksel'rud \Bet Shmu'el\ Kinnui: *Itsel*

Akshil'rod {Bet Shmu'el} Kinnuim: *Bendet,*[8] *Bendid, Bendit, Bindit, Bishuf, Bunfant, Bunfat*

Akuv \Akiv\ {Nehemiah 7:45}

Al'bert [B, L, P] Adopted German name, a short form of Adalbert.

Al'brekht [L] Adopted German name, an early form of Albert.

Al'fred [B, L, P] Adopted Old English name.

Aleksa {Talmud} Assumed to have been derived from Alexander.

Aleksandr {Tamid 31b} Kinnuim: *Senda, Sender* [L, P], *Senderla, Senderlajn, Senderman, Shender* [P], *Shiskin* [L], *Suse, Zindl.* Derived from Zyus'kind. (O.R.), *Zisa, Ziskind,*[9] *Zisl, Zusa, Zusl, Zuslin, Zusman, Zusya, Zysha.* Variant: *Aleksandor*[10] [L]

Alzguto {Bet Shmu'el} *See* feminine Gutlin.

Amado *Amato*

Amasiya \Amasio\ {II Chronicles 17:16}

Aminadov \Aminudov\ {Exodus 6:23}
Variant: *Aminodov*

Ammiil \Amiejl'\ {Numbers 13:12}
Variant: *Ammieil*

Ammiud \Amigid\ {Numbers 34:20}
Variant: *Ammihud*

Amnon {II Samuel 3:2} [P]

Amos \Umojs\ {Amos 1:1} The name of
this prophet was not used by Russian
Jews in the nineteenth century.

Amram \Amrom\ {Exodus 6:18} Variant:
Ameram

Amron {Shulkhan Gama'arekhet} A
variant of Amram but cited by
Kulisher as an independent name. The
final *m* was replaced by *n* in Arab
countries.

Amshej {Pg.} *Amasaj, Amashsaj,
Amessaj, Amush, Amushaj*. This name
is a confluence of the three names:
Amasaj-Amushaj {I Chronicles 6:10},
Amessaj-Amosho {II Samuel 20:4} and
Amashsaj {Nehemiah 11:13}.

Anameil \Khanam-ejl\ {Jeremiah 32:7}

Anan \Onon\ {Nehemiah 10:27} Variant:
Inam

Ananeil \Khanan-Ejl\ {Jeremiah 31:38}
Khune. Abbreviations: *Khanon*,[11]
Khonon. Variant: *Khananejl*.[12]

Ananiya \Khananio\ {Jeremiah 36:12}
Abbreviations: *Khanon* [V], *Khonon*,
Khune, Khunen

Anatol [P]

Anatolij [B]

Anboaz {Shulkhan Gama'arekhet}
Longer version of Boaz.

Anbonit {Shulkhan Gama'arekhet}

Andrej Variant: *Andzej* [P]

Anmojshe {Shulkhan Gama'arekhet}
Longer version of Mojshe.

Anruvin {Shulkhan Gama'arekhet}
Longer version of Ruvin.

Anshlojma {Shulkhan Gama'arekhet}
Longer version of Shlojma.

Anton [P]

Antonij [P]

Ar'ej {Kav Nuki} Kinnuim: *Abush,
Ariya-Lejb, Ariyash* [L], *Iuda-Ariya*.[13]
Variants: *Ar'e* [L], *Ar'ya*,[14] [B, L]
Aria [B, L], *Ariam* [L], *Arij, Ariya,
Ariyash*

Artur [B, L]

Asa {I Kings 15:8}

Asail \Asuejl\ {II Samuel 2:18} Variant:
Ashoel.[15]

Ashkar {Bet Shmu'el} Means red in
Turkish (TG).

Ashlan {Shulkhan Gama'arekhet}

Ashtruk {Bet Shmu'el} Means
astronomer in Greek.

Asir \Ushejr\ {Genesis 30:13} Kinnuim:
Amsel' [L], *Amsl*,[16] *Anchil, Andzel*
[P], *Anselm* [P], *Antsel* [B], *Antshil,
Anchel'* [L, P], *Anshel'* [L], *Anshil',
Anshl, Enzkhil, Enskhin, Enshkhin,
Enzil', Gendzel'* [V], *Gensl, Gentshil,
Iojzlo, Kosher, Lam, Lemil', Leml,
Lemko* [V], *Lemlin, Mani, Muni, Mekl,
Mukil, Mukl, Onuel', Zelig, Zeligman,
Zelik, Zelikin, Zelikman, Zigmund* [L,
P], *Zigmunt* [P]. Variants: *Asher* [L],
Assir[17] [L], *Assur* [P], *Oser* [B, L, P],
Osher [L, V], *Usher* [L, V]

Asriejl \Asriil\ {Numbers 26:31} Variant:
Asriel'.[18]

Atsel {I Chronicles 8:37} Kinnui: *Itsel*.
Variants: *Azel, Otsel*

Avadia \Ovad'e\ {Obadiah 1:1} *Avdia*

Avdiil' \Avdejl'\ {Jeremiah 36:26}

Avdon {Shulkhan Gama'arekhet}

Avel' \Gevel'\ {Genesis 4:2} Kinnui:
Abele. Russian Jews used only the
European translation of the name,
Abel' (Pg.).

Avenir \Avnejr\ {I Samuel 17:55}
Variant: *Abner*

Avesalom \Avshulojm\ {II Samuel 3:3}
Variants: *Absalom, Avisalom,
Avsholoum*

Avessa \Avishaj\ {I Samuel 26:6}
Variant: *Avesaj*

Avi Goezer \Avi Guezer\ {Bet Shmu'el}
See Aviezro.

Aviezer \Aviezer\ {Joshua 17:2}
Kinnuim: *Zelig, Zeligman, Zelik,
Zelikin, Zelikman*

Aviezro \Aviezro\ {Bet Shmu'el}

Avigdor Abbreviation: *Vigdejr*.
Variants: *Abigdor, Avigdour*. This
name was incorrectly translated as
Victor into Russian. The Hebrew name
means Gedor's father {I Chronicles

4:4} and was created in the Middle Ages.

Avigeja Variant: *Avgali*

Avishir {Shulkhan Gama'arekhet}

Avisholoum \Avshulojm\ {Bet Shmu'el}

Avishu {Be'er Yitzchak} Variant: *Abusia* [P]

Avishua {I Chronicles 8:4} Variant: *Abishua*

Avishur \Avishir\ {I Chronicles 2:28} Variant: *Abishur*

Avraam {Genesis 17:5} Abbreviation: *Avromko*. Kinnuim: *Abarlima, Abarlina, Aberl', Aberlan, Aberle, Aberman, Aberman, Abish, Abisha, Abli, Abo, Abrash, Abrashka, Abril', Abrul', Abrumchik* [V], *Abrush, Abrushka, Abrushke, Abtsi, Abush, Adol'f, Adol'fo* [L], *Albert* [P], *Avadia, Avram, Avrum*. This name was also used by Christians in the Middle Ages (O.R.)., *Avrumchik* [V], *Avrumko* [V], *Avrunko, Bkhor, Burgel', Eber* [V], *Eberl'* [P], *Eberlajn, Eberlan, Eberlin, Ebermajn, Eberman, Ebril', Ebrush, Ejber* [V], *Iber* [V], *Ibragim* Arabic equivalent of Avraam (Sh. Gam.), *Ivri, Kalman, Kgetsl, Khokhom, Mamu, Mirkadu, Morejnu, Papu, Prisadu, Pulu, Shafmi, Shabsuli, Shamsuli, Temerlin, Zalman, Zalmen, Zel'kin, Zel'kind, Zeligin, Zeligman, Zelik, Zelikman, Zelko*. Variants: *Abragam* [L], *Abram, Avragam* [B], *Avrakam* [B], *Avram* [L], *Avramets* [L], *Avremchij, Avremij* [L], *Avrogam, Avrogom* [B], *Avrum*

Avvakum \Khavakuk\ {Zh.R.}

Ayid {Ezrat Nashim}

Azariya \Azar'e\ {II Kings 14:21} Kinnui: *Zusa*. Variants: *Avdenago, Azario, Ezra*

Azon [L]

Azriil \Azriejl\ {I Chronicles 5:24} Kinnuim: *Lemlin, Zelig, Zeligman, Zelik, Zelikin, Zelikman, Zusman*. Variants: *Azreil'* [V], *Azriel* [L], *Azriel', Azril'* [V]

Azyas {Ezrat Nashim} [L]

Baboku {Shulkhan Gama'arekhet}

Bagbag {Shulkhan Gama'arekhet}

Bardalo {Bet Shmu'el} Variant: *Dalo*

Barkhiel' \Barkhiejl'\ {Shulkhan Gama'arekhet}

Bati {Bet Shmu'el}

Batko \Bat'ko\ [L]

Bebaj \Bejboj\ {Ezra 2:11} Kinnui: *Bejbe*.[19] Variants: *Bajrakh* [P], *Bejrakh, Birakh* [V]

Bendavid [P]

Bentsion \Bentsiejn\ {Talmud} Variants: *Bension* [B], *Bentsa* [B], *Bentsel'* [B, L], *Bentsen* [B], *Bentsian* [P], *Bentsio* [V], *Ben-Tsion*

Berakha \Brokho\ {I Chronicles 12:3} Variants: *Brukha, Brukhche, Bryukha*

Berekhiya \Berekhio\ {I Chronicles 9:16} Kinnuim: *Bejrakh, Berkhen, Berman*. Variants: *Berakh'ya, Berakhie* [L], *Berekhio, Brakhia* [P], *Varakhia*

Bertgol'd [B]

Bibenshits [L]

Binekh [P]

Binet {Bet Shmu'el}

Bkhaj {Shulkhan Gama'arekhet}

Boaz {Ruth 2:1}

Bogdan [V] Slavic translation of Nataniel

Boleslav [P]

Bonaventura [P]

Bronislav [P] From Polish: Bronislaw

Bruno [B]

Brushan {Shulkhan Gama'arekhet}

Bulakhsin {Kneset Hagedolah}

Buna \Bino\ {I Chronicles 2:25}

Bundiun {Shulkhan Gama'arekhet}

Bundyan {Shulkhan Gama'arekhet}

Bunfet {Bet Shmu'el}

Bunvet {Bet Shmu'el}

Buva [V]

Chanko [L]

Dafan \Duson\ {Numbers 16:1} Abbreviation: *Dose*

Dan \Don\ {Genesis 30:6} Kinnuim: *Denil, Denzajl, Donki*

Daniil \Daniejl\ {Daniel 1:6} Kinnuim: *Dankhel, Danki, Ganir*. Variants: *Dan'el* [P], *Danel'* [L, P], *Danil* (The name of the prophet also known as Baltasar), *Danila*

David \Duvid\ {I Samuel 16:13}

Kinnuim: *Bdaus, Budan, Budin,*
Daud, Dav'yu [P], *Davidko, Davitka,*
Davitki, Dode, Dodi, Dodl, Donki,
Dovetki, Dovid [L], *Dovidl, Dovitki,*
Duda, Dudi, Dudil, Dudl, Dunda,
Dun'ka, Dun'ki, Dunika, Duvidl,
Frefir, Khrefir, Khrefr, Krefir, Krefr,
Muki, Sheftil, Sheftl, Tejbel' [P],
Tejvel' [P], *Tevel', Tevil'* [P], *Tevla*

Dejsha [P]

Demyan [L]

Dionizij [P]

Dodo \Dojdoj\ {I Chronicles 11:26}

Dov \Dojv\ Kinnuim: *Baer* [B, L], *Barche*
[P], *Bejrish* [V], *Ber* [B], *Bera, Berek*
[P], *Berel'* [L, P], *Berend, Berish,*
Berka [V], *Berkhen, Berko* [L, V], *Berl*
[V], *Berlin, Berman*. This name was
also used by Christians in the Middle
Ages (O.R.), *Bernard* [L], *Bernat* [L],
Berngard [B, P], *Bersh, Bertol'd* [L],
Bertsya, Berush [L], *Boris* [L, P, V],
Dujnika, Perko [P], *Verendt* [L]. Dov
has replaced Issakhar's biblical
nickname, ass, a derogatory word
among Europeans. Even in the Bible
this name has been used to describe
endurance rather than wisdom. The
name Dov is rarely used in the
Issakhar-Dov combination.

Duran {Shulkhan Gama'arekhet}

Eber \Heber\ {Genesis 10:24} Variants:
Ejver, Ever

Edidia \Edidie\ {II Samuel 12:25} *Lyuba,*
Vajvish

Edmund [L, P]

Eduard \Edvard\ [L, P]

Efer \Ejfer\ {Genesis 25:4} Variant: *Afir*

Efrem \Efraim\ {Genesis 41:52}
Abbreviations: *Frajko, Fraim* [L],
Froim, Frojka. Kinnuim: *Afrash* [L],
Efrashka, Fish, Fishka, Fishko, Fishl,
Frajko, Frajmush [P], *Franek* [P],
Froim [P, V], *Frojka, Gimpikht,*
Gimpil', Gumf, Gump, Gumpil,
Gumpl', Gumprekht, Gumprikht,
Karpil, Kerpl, Shejnman, Vajdel',
Vish, Vishl, Zal'men, Zalman,
Zel'kind, Zeligin, Zeligman, Zelik,
Zelikman, Zelkin, Zelko. Variants:
Afroim [L], *Efraim* [L, V], *Efroim* [V]

Egon [B]

Ejkhen [L]

Ejkhor [V]

Ejz {Shulkhan Gama'arekhet}

Ejzhen [B]

Ekhio {Ohalei Shem}

Ekufiil \Ekusiejl\ {I Chronicles 4:18}
Kinnuim: *Ksiel', Kusiel', Laza, Lazo*

Eldod {Pg.}

Eleasa \Elosho\ {Jeremiah 29:3}

Eleashiv \El'yushiv\ {I Chronicles 3:24}
Variants: *Eliashiv, Eliasiv, Elioshiv*

Eleazar \Eluzor\ {Exodus 6:23}
Kinnuim: *Bukish, Buks, Buksh,*
Fabuli, Fajbush [V], *Lazar, Lazar',*
Lezer, Libman, Lipko [L], *Lipman,*
Lozon, Viblan, Zal'kind, Zalkin,
Zalman [L]. This name was also used
by Christians in the Middle Ages
(O.R.), *Zel'kind, Zel'man* [L, P, V],
Zeligin, Zeligman, Zelik, Zelko,
Zil'man [P], *Zusa*. Variants: *Elazar*
[P], *Elozor*. Elozor, אלעזר, is often
confused with the etymologically
identical אליעזר or Eliezer.

Eliakim \El'yukim\ {II Kings 18:18}
Kinnuim: *Anastas, Anastazij* [P], *Ekev,*
Ekl, El'yukim, Fajvel, Fajvish, Gets,
Getshlik, Getsil, Getsil' [P], *Getsko* [L],
Getsl, Getsla, Getsli, Guts, Gutsel',
Gutsl, Gutsla, Gutslak, Gutsli, Gutslik,
Gutsmak, Iatsa, Lebl, Leblan, Leblin,
Lib, Liblin, Libo, Livb, Livi, Livo,
Nutsli, Nutslik, Shtenglin, Vajvel,
Vajver, Vajvish, Viblan, Vibli, Viblin,
Zal'kind, Zalkin, Zalman, Zeligin,
Zeligman, Zelik, Zelikman, Zelka.
Variants: *Eliakim, Eliokim, Eliokum*
[L], *Elyakum* [L], *El'yukim*

Eliezer \Eliezer\ {Genesis 15:2}
Kinnuim: *Bukhsh, Bukish, Buksh,*
Fabuli, Fajv, Fajvish, Fajvl, Fuks,
Iozibl, Krup, Laza, Lazan, Lazar,
Lazar', Lazarus [P], *Lazer* [P], *Lazl,*
Lazor [B], *Lejzer* [L, V], *Lejzl, Lejzor*
[P], *Lezl, Liber* [P], *Liberman, Lipa,*
Lipko [L], *Lipman* [L, P], *Litman* [V],
Lozer [B], *Lozor* [L], *Luzer* [P], *Lyajzer*
[P], *Lyazer* [P], *Lyuzer* [P], *Papu,*
Vajvish, Vajvl, Zalman, Zisman, Zusa,
Zusman. This name was also used by

Christians in the Middle Ages (O.R.).
Variants: *Elazar* [P], *Elezer* [P],
Elezerek [P], *Eliazar* [B, L], *Eliazer*
[P], *Eliezer*

Elimelekh \Elimelekh\ {Ruth 1:2}
Abbreviation: *Majlekh* [P, V], *Malko*
[L], *Mejlakh* [L, V], *Mejlekh* [L],
Mejlikh [L], *Melekh, Mojlekh* [P].
Kinnuim: *Pilte, Plit.* Variants:
Elimalakh [B]

Elioenaj \El'ejejnaj\ {I Chronicles 7:8}
Variants: *Eliejnaj, Elionaj.*

Elisej \Elisho\ {I Kings 19:19} Kinnuim:
Lejshe, Lejshke. Variants: *Elisej* [P],
Elisha [B, L], *Elishe* [B], *Lisha* [P]

Elitsafan \Elitsufon\ {Numbers 3:30}
Variants: *El'tsofon, Elisafan, Elitsfan,*
Elitsofon, Eltsafan

Elkana \Elkuno\ {Exodus 6:24}
Kinnuim: *Aliko, Ilko, Kana, Kane,*
Konyuk [L], *Kuna* [P], *Kune, Kuni.*
Variants: *Alkon* [V], *Alkuna* [V],
El'kon [B], *Elkona* [V], *Elkono, Elkune*

Elkhanan \Elkhunon\ {II Samuel 23:24}
Abbreviations: *Khanon* [P], *Khonel'*
[B], *Khono, Khonon, Khuna* [V],
Khunon [B, V]. Variants: *Eleanan,*
Elkhanan, Elkhanon [P], *Elkhonon,*
Elkhune, Elkhuno [P]

Elnafan \Elnuson\ {II Kings 24:8}
Variants: *El'noson, Elanasfan,*
Elanassan

Eman \Gejmon\ {I Kings 5:11} Variants:
Emuan, Gajman [P], *Gejman* [P]

Emilyan [L]

Emmanuil \Imuniejl\ {Isaiah 7:14}
Kinnuim: *Mannel, Men'khin, Zusman.*
Variants: *Amniel, Emaniel'* [L],
Emanuel [B], *Emanuel'* [B, L],
Emanuil [B], *Immanuil, Imonuel',*
Manuil

Enanij [B]

Endl {Shulkhan Gama'arekhet}

Enokh \Khanojkh\ {Genesis 4:17}
Kinnuim: *Ejnokh, Gejnokh* [V],
Genakh [B, L], *Genek* [P], *Genokh* [L,
P], *Genukh, Ginokh* [V], *Grasajanu,*
Zendel, Zindl, Zundel' [V]. Variants:
Khanokh, Khenokh [P]

Enos \Enojsh\ {Genesis 5:6}

Eorg [B]

Eremiya \Irmijogi\ {Jeremiah 1:1} *Erma*

Erikh [B]

Ernest \Ernst\ [B, L]

Erukhom {I Samuel 1:1} Kinnui: *Vishli*

Erzhij [P]

Eten [B]

Etio {Shulkhan Gama'arekhet}

Eugen \Eugenio\ [L]

Evdokim [L]

Ewgeniusz [P]

Evgenij [B]

Evidi {Kav Nuki}

Ezdra \Ezro\ {Ezra 7:1} Abbreviation:
Ojziro. Kinnuim: *Ojzejr, Ojzer.*
Variants: *Ezra, Ezro*

Ezekie \Khazkie\ {II Kings 18:1}
Kinnuim: *Fajvish, Fajvl, Ges, Vajvish,*
Vajvl. Variant: *Khizkiya*

Ezekiil \Ekhezkijl\ {Ezekiel 1:3}
Kinnuim: *Gisikis, Kgisel', Vajl*

Ezel' [L, P]

Eziz {Ezrat Nashim}

Ezkhea [V]

Fabian \Fabiyan\ [P]

Fajbuzia [P]

Fajfel' [P]

Fajtsh {Ma'agalei Teshuvah}

Faleg \Peleg\ {Genesis 10:25} Variant:
Falek

Fallu \Pali\ {Genesis 46:9}

Falma \Talmaj\ {II Samuel 3:3} Variant:
Folmaj. Folmaj is not Jewish. It was
the name of a king of Geshur, an
ancient kingdom in the Middle East,
and of fifteen pharaohs in the fourth
through first centuries B.C.E. Its most
famous bearer was Cladius
Ptolomeaus, an Alexandrian
astronomer who lived in second
century C.E.

Faltiil \Paltiejl\ {Numbers 34:26}
Kinnuim: *Pal'tiel', Paltij, Pel'te* [P],
Pil'to. Variants: *Pal'tiel'*

Famakh \Temakh\ {Ezra 2:53} Variant:
Fomakh

Fares \Perets\ {Genesis 38:29} Kinnuim:
Pertsi [B], *Pertsin.* Variant: *Perets*

Feb [L]

Fedaia \Pdojo\ {Nehemiah 3:25}

Feliks [L, P]

Fendel' [L]

Ferdinand [P]

Filipp \Filep\ {Talmud} [L, V]

Finees \Pinkhos\ {I Samuel 1:3}
Kinnuim: *Pina* [L], *Pinel', Pini, Pinio*
[V], *Pinko* [P], *Pinya, Puntsha, Zelig,*
Zeligman, Zelik, Zelikin, Zelikman.
Variants: *Pinhkus* [L], *Pinkas* [V],
Pinkhas, Pinkus [L, P, V], *Pinkvas*
[P], *Ponkhes* [P]

Fishel' [P]

Fisher [P]

Flem \Flejme\ {Talmud}

Frants [L]

Frantsisk \Francyszek\ [P]

Frederik [L]

Friderik [P]

Fridrik [P]

Frika [P]

Frimt [P]

Fua \Pio\ {I Chronicles 7:1}

Futiil \Pitiil\ {Exodus 6:25}

Gabor [L]

Gabusia [P]

Gad \God\ {Genesis 35:26} Kinnuim:
Gedil, Gidel, Gode, Godil, Godl, Godli

Gadriel' \Gadriejl'\ {Shulkhan
Gama'arekhet}

Gaj \Aj\ {Bet Shmu'el} One of the
seventy apostles, corresponding to the
seventy peoples of the world.

Gajman \Gejmon\ [L, P]

Gakkatan \Gakuton\ {Ezra 8:12} The
same name as Paulus in Latin, Petit
in French, meaning small/short/little
in Russian (Pg.).

Gamaliil' \Gamaliejl\ {Numbers 1:10}
Variants: *Gamaliil', Gamliel'*

Ganko \Gonko\ [L]

Garol'd \Harold\ [L]

Garrik [B, L]

Gartvig \Girts\ [L]

Gavriil \Gavriejl\ {Daniel 8:16} Variants:
Gabriel' [L], *Gadi, Gavriel'* [B, L, V],
Gavril' [P, V], *Gavrila*

Gedalya \Gedal'e\ {Zephariah 1:1}
Kinnuim: *Gadala, Gdale, Gdush,*
Gvursman. Variants: *Gedaliya, Igdal,*
Igdalyugi.

Gelias \Geliash\ [L, P]

Gemali \Gmali\ {Numbers 13:12} The
name means camel, *gamillus* in Latin.

Genrik [P] Variants: *Gejnrikh* [B],
Genrikh [B, P, V]

Georg \Georgij\ [L, P]

Gerasim [B] *See* Girson.

Gerbert [B]

Gerford [L]

Gerig [P]

Germam \Hermam\ [L]

German [B, P] *See* Khermon.

Gesikis {Shulkhan Gama'arekhet}
Variants: *Gis, Gisikis, Khis, Khiz*

Giddel' \Gidejl\ {Ezra 2:47} Variants:
Gaddail, Giddel', Gidel [L] Aramaic
version of Hebrew *Gadol* (great); Latin
form is Magnus, Greek form is Megas.

Gideon \Gidojn\ {Judges 6:11} Variant:
Gid'on

Gieronim \Geronim\ [P]

Gil'ejl {Shulkhan Gama'arekhet}

Gil'mar [P]

Gilarji \Gilyarij\ [P]

Gilibun {Shulkhan Gama'arekhet}

Gillel \Gilejl\ {Judges 12:13}
Abbreviation: *Gile*. Kinnui: *Gulik*.
Variants: *Ellikh, Gerson, Gil'* [V],
Gil'ka [P], *Gil'ko* [L], *Gila* [P], *Gilel,*
Gilel' [L], *Giler* [V]

Gipolit [P]

Giroriya [P]

Girshom \Gershojm\ {Exodus 2:22}
Kinnuim: *Gumprikht, Kurshman,*
Mefantslik, Mentslin, Monush,
Zelikman. Variants: *Gershom, Girsom*

Girson \Gershojn\ {Genesis 46:11}
Kinnuim: *Girshon, Girson, Kirshman,*
Kurshman, Manis, Mendl, Mendlan,
Mendlin, Menlin, Monis, Monish,
Zelig, Zeligman, Zelik, Zelikin,
Zelikman. Variants: *Gershon* [V],
Gershun [V], *Gerson* [B, L], *Girshon,*
Kershon [L]

Glebko \Gleb\ [L]

Gmalin {Bet Shmu'el}

Gniva {Shulkhan Gama'arekhet}

Godfrid [P]

Godl \Godl\ *Godya*

Godoliya \Gdal'yugi\ {Jeremiah 38:1}
Kinnuim: *Gdal'* [P, V], *Gdale, Gdush,*
Gdushman, Gedil, Gidajl, Gidol,
Godajl [L], *Godel'* [P, V], *Godil, Godol*
[L], *Godush, Grojsman, Gvursman.*

Variants: *Gadala* [P], *Gdal'yu* [L],
Gdaliya [P], *Gdalyash* [L], *Gedal'e* [L],
Gedaliya [P], *Gedalya* [P]
Gofoniil \Osniejl\ {I Chronicles 4:13}
Variant: *Asniel*
Golosh [L]
Gorko [L]
Gorojn \Gurojn\ {Shulkhan
Gama'arekhet}
Goroz [P]
Goshaia \Gojshaio\ {Nehemiah 12:32}
Kinnui: *Shaya*. Variant: *Goshaya*
Gozias [B]
Guglel'mo \Gugliel'mo\ [L]
Gugo [B]
Guna \Gino\ {Bet Shmu'el}
Gur \Gir\ {Shulkhan Gama'arekhet}
Variants: *Gur'yan*, *Gurij*
Gurion \Gir'ejn\ {Talmud}
Gustav [L, P]
Gutel' [B, L]
Guter [P]
Iafet \Efes\ {Genesis 5:32}
Iafniil \Iasniejl\ {I Chronicles 26:2}
Iair \Yuir\ {Judges 10:3} Kinnuim: *Yura*,
Yuro
Iakim {I Chronicles 24:12} *Yakhim*,
Yakim. Spanish Jews used it as a
short version of Eliakim (Shulkhan
Gama'arekhet).
Iakov \Yakov\ {Genesis 25:26} Kinnuim:
*Bishuf, Bundit, Bunfant, Bunfat,
Bunfil', Ejkev, Ekalets* [L], *Ekef* [V],
*Ekev, Ekir, Ekl, Encha, Gulek,
Gumprikht, Iakush, Iekel', Iojkev,
Iojkiv, Iokel', Iokish, Iokush, Iokushko,
Iuka, Kobke, Kofman* [V], *Koftsya,
Kojfan, Kojfman, Kojpa, Kokhman* [L],
*Kop, Kopal, Kopalman, Kopgan, Kopil,
Kopl*. This name was also used by
Christians in the Middle Ages (O.R.).,
*Koplman, Kreplan, Kufin, Kuli, Kulik,
Kupilman, Kuplman, Kuvin, Papu,
Sheftel', Tuki, Yaakov, Yakef* [V], *Yakl,
Yakob, Yakovko, Yakub* [L], *Yanash*
[P], *Yanche* [P], *Yanin, Yankl, Yantsi,
Yanush* [L], *Yaska* [L], *Yatsa, Yatsi,
Yatsko, Yukef* [P], *Yukel', Yukir, Zelig,
Zeligman, Zelik, Zelikin, Zelikman*.
Variants: *Yakov, Yankel', Yankev*
Ianaj \Iaani\ {I Chronicles 5:12}

Iavis \Iavejts\ {I Chronicles 4:9}
Ido \Idoj\ {Ezra 8:17}
Idor {Shulkhan Gama'arekhet}
Iedaiya \Edae\ {Nehemiah 11:10}
Iedidia \Edid'e\ {II Samuel 12:25}
Kinnuim: *Gotlib, Gutlib, Gutlif,
Gutlipo, Lyuba*. Variants: *Did'ya* [P],
Edid'ya, Edidiyash [L], *Eididio*,[20]
Ejdidio, Iedidiya [L]
Iefeaj \Iftokh\ {Judges 11:1}
Iegallelel \Iegalel'ejl\ {I Chronicles 4:16}
Iegojosh {II Kings 12:1} Variant of Ioas.
Iekhiil \Ekhiejl\ {I Chronicles 23:8}
Abbreviation: *Ikhl, Khiejl, Khil'* [P,
V]. Kinnuim: *Buni, Bunian, Bunin,
Buniun, Ikhel, Ikhel', Ikhil', Mekl,
Mikhl, Mikhush, Mikl, Mokhl*.
Variants: *Ejkhel'* [V], *Ekhiel, Ekhiel'*
[V], *Iakhel'* [L], *Iekhiel', Ikhiel'* [L],
Iokhel' [L]
Iekhoniya \Ekhon'e\ {Esther 2:6}
Kinnui: *Iokonia*
Iekufiil \Ekisiejl\ {I Chronicles 4:18}
Abbreviation: *Kusiil'*. Pet form of
Iejkusiil, *Kusya*. Pet form of Kusa.
Kinnuim: *Kojfman, Kopilman, Kusa,
Kusha, Kusheliel', Kushko, Kuski,
Kusko, Kusman, Laza, Lazal, Lazo,
Zalman, Zelig, Zeligin, Zeligman,
Zelik, Zelikin, Zelikman, Zelkin,
Zelkind, Zelko, Ziskind, Zusa, Zusi,
Zusman*. Variants: *Ekhfiil, Ekisiel,
Ekufiil', Ekutiel, Ekutiel'* [P], *Iejkusiil,
Iekisiel* [P], *Iekufiil', Kasiel* [P], *Kesil'*
[V], *Kishel'* [P], *Kishlak* [L], *Kisiel,
Kisiel'* [B, P], *Ksiel'* [L, V], *Kusel'* [L],
Kushel' [L], *Kushiel'* [B], *Kusiel'* [L]
Iemuil \Emiejl\ {Genesis 46:10}
Variants: *Emil'* [B, P], *Emiliya* [L]
Ier [P]
Ierakhmeil \Erakhmejl\ {I Chronicles
2:9} Kinnuim: *Guchlek, Gutslik,
Ziskind, Zuse, Zusman*. Variants:
Iejrakhmiel', Ierakhmiejl [L],
*Ierakhmiel', Ierakhmiil, Ierameil,
Rakhmael* [L], *Rakhmiel, Rakhmil'*
Ieremiya \Irmijogi\ {Jeremiah 1:1}
Variants: *Eremiya* [B, V], *Erma* [B, V],
Ermash [L], *Iarma* [P], *Ieremiash* [P],
Ieremiyash [P], *Iirmio, Irma* [V],
Yarmush [P]

Iersi [P]

Ierukhom \Erikhom\ {I Samuel 1:1}
Kinnuim: *Fishel*, *Vishel*, *Vishli*.
Variants: *Erikhem*, *Erukhim* [L],
Ierokham, *Ierukhem* [B]

Ieshuo {Bet Shmu'el} Kinnui: *Fargon*

Iessej \Ishaj\ {I Samuel 16:1}

Ieush {I Chronicles 23:10}

Iezekiil \Ekhezkejl\ {Ezekiel 1:3}
Abbreviations: *Khaskel'*, *Khatse*,
Khazkl. Kinnuim: *Fajvish*, *Fajvl*, *Ges*,
Geshl, *Gesikis*, *Gisikis*, *Kgizel'*,
Khatskel', *Vajvish*, *Vajvl*. Variants:
Ekhezkel, *Ezekhil* [L], *Ezekiel'* [P],
Gaskiel' [P], *Iekhezkel'*, *Iekhezkiel'*
[P], *Iezekhil*, *Iezekiel'* [B, L, V],
Iezekiil, *Iokhezkiel'* [L], *Khaskiel'* [P]

Ifamar \Isumor\ {Exodus 6:23} Kinnui:
Sumer. Variants: *Isumer*, *Itamar*,
Isomor

Iga \Igia\ {Shulkhan Gama'arekhet} *See*
Ojshij.

Iisus \Iegojshia\ {Exodus 17:9}
Abbreviations: *Gojshia*, *Goshea*,
Iojsha, *Shia* [P], *Shiela*, *Shika*, *Shua*,
Shuela, *Shueli*. Kinnuim: *Falek*, *Falk*,
Geshel', *Geshika*, *Geshil'*, *Geshka*,
Gojshil, *Gojshko*, *Gojshl*, *Goshko*,
Goshla, *Goshman*, *Gushl*, *Gushma*,
Gushman, *Ioshko*, *Ishka*, *Iushko*, *Ushl*,
Valk, *Zelig*, *Zeligman*, *Zelik*, *Zelikin*,
Zelikman, *Zisel* [L], *Ziska* [L], *Zisman*
[L], *Zusa*, *Zusel*, *Zusi*, *Zusko* [L],
Zuslan, *Zuslin*, *Zusman* [L]. Variants:
Avsej [B], *Egoshiya* [L], *Egoshua* [P],
Ejshua, *Eshia* [V], *Eshiel'* [V], *Eshii*
[L], *Eshij* [L], *Eshua*, *Eshuj* [V],
Eshuya [B], *Esua* [L], *Evsej* [V],
Goshiya [V], *Govsej* [B, L], *Govshiya*
[V], *Iegoshia* [L], *Iisuj*, *Ioshua* [V],
Ioshuva [V], *Iosiaz* [P], *Iosie* [P], *Ishia*
[V], *Ovsej* [L, V], *Ovshej* [V], *Ovshij*
[V], *Ovshiya* [L], *Ovsiej* [P]

Ikhel' \Iekhiil\ {I Chronicles 15:18} *Ikhel*

Il'ya \Ejliyugi\ {I Kings 17:1} Kinnuim:
Elash [P], *Elias* [B, L], *Eliash* [L, P],
Elik, *Elios* [B], *Eliyas* [P], *Elyash* [L],
Il'ko, *Ilish*, *Iliyash* [L, P, V], *Ilyash*
[L], *Khejn*, *Kidor*, *Ol'e*, *Svechki*.
Variants: *El* [V], *El'ya* [L, V], *El'yu*
[V], *Eli*, *Elia* [L, P], *Elian* [V], *Elie*

[V], *Elij* [L], *Eliogu*, *Eliya*, *Eliyagu*,
Eliyu [V], *Elyam* [B], *Il'ya*, *Ilya* [V]

Invidal {Shulkhan Gama'arekhet}

Ioakhal \Iikhal\ {Jeremiah 38:1}
Variant: *Iyukhal*

Ioakim \Egoyukim\ {II Kings 23:36}
Kinnuim: *Yakim*, *Iokim*

Ioas \Iojosh\ {Judges 6:11} Kinnui:
Gojvesh

Ioav \Iojov\ {II Samuel 2:13}

Ioets \Iojejts\ {Bet Shmu'el} Kinnuim:
Gotlib, *Iolets*, *Shalman*, *Shulman*,
Yulin. Variant: *Ioach'*

Iofoniya \Iefine\ {Numbers 13:6}
Kinnui: *Bunya*. Variant: *Iefuno*

Ioil \Iojejl\ {Joel 1:1} Kinnuim: *Fajvish*,
Fajvl, *Iatsa*. Variants: *Ejlik* [V], *Evel'*
[L, V], *Ioel* [L]

Ioil' \Iojejl'\ {Joel 1:1} Kinnuim: *Ejlik*
[V], *Evel'* [L, V], *Fajvish*, *Fajvl*, *Iatsa*,
Vajvish, *Vajvl*, *Zisa* [P], *Zisla* [P],
Zislan, *Zislin*, *Zusa*, *Zusel'* [P],
Zuslan, *Zuslin*, *Zusman*. Variants:
Ioel', *Ioil*, *Iojel'*, *Iovel'* [L], *Iuliush* [P],
Ovel' [L], *Yul'ius* [B, L, P], *Yulius* [B,
P], *Yuliyan* [P]

Iojsha {Ohalei Shem}

Iojskhin {Shulkhan Gama'arekhet}

Iojzzhe [P]

Iokha \Iojkho\ {I Chronicles 8:16}
Variant: *Iojkhoj*

Iokhaf \Iakhas\ {I Chronicles 6:5}

Iokhanan \Iojkhonon\ {II Kings 25:23}
Abbreviation: *Khanon*, *Zheke*.
Kinnuim: *Grasajanu*, *Iokhna*, *Iulin*,
Shul'man. Variants: *Ioanan*, *Ioann* [L,
V], *Ioen* [P], *Iojkhanan*, *Iokhan* [L],
Iokhanan, *Iokhen* [P], *Iokhenen* [B, P],
Iokhonan, *Iokhonon* [B, P], *Ivan* [L],
Yan [P], *Yane* [P], *Yukhno* [L]

Iokim {I Chronicles 4:22} Variant:
Yakim

Iokor \Iakir\ {Bet Shmu'el} Kinnuim:
Ajzl, *Beliklajn*, *Fajtel'*, *Seliklajn*,
Vajdel', *Zelikman*. Variants: *Yakar*,
Yaker [L, V]

Ioktan \Iokton\ {Genesis 10:25}

Iom-Tov \Iojm-Tojv\ {Bet Shmu'el}
Kinnuim: *Bajras*, *Bakhram*, *Bendet*,
Bendid, *Bendit*, *Bindit*, *Bnet*, *Buan-
Gojren*, *Bundio*, *Bunet*, *Danun*, *Id*,

Iomtl, Iontl, Lipa, Lipman. Iom-Tov
replaced the ancient name Khagi,
meaning holiday.

Iona \Iojno\ {Jonah 1:1} Kinnuim: *Ionik,
Ionikil*. Variants: *Ejna* [V], *Evna* [V],
Evno, Evnos [P], *Ina* [V], *Ionas* [L],
Ionash [B, L, P], *Ionko* [L], *Yanos* [B,
L], *Yanot* [B], *Yavnin* [B], *Yavno* [L].
Translated as Columbus into Latin
(Pg.).

Ionafan \Iegojnuson\ {I Samuel 13:2}
Abbreviation: *Noson*. Kinnuim: *Falk,
Valk*. Variants: *Iojnesen, Iojnoson,
Ionatan*

Ioram \Iegojrom\ {II Kings 1:17}

Iorosej [L]

Iosif {Genesis 30:24} Abbreviations:
*Es'ka, Esko, Iojs'in, Iojsele, Iojsi,
Iojsko, Iojzlin, Ios'* [V], *Ios'man,
Iojsko, Iosek* [P], *Iosh* [V], *Yusko* [L],
Iosele, Iojsiya [P], *Iosya* [V], Kinnuim:
Ejzap [L], *Eslo* [L], *Ezif* [L], *Gezl,
Gilik, Gotlipo, Goz, Gutlib, Gutlif,
Gutlipo, Iezel', Iojpl*-Most likely is a
misspelled *Iojzpl, Iojsif'e, Iojsin,
Iojslin, Iojzefij* [L], *Iojzel', Iojzik* [V],
Iojzip [V], *Iojzpl, Iojzpo, Iojzvel',
Ios'ko, Iosef, Iosek, Iosel', Iosfis, Iosha*
[L], *Ioshi, Iosif, Iosij, Iosil', Iosiya* [P],
Ioskhin, Iosko, Iosl, Ioslin. This name
was also used by Christians in the
Middle Ages (O.R.)., *Iozef* [B, L, P],
*Iozeppe, Iyushke, Lupis, Manla,
Mansa, Minman, Munkhin, Muts,
Pandiro, Pul'zuto, Yuzef* [P], *Yuzheva*
[L], *Zundel'*. Variants: *Iojsif, Iosif,
Iosip* [B, L], *Osip* [B, L]. Iosif is
pronounced Yojsef in the first source
and Yehojsejf in the second one. It is
spelled Iegojsif in some editions of the
Russian Orthodox Bible (Zh. R.)

Iosiya \Iojshiyugi\ {II Kings 21:26}
Variant: *Ioshie*

Ira \Iro\ {II Samuel 20:26} Variant: *Iras*

Irad \Irod\ {Genesis 4:18}

Iri {I Chronicles 7:7} Kinnuim: *Fajbush,
Fajvl, Feul, Gumo, Gumplin, Vajvish*

Irigrus Kinnui: *Viblan*

Irshrago Kinnuim: *Fajbus, Fajbush,
Fajbush, Fajsh, Fajtel, Fajve, Fajvish,
Fajvl, Fejbus, Filill, Vajvl*

Isaak \Itskhok\ {Genesis 21:5} Kinnuim:
Ajza, Ajzik, Ajzika [P], *Ajzman, Ber,
Beril', Berkhin, Berlin, Berman, Bero,
Durant, Ejzik* [V], *Ejzyk* [P], *Ignat* [L],
Ignatij [P], *Ignatsa* [P], *Ignatts,
Isaakij, Isachko* [L], *Isak, Isakub* [P],
Ishak, Itse [V], *Itsek, Itsekl, Itsi, Itsig*
[P], *Itsik, Itsili, Itsko* [L, V], *Itskol,
Itsl, Itsli, Itsya, Ittsig* [P], *Iza, Izak,
Izash* [L], *Izlan, Izlin, Khakin,
Khakinat, Khokhom*,[21] *Kitin, Kitojn,
Krojli, Krula, Leblang, Leblangen,
Leblig, Lyuba*,[22] *Pitsa, Puga, Pulder,
Putsi, Sak* [L], *Zak*. Derived from
Ajzik, *Zaklin, Zejlig, Zejlik* [V], *Zekil',
Zekl, Zeklin, Zelig, Zeligman, Zelik,
Zelikin, Zilig* [V], *Zuslin*. Variant:
Iitskhok. This name became Izak in
Germany and Isaac in England. The
latter form was widely used in Russia
(O.R.), *Iskhak* [L], *Itskanko* [L],
Itskhak [L], *Itskhol'* [V]

Isaia \Ieshaiugi\ {Isaiah 1:1}
Abbreviation: *Shaiya, Shaya*.
Kinnuim: *Saadiya, Shajka*. Variants:
Eshaia, Ezaes [B], *Ieshaje, Isaj* [L],
Isaya [P], *Izayash* [P]

Ishmaia \Ishmaiugi\ {I Chronicles 27:19}

Ishrugu {Ezrat Nashim}

Ishtrugu {Ezrat Nashim}

Isikis \Gisikis\

Issakhar \Isoskhor\ {Genesis 30:18}
Kinnuim: *Ber, Beril, Berkhen, Berlin,
Berman, Bero, Dov, Perlajn, Perman,
Permun, Taus, Tsakhrajs*. Variants:
Iisskher, Iisukher, Isakhor [P], *Isokhor
, Isukhor* [V], *Sakhar* [P], *Sokhor* [V],
Soskher [V], *Sukher* [V]

Istrugu {Ezrat Nashim}

Iuda \Egido\ {Genesis 29:35} This name
gave rise to one of the names of the
Jewish people - Iudei (Russian).
Eguda, Nejme. Kinnuim: *Ashman,
Aslan, Atslan, Avirlin, Gudl, Gushma,
Gutska, Idel', Iodal, Iud*. This name
was also used by Christians in the
Middle Ages (O.R.)., *Iudel', Kunfradu,
Laba, Labish, Labush, Lajb* [P],
Lajbele [P], *Lava, Lavish, Leb* [L, P],
*Leba, Leber, Lebil', Lebl', Leblan,
Leblin, Lebus* [L], *Lejb, Lejba, Lejbche*

[P], *Lejbel'* [P], *Lejbesh, Lejbi* [P],
Lejbish [V], *Lejbka, Lejbko* [V], *Lejbli,*
Lejblin, Lejbus [P], *Lejbush, Lejme,*
Lejvi, Lejvo, Leo [L]- Translation of
Lejb, *Leon*-Translation of Lejb,
Leonard [P], *Leopol'd* [B], *Lepol'd, Lev*
[L]-Iuda's (Juda's) nickname., *Levan*
[B], *Levek* [P], *Levik* [B], *Levin, Levka*
[P], *Levko* [L], *Levon* [L], *Liber,*
Liberman, Liman, Limo, Lionush,
Liovo, Liv, Livb, Livn, Livo, Lyuba [L],
Pulikhruni, Pulikhrunu, Trajt, Tratl,
Vruman, Yuda, Yude [V], *Yudka* [L, P,
V], *Yudko* [V], *Zelek* [P], *Zelig,*
Zeligman, Zelik, Zelikin, Zelikman,
Zelko, Zundel'. Variants: *Egide,*
Ieguda [L], *Iguda* [L], *Igudko* [L],
Ikhudko [L]

Iuziya \Oziya\ Kinnui: *Eneil*

Iyames [L]

Iziil \Iziejl\ Kinnui: *Labush.* Variants:
Aziel', Oziil

Izmail \Ismail\ {Genesis 16:11} Kinnui:
Maliku. Variants: *Ismael', Izmail'*

Izrail \Isruejl'\ {Genesis 32:28}
Kinnuim: *Iser, Iserl, Isidor* [L, V],
Isidore [L, V], *Isor* [V], *Isser* [L], *Izar*
[P], *Izidor, Izor* [P], *Pufir, Pupu, Zusa,*
Zuskind. Variants: *Iisrael', Isroel'* [L,
P, V], *Isrol, Isruel, Izrael'* [B, L, V],
Izrajlo [L], *Izral'* [L], *Srol'* [L, P, V],
Srul' [L, P, V], *Srulik, Zrael'* [L],
Zrail' [L]

Kaas \Kgos\ {Genesis 46:11} Kinnuim:
Kgisl, Kgosl

Kaem Means sturdy, an expression of a
desire to see the newborn healthier
than his father or mother, especially
in the case of the father's death before
the birth of the baby or the death of
the mother in childbirth (Zh.R.).

Kagane {Bet Shmu'el}

Kaiel' [P]

Kal'vin [L]

Karl [L, P]

Karmi {Genesis 46:9}

Karol' [P]

Kashriel' \Kashriejl'\ {Shulkhan
Gama'arekhet}

Kashtu {Bet Shmu'el}

Kaspar [L]

Kasriil \Akasriel'\ {Bet Shmu'el}
Variants: *Kasriel', Kasril'* [L, V].
Cabalistic name, means God is my
crown. It was not used in the Bible,
like the name of Gabreil. It's root
name Akasriel was not used in
everyday life because of the holiness of
the God's name.

Kavrill \Kavriejl\ {Nakhlat Shiv'ah}

Kazhen [P]

Kazimir [P], Variant: *Kazhimir,* From
Polish: Kazimierz

Kedorloamer \Kdorloojmer\ {Genesis
14:1}

Kelugi \Klugi\ {Ezra 10:35}

Khaim Kinnuim: *Fajvish, Fajvl, Vajvish,*
Vajvl, Vidal, Vitalij [V]. Variant: *Efim*
[V] Khaim, or its English equivalent,
Chaim, is one of the most popular
names. Although not a biblical name,
the word was used as an adjective in I
Samuel 17:26 (". . . living God").
Historically it was often bestowed
upon a critically ill person in the hope
that he will be restored to good health
(Kolatch 1984:53).

Khaj {Shulkhan Gama'arekhet}

Khajman [P]

Khajno {Kav Nuki}

Khakhmojn {Shulkhan Gama'arekhet}
Variant: *Khokhman* [P]

Khakim {Shulkhan Gama'arekhet}

Khalafta {Shulkhan Gama'arekhet}

Khalev \Kulejv\ {Numbers 13:6} Kinnui:
Vavil. Variant: *Kolev*

Khalfon \Khalfojn\ {Bet Shmu'el}
Kinnui: *Evats*

Khalfuj {Bet Shmu'el}

Khalifa {Tuv Gittin} Variant: *Alfej*

Khalifo {Kav Nuki}

Khamel' [P]

Khaniil' \Khaniejl\ {Numbers 34:23}
Variant: *Khanniil'*

Khanina {Bet Shmu'el}

Khanuka \Khaniko\ {Shulkhan
Gama'arekhet} This name was given
to babies of either gender born during
Hanukkah.

Khanun {Nehemiah 3:13} Kinnuim:
Khone, Khune. Variant: *Khanon* [V]

Khasan {Shulkhan Gama'arekhet}

Khasmonej \Khashmojnui\ {Shulkhan Gama'arekhet} Kinnui: *Mirkadu*

Khedkel' [L]

Khelbo {Shulkhan Gama'arekhet}

Khelkiya \Khilkiyugi\ {I Chronicles 6:30}

Kheresh {I Chronicles 9:15}

Khermon \Khermojn\ {I Chronicles 5:23} This name appears as a name of a mountain in the Tanakh, but in no other context. It has been used as a given name and is mentioned in Seder Hadorot (Pg.)

Khie {Talmud}

Khisda \Khisdoj\ {Talmud}

Khisil' {Shulkhan Gama'arekhet}

Khlavno {Kav Nuki} Variants: *Khlavn, Khlouno*. This name is a distorted pronunciation of *golovnya* the Russian translation of the Hebrew name Lapidot (O.R.).

Khlavo {Shulkhan Gama'arekhet}

Khlavun {Kav Nuki}

Khlojna {Kav Nuki}

Khobaiya \Khovoio\ {Ezra 2:61} Kinnui: *Khev'e*. Variant: *Ovaia*.

Kholef {Shulkhan Gama'arekhet}

Khonin {Shulkhan Gama'arekhet}

Khorosk [L]

Khovij {Bet Shmu'el}

Khoviv {Shulkhan Gama'arekhet}

Khristian [L]

Khuni {Kav Nuki}

Khusij \Khushaj\ {II Samuel 15:32} Kinnui: *Gushi*

Kis \Kish\ {I Samuel 9:1}

Klaude [L]

Klemens [L]

Klojkhi {Bet Shmu'el}

Klojnimus \Kolojnimus\ {Avoda Zara 11a} Kinnuim: *Kaliman* [L], *Kalma* [P], *Kalman* [V], *Kalmekhin, Kalmen* [B], *Kalmon* [L], *Kel'ma* [P], *Kel'man* [L, P], *Kel'mon* [P, V], *Kelmekhin*. Variants: *Klejnimus, Klonimes*

Kodojsh {Bet Shmu'el} Variants: *Kadesh* [L], *Kadish* [B], *Kadosh* [L]

Kogen \Kojgen\ {Kav Nuki} Variant: *Kagan*

Kono {Ohalei Shem}

Konrad [L]

Konstant [P]

Konstantin [B]

Kornel' [L]

Kosman [L]

Kostush [P]

Krishkash {Bet Shmu'el}

Krivon [L]

Krivonya [L]

Kron [B]

Ksaverij [P]

Kulo {Bet Shmu'el} Variant: *Kulu*

Kundejr [B]

Kurti {Bet Shmu'el}

Kushaia \Kishuyugi\ Kinnuim: *Kuse, Kushe*

Kyadiya [L]

Lambert [L]

Lamekh \Lemekh\ {Genesis 4:18} Kinnui: *Lemil'*

Lapidof \Dalidojs\ {Judges 4:4} Kinnui: *Khlafna*. Variants: *Lafidof, Lapidejsh*

Lejshekh [B]

Lejv {Shulkhan Gama'arekhet}

Levij \Lejvi\ {Genesis 29:34} Kinnuim: *Lejvik, Level', Levlin*. Variants: *Levi* [L], *Levie* [P],

Levitas {Talmud}

Liberl {Shulkhan Gama'arekhet}

Libkind \Lipkind\ {Bet Shmu'el} This name was also used by Christians in the Middle Ages (O.R.).

Linman [B]

Livts {Kav Nuki}

Lojntij {Talmud} Variant: *Leontij*

Loli [L]

Lorents [L]

Louis \Lui\ [B, L]

Lutsian \Lyutsian\ [L, P]

Lyudvig \Lyudvik\ [L, P]

Maakha \Maakho\ {I Chronicles 3:2}

Maassiya \Maaseiyu\ {Nehemiah 8:4}

Maes [P]

Mafnaj \Matnaj\ {Nehemiah 12:19}

Mafusal \Msishelakh\ {Genesis 4:18} Kinnui: *Zavil*. Variant: *Metush*

Majmun {Bet Shmu'el} Variant: *Muemin* [L]

Majnko {Kav Nuki}

Makheleil \Makhalejl\ {Genesis 5:12}

Makhir \Mukhir\ {Genesis 50:23} Variant: *Mokhir*

Makhluf {Kav Nuki}

Makhola [P]

Maksimilian [B, P]

Malakhiya \Malukhi\ {Malachi 1:1}
Variant: *Mal'akhiya*

Malkhiil \Malkiejl\ {Genesis 46:17}
Variants: *Mal'kiel, Mal'kiil, Melkhiil*

Mallukh \Malikh\ {Nehemiah 10:5}
Kinnui: *Mejlakh*

Malul {Shulkhan Gama'arekhet}

Mamfl {Bet Shmu'el}

Mamri {Shulkhan Gama'arekhet}

Man \Manush\ Variant: *Man*

Manassiya \Mnashe\ {Genesis 41:51}
Kinnuim: *Man, Man'*. Variants:
Manasha [L], *Manasse* [P], *Manosse*
[L], *Menash* [P], *Menasha* [P],
Menashe [V], *Menassa* [P], *Monashko*
[V], *Nashka* [V]

Mangejm [P]

Mani {Judges 13:2}

Manoj \Manojakh\ {Judges 13:2}
Kinnuim: *Gandl, Gendel', Man*. This
name was also used by Christians in
the Middle Ages (O.R.), *Mendel',*
Mendl,[23] *Mendlan, Mendlin,*
Trishtal'. Variant: *Monoakh*

Mantsojr {Ezrat Nashim}

Mardokhej \Mordkhaj\ {Esther 2:5}
Kinnuim: *Fatsejk, Gilibi, Gimpel',*
Gimpli, Gimtsel', Golibi, Gumo,
Gumpes, Gumpil, Gumpl, Gumplajn,
Gumplin, Gumprekht, Imordokh,
Majko, Majzil, Mako, Maks, Mane [B],
Mani, Mardi, Mardya, Marechko [P],
Marek [L, P], *Mark* [L, P, V], *Markaj,*
Markelij [P], *Marki, Markil', Markl,*
Marko, Markus, Matel' [P], *Mauris*
[P], *Mauritsij* [L, P], *Mejcha, Mekl,*
Menlin, Merel', Mergel', Merkel',
Mijzil, Mikl, Mintish, Mirku, Mizil,
Modil, Modl, Mojdl Variation of Modl
(O.R.), *Mojzil, Mojzl, Mordash* [L],
Mordesh, Mordish [L], *Mordosh* [L],
Mordus [L], *Mordush, Moris* [B, P],
Morits, Mot' [V], *Mota* [L], *Mote* [V],
Motek [P], *Motel', Motka* [L], *Motl* [V]-
Variation of Motel (O.R.), *Motya,*
Mukil', Muni, Murkel', Murkil', Revil,
Ziskind, Zuskind. Variants: *Mardko*
[V], *Mardokaj, Mardokhaj* [P],

Markhaj [L], *Mertkhaj* [L], *Mordekhaj*
[L], *Mordka* [P], *Mordkhaj* [L, V],
Mordkhe, Mordkhel' [B], *Mordko* [L,
P, V], *Mordokh* [L, P], *Mordukh* [L,
P], *Morkha* [L], *Mortek* [P], *Mortkhel'*
[B]

Marian [P]

Martin [L]

Martish [L]

Marton [L]

Martselij [P]

Martsin [P]

Masid \Masud\ {Tuv Gittin}

Masur [P]

Mata {Kav Nuki}

Matfan \Maton\ {Jeremiah 38:1}
Variants: *Matan, Nafan*

Matfifiya \Matis'e\ {Ezra 10:43}
Abbreviation: *Mas'e, Matas, Mates* [L,
P], *Matesh* [V], *Matias* [L, P], *Matois,*
Matous', Matoush [P], *Matus* [V],
Matys [L, P]. Variants: *Matafiya,*
Matas'ya, Matash'e, Matfafiya, Matfej,
Matfij, Matis'ya [P], *Matis'yaga* [P],
Matit'ya, Mattafiya, Mattifiya, Matvej

Matsliakh {Tuv Gittin} Kinnuim:
Projsferu, Prosfer

Matso \Mojtso\ *Mejche*

Mavrikij [P]

Mazol-Tov {Shulkhan Gama'arekhet}
Used as both a masculine and
feminine name.

Mechislav [P]

Meguyail \Mkhiyuejl\ {Genesis 4:18}

Meir {Bet Shmu'el} Kinnuim: *Libertrojt,*
Magaram, Majir, Majko, Majrim [B],
Marim, Metsl, Metso, Metsu, Mitsi,
Mitsu, Vivlman. Variants: *Maier* [L,
P], *Majer* [P], *Majre* [L], *Majrek* [P],
Mayarka [V], *Meer* [L, V], *Mejchik* [L],
Mejer [L], *Mejir, Miron* [V], *Morek* [P]

Mejna [B]

Melkhiram \Malkirom\ {I Chronicles
3:18}

Memuilam \Mshilom\ *Zelkin*

Menaim \Mnakhejm\ {II Kings 15:14}
Kinnuim: *Ikel', Majnshter, Majnsterl,*
Majnsterlan, Man, Mana [L], *Mane* [B,
L], *Manel'* [P, V], *Manes* [L, V], *Mani,*
Manik, Manil [P], *Manis, Manish,*
Manke [L], *Mankhen, Mankhin,*

Manli, Manlo, Manos [B, P], *Mansh, Manshir, Manus* [L, V], *Menas* [B], *Mendel'* Often used as a second name with Manail (Pg.), *Mendko* [L], *Mendlan, Menishan, Menkhen* [L], *Menkhin, Menki, Menko, Menli, Menlin, Menlo, Menshin, Minko* [L], *Minster, Mnuejl, Monash* [V], *Monits, Monsh, Monush, Mulem, Munish* [V], *Nakhlo, Nakhum, Nojm, Noim, Nokhum, Nukhim* [V], *Shunman, Trojshtam*. Variants: *Manaim, Menakhem* [L], *Menakhim* [L], *Mnakhem*

Meshelemiya \Mshelem'e\ {I Chronicles 9:21} Abbreviation: *Mesel', Meshel'.* Variant: *Meselemiya*

Meshezavel \Mshejzavejl\ {Nehemiah 10:22} Kinnui: *Zavil.* Variant: *Mshezavel'*

Meshuilam \Mshilom\ {II Kings 22:3} Kinnuim: *Durant, Fajvish, Kaufman, Koftse.* Derived from Kaufman (O.R.), *Koftsya, Kojfilman, Kojfman, Mvajt, Vajbush, Vajvil, Zal'men, Zeligin, Zeligman, Zelik, Zelikind, Zelikman, Zelkin, Zelko, Zemil', Zeml', Zimel', Zimlin, Zis'e, Zisel', Zumlin, Zumm, Zusa, Zusman.* Variants: *Mashulem, Meshilam, Meshulam, Messolam, Mshilom, Mshulom*

Mevorakh \Mvojrokh\ {Shulkhan Gama'arekhet}

Mikhne [L]

Mikhush {Shulkhan Gama'arekhet} According to O.Sh., it is a calque of Iekhiel'.

Miklos [L]

Mikolaj [P]

Miksa [L]

Milalaj {Nehemiah 12:36}

Miniamin \Minyumin\ {Nehemiah 12:41}

Mir [B]

Misail \Mishuejl\ {Daniel 1:6} Variant: *Mishoejl*

Miyamin \Miyumin\ {Nehemiah 10:8} Variant: *Miiamin*

Mnuejl \Mniejl\ Most likely derived from Immanuil (Tuv Gittin).

Mnukha \Mnikho\ {Bet Shmu'el}

Moisej \Mojshe\ {Exodus 2:10} Kinnuim: *Abigedor, Abisooh, Abizoog, Ajtel'khen, Durant, Eber, Evits, Fihsl, Gutman, Guva, Iekutiel', Iered, Karmi, Ketsil, Khojvo, Krumplig, Krumpling, Kunfradu, Kush, Kushman, Kusht, Lava, Lebl, Leblan, Leblin, Lejb, Lejba, Lejblin, Lejvb, Lejvo, Levi, Majzish* [L], *Majzus, Mazis, Meshil', Meshl, Meshulem, Mirush, Mishl, Mojkhno, Mojshe, Mojshele, Mojshl, Mojshno, Mojsi, Mojzesz* [P], *Mojzis, Mokhno, Moni, Moshke, Moshko, Moshl, Moshno, Moshuta, Mosya, Moze* [L], *Mozes* [B, L], *Mozesh, Mozez, Mozis, Mozus, Mukaj, Muki, Mulin, Muna, Mune, Mushel', Mushman, Muzes* [B], *Mvajt, Natanel', Papilo, Papulo, Pilu, Potku, Shemaiya, Shiman, Shlemkhaj, Shliman, Shniur, Shotur, Shoturl, Shtiur, Soferl, Sosojn, Susi, Tovij, Vajvish, Vishl, Vruman, Zalman, Zeml, Zusman.* Variants: *Masej* [L], *Mejsha* [L], *Mejshe, Mishko* [L], *Mojshej* [L], *Mosek* [P], *Mosha* [L], *Moshe* [L, V], *Moshej* [L], *Moshek* [L, P], *Moshekil* [P], *Moshij* [B, L], *Mosko* [L], *Movsha* [P, V]

Mol' [V]

Mola {Ma'agalei Teshuvah}

Molo {Shulkhan Gama'arekhet}

Monush {Bet Shmu'el} Kinnuim: *Man* [B, V], *Man'* [B, V]

Morais \Mor\ [L]

Motsa \Mojtso\ {I Chronicles 9:43} Kinnuim: *Mejche, Mejke.* Variant: *Mesa*

Msayejl' {Bet Shmu'el}

Muni {Bet Shmu'el}

Muno {Tuv Gittin}

Mushi {Exodus 6:19}

Mushku {Shulkhan Gama'arekhet}

Myukhos {Shulkhan Gama'arekhet}

Naaman \Naamon\ {Genesis 6:21}

Naason \Nakhshojn\ {Exodus 6:23} Variant: *Nakhshon* [V]

Nadav \Nudov\ {Exodus 6:23} Variant: *Nodov*

Nafan \Nuson\ {II Samuel 5:14} Kinnuim: *Karpil', Nosi, Nota, Notel'* [L], *Notka* [L], *Notki* [L], *Nusa, Nuse,*

Nute, Nutya [V], *Shvartsmon, Zanvil',*
Zavlin, Zelik, Zunvil'. Variants: *Nasel'*
[P], *Natan* [L, P], *Nosan* [P], *Nosel'*
[L], *Noson* [B], *Nus'* [V], *Nusen* [V],
Nusin [P, V], *Nusya* [V]

Nafanejl' \Nafanail\ {Numbers 1:8}
Abbreviation: *Sana, Sane* [P], *Sanejl',*
Sanel' [L, P], *Sani, Sanio, Sanko* [L],
Sano. Kinnui: *Sender*. Variants:
Nataniel, Nataniya, Slavic translation
is Bogdan or God gave (O.R.),
Nataniil, Nesanejl, Nesanel

Naftalim \Naftuli\ {Genesis 30:8}
Abbreviation: *Toli*. Kinnuim: *Garsh,*
Garts. This name was also used by
Christians in the Middle Ages (O.R.).,
Gersh, Gershl, Gerts, Gertsko, Gertsl,
Gertso, Girsh. This name was also
used by Christians in the Middle Ages
(O.R.)., *Girshil, Girtsil, Girtsl, Girtso,*
Girtsship, Ziml. Variants: *Avtuli* [V],
Naftala, Naftalim [P], *Naftel'* [P],
Naftol [P], *Naftola* [L], *Naftul'* [L],
Naftula [V], *Navtal* [P]

Najlikh [P]

Nakhaf \Nakhas\ {Genesis 36:13}

Nakhamu {Shulkhan Gama'arekhet}

Nakhlifo {Shulkhan Gama'arekhet}

Nakhmanij \Nakhmuni\ {Nehemiah 7:7}
Kinnui: *Nakhmenke*. Variants:
Nakhman, Nakhmani, Nakhmanie [P]

Nakhmish {Shulkhan Gama'arekhet}

Nakhmon {Bet Shmu'el} Kinnuim:
Gebel, Nakhli, Nakhlo, Nakhmanki,
Nekhil', Nekhl. Variant: *Nakhmen* [L].
Nakhmon is derived from Nahmani as
a new independent name (Pg.)

Napoleon [P]

Nasanmok [P]

Natrojno {Bet Shmu'el} Kinnui:
Shuman. Variants: *Natrejn, Natrejne*

Natsejr {Shulkhan Gama'arekhet} This
may be a kinnui derived from Azariya,
Ezra, Eleazar (Sh. Gam.).

Naum \Nakhim\ {Nahum 1:1} Variants:
Nakhim [L], *Nokhim* [L, P, V],
Nokhum [L], *Nukhem, Nukhim* [P, V],
Nukhimche [P]

Navin \Nin\ {Exodus 33:11}

Nazariya [P]

Nedel [P]

Neemiya \Nkhem'e\ {Nehemiah 1:1}
Kinnuim: *Fajvish, Fajvl, Khuts,*
Trejstlajn. German translation of
Neemiya., *Truslin, Vajvish, Vajvl,*
Vruman. Variants: *Khemia* [B, P],
Khemiya [B, P], *Nakhmias* [L],
Nekhamiyashch [P], *Nekhemia* [P],
Nekhemie, Nekhemij, Nekhemiya [P],
Nekhemiyash [L], *Nokhemiya*

Nefaniya \Nesanio\ {II Kings 25:23}
Abbreviations: *Sana, Sani, Sanio*.
Kinnuim: *Teodorus, Tod, Tode*.
Variant: *Nafaniya*. Since the name
means God's gift, it was translated as
Feodoros, Feodotsios and Doroteos in
Greek; Deodatus and Diodorus in
Latin; Deudonne in French; Gottlieb
in German; Bogdan and Bogdana in
Slavic languages. Its Yiddish variant is
Todros.

Negojroi {Shulkhan Gama'arekhet}

Nekhomo {Shulkhan Gama'arekhet}

Nekhunio {Kav Nuki}

Neus [B]

Nikodem [P]

Nikolaj [B, P, V]

Nikomojkhi {Talmud}

Nir \Nejr\ {I Samuel 14:50}

Niriya \Nejrio\ {Jeremiah 32:12}
Variants: *Nerio* [P], *Niriin*

Nisim {Bet Shmu'el}

Nison {Esther 3:7} Variants: *Nesel'* [V],
Nis [V], *Nisale* [P], *Nisek* [P], *Niska*
[L]. According to *Shulkhan*
Gama'arekhet, all males born during
the month of Nisan receive this name.

Noj {Genesis 5:29} Kinnui: *Majsterl*.
Variants: *Nevakh* [P, V], *Noakh* [P],
Noan [L], *Noe* [P], *Novakh* [P],
Noyakh [V]

Norbert [L, P]

Nover [B]

Oded \Ojdejd\ {II Chronicles 15:1}
Variants: *Adad, Ejded*

Ogij \Ojgij\ {Bet Shmu'el}

Ojshie \Ojshio\ {Bet Shmu'el}
Abbreviation: *Tiviomi, Trajt, Trajtl*

Ojvedi {Kav Nuki}

Ojvidi {Ohalei Shem}

Olev [V]

Onezimus [L]

Orem [P]

Osiya \Gojsheja\ {Hosea 1:1} *Gojshika*.
Kinnuim: *Gejshil, Gesel'* [L, V],
Geshel' [L], *Geshil, Geshl, Gesiya,*
Gojshika, Gojshil, Gojshka, Gojshma,
Gojshman, Goshki, Goshko, Goshma,
Goshman, Gosko [L], *Gozhko* [L],
Iojshka. Variants: *Gosha, Osha* [P, V]

Oskar [L, P] Assumed to have derived
from Ovsej.

Osof \Usof\ {I Chronicles 6:24}

Otor {Shulkhan Gama'arekhet}

Otto [B, L]

Ovadia \Ojvad'e\ {Obadiah 1:1}
Variants: *Avadia* [B], *Avdij, Avdiya*
[B], *Evad'ya* [V], *Evadij, Evadio,*
Evadiya [V], *Evdij* [V], *Ojvedi,*
Ovadiya, Ovodia [P], *Ovotsiya* [L],
Ovotya [L], *Vadia* [B]

Oved \Ojveid\ {Bet Shmu'el}

Ozer \Ojzer\ {Bet Shmu'el} Variants:
Auzer [L], *Azur* [B, L], *Ejzer* [B, L],
Ovzer [L]. Ozer may be an
abbreviation of Azariya (Sh. Gam.)

Pade \Pad\ {Talmud}

Paguil \P'yejl\ {Numbers 1:13}

Pajlets [P]

Pantelej [L]

Papa \Papi\ {Shulkhan Gama'arekhet}

Parnejs {Shulkhan Gama'arekhet}

Paseakh \Pusejakh\ {I Chronicles 4:12}
Variants: *Feesiya, Pajsha* [V], *Pejsak*
[B, L, P], *Pejsakh* [L], *Pejsha* [V],
Pejshke [L], *Pejsya* [V], *Pesakh* [L],
Peshak [L], *Petakh*. It is possible that
the Biblical name Paseakh became
Pesakh because of incorrect reading,
or because it gained legitimacy
because of the holiday of Peisakh
(Passover). Lastly, it is also possible
that the name Pesakh is a Hebrew
translation of the medieval name
Pascalius (Pg.).

Paul \Paul'\ [B, L, P]

Pavel [B, P]

Pedatsur \Pedotsur\ {Numbers 1:10}
Variants: *Fadassur, Fedassur,*
Pdochur

Pejlet [L]

Pekhturts [L]

Pelter [P]

Pelyutka [L]

Pesnyj [L]

Petakhiya \Psakh'e\ {I Chronicles
24:16} Kinnui: *Tsakhrajm*.[24]
Variants: *Fefeiya, Psakhiya*.

Peter {Shulkhan Gama'arekhet}

Prakhiya \Prakhio\ {Shulkhan
Gama'arekhet}

Prejdel' [B]

Prigrus {Ohalei Shem} Kinnui: *Viblan*

Prikhodosh {Shulkhan Gama'arekhet}

Prufito {Get Pashut}

Puntsko {Bet Shmu'el}

Puss [P]

Rabo {Shulkhan Gama'arekhet}
Variant: *Rabej* [L]

Raguil \R'yejl\ {Exodus 2:18} Kinnui:
Rul'ke. Variants: *Rejuel, Reuil,*
Riel'[P]. This name gave rise to
feminine Rulya.

Rakhail \Rakhaiel'\ [V]

Rakhamim \Rakhmim\ {Shulkhan
Gama'arekhet}

Rakhmiil \Rakhmiejl\ {Shulkhan
Gama'arekhet} Variants: *Rakhmel'*
[L], *Rakhmil'* [V]

Ramiro [L]

Rampa [P]

Reaiya \Reuio\ {Ezra 2:47}

Rechejka [L]

Refail \Refuejl\ {I Chronicles 26:7}
Kinnuim: *Fejle, Fole*. Variants: *Rafael'*
[L, P], *Rafail* [B, P, V], *Rafal'* [P],
Rafel' [L], *Rafol'* [P], *Rafuel'* [V],
Raful' [V], *Refael'* [V], *Refoel'* [V],
Refoil, Refuel' [V]

Refuo \Refio\ {Shulkhan Gama'arekhet}

Rekhaviya \Rekhav'e\ {I Chronicles
23:17} Abbreviation: *Ravio, Rakhav*.
Kinnui: *Khovel'*. Variants: *Rakhaviya*
[L], *Rekhavio, Rokhval* [L]

Rekhemio {Ohalei Shem}

Rekhovo \Rekhuvo\ {Shulkhan
Gama'arekhet}

Rekhum \Rekhim\ {Ezra 2:2} Variants:
Rejkhum, Reum

Rikhard [L]

Rimon {II Samuel 4:2} [B]

Roguil *Rejdel'*

Roman [P]

Romio {Get Pashut}

Romuald [P]

Rosh \Rojsh\ {Genesis 46:21}

Rovo \Ruvo\ {Shulkhan Gama'arekhet}

Rubik [B]

Rudol'f [B, L, P]

Runi {Tuv Gittin}

Ruvim \Rivejn\ {Genesis 29:32}
Kinnuim: *Fraden* [V], *Fridl, Rejze,
Robert* [B], *Rovn, Vridl, Zelig,
Zeligman, Zelik, Zelikin, Zelikman*.
Variants: *Reiben* [L], *Reiven, Rejben,
Revan* [P], *Rovel'* [V], *Ruban* [L],
Rubin [B, L, P], *Ruvel'* [B, P], *Ruven*
[L, P, V], *Ruven'* [L, P, V], *Ruvin,
Ryven* [P]

Ruzha [P]

Ruzin {Shem Aryeh}

Saad'ya \Saad'e\ {Bet Shmu'el}
Kinnuim: Khlavne, Soid

Saada {Shulkhan Gama'arekhet} Used
by Jews in Arab lands (Sh. Gam.).

Saadon \Saadojn\ {Kneset Hagedolah}

Sablika [L]

Sadok \Tsodojk\ {I Chronicles 12:29}
Variants: *Tsaduk* [B], *Tsodik* [L, V],
Tsodok [L], *Tsoduk* [L], *Tsudek,
Tsudik* [P], *Tsudya* [V]

Safatiya \Shfat'e\ {II Samuel 3:4}

Safronij [L]

Sagulo {Shulkhan Gama'arekhet}

Said {Shulkhan Gama'arekhet} Used by
Jews in Arab lands (Sh. Gam.); may
also be a kinnui for Saadya (Zh.R.).

Sal'nik [P]

Salafiel \Shaltiejl\ {Haggai 1:1} Kinnui:
Ajzik

Salam {Shulkhan Gama'arekhet} Used
by Jews in Eretz Israel (Sh. Gam.)

Salim {Shulkhan Gama'arekhet} Used
by Jews in Arab lands (Sh. Gam.).

Salmon \Salmojn\ {Ruth 4:21}

Samshel' [P]

Samson \Shimsojn\ {Judges 13:24}
Kinnuim: *Fabil, Fabul, Fabuli,
Fajvish, Fajvl, Fakhul', Vajvish, Vajvl*.
Variants: *Sampson, Shamshel'* [V],
Shamshon [V], *Shamson* [B, P, V],
Shimshejn, Shimshon [L], *Simson* [B,
P], *Sumshin* [L]

Samuil \Shmiejl'\ {Numbers 34:20}
Abbreviations: *Muli, Mulo*. Kinnuim:

*Bindit, Bishuf, Bonfant, Bundit,
Bunem, Bunfat, Fajvish, Fajvl,
Fajvuli, Fishel', Fishli, Flajshl,
Gankhin, Gel'man, Geronim* [P],
*Gil'man, Grojnem, Grojno, Kajaml,
Kunfradu, Muejd, Muejl, Muna,
Munie, Mutin, Mutun', Pashtir,
Pashtur, Shalmun, Shmelko, Shmilik*
[V], *Shmuejlo, Shmuli, Shmulik* [L],
*Shtajr, Shtir, Vajbus, Vajvish, Viblan,
Vishlajn, Vishlan, Vishli, Vishlin,
Vlajshl, Zajvel, Zajvl, Zanvel'* [V],
*Zanvil', Zanvl, Zavl, Zavlin, Ziml,
Zuml, Zumlin, Zunvil*. Variants:
Samoil [V], *Samuel'* [P], *Shemiel,
Shemiuel, Shmiel, Shmil* [L], *Shmojlo*
[B, L], *Shmuel* [B, L], *Shmuel',
Shmuil* [L], *Shmul'* [B, L, V],
Shmul'ke [V], *Shmul'ko* [V], *Shmulo*
[L], *Simuil* [B, L], *Smuel'* [B, L, P],
Zamuel' [B]

Santel' [B]

Sanvel' \Sanel'\ [B, L]

Sar-Sholojm \Sar-Shulojm\ {Bet
Shmu'el}

Saraf \Surof\ {II Chronicles 4:22}

Saul \Shuil\ {I Samuel 9:2} Kinnuim:
Shejlil, Shojejl, Shojl. Variants:
Savelij [B], *Shaul, Shaulko* [L], *Shejl'*
[V], *Shoel, Shoel'* [P], *Shoul*

Savej \Sheva\ {II Samuel 20:1}

Sebast'yan [P]

Sedekiya \Tsidkijo\ {II Kings 24:17}

Sejman [P]

Selemiya \Shelem'e\ {Jeremiah 37:3}

Semakhiya \Smakh'yugi\ {I Chronicles
26:7} Variants: *Sevakhiya, Smakhio*

Semej \Shima\ {II Samuel 16:5}

Sergij [B, V] Variants: *Sergej, Sergiusz*

Seruya \Tsruya\ {II Samuel 16:9}

Seudi {Shulkhan Gama'arekhet} Used
by Jews in Arab lands (Sh. Gam.).

Severin [P]

Sevna \Shevno\ {II Kings 18:18}

Shabos {Kneset Hagedolah}

Shabso {Bet Shmu'el}

Shabsoj {Shulkhan Gama'arekhet}

Shafat \Shufot\ {Numbers 13:5}
Variant: *Safat*

Shakhno {I Chronicles 3:21} Variants:
Sakhno, Shakhna [P]. May be kinnui

derived from Sholojm (Zh.R.), *Shakhne* [P]

Shalmo {Be'er Yitzchak}

Shalshel' \Shalshel\ [V]

Shalum \Shalim\ {I Chronicles 9:17} Variant: *Salum*

Shamkho {Shulkhan Gama'arekhet}

Shammaj {I Chronicles 2:28} Kinnui: *Shamkhe*. Variants: *Sammaj, Shame*

Shar'e [B]

Shavfaj \Shabsaj\ {Ezra 10:15} Abbreviations: *Shabsil, Shibi*. Kinnuim: *Gendil', Karashkat, Shabati, Shabsuli, Shapatan, Sheban, Sheftil, Shepe, Sheps, Shepsil, Sheve*. Variants: *Sabbataj, Savvafaj, Shaba* [V], *Shabsa* [P], *Shabse* [L], *Shabsel'* [B, V], *Shapsa* [P], *Shapsel'* [V], *Shapsiya* [V], *Shebsel'* [L], *Shepsel'* [L], *Shepsyu* [P]

Shebl' {Shulkhan Gama'arekhet} A new name, derived from Shabfaj.

Shejshes {Shulkhan Gama'arekhet}

Shem-Tojv {Bet Shmu'el}

Shema {I Chronicles 2:43} Variants: *Samaa, Shejma, Shima*

Shemaiya \Shmayugi\ {I Kings 12:22} Kinnui: *Shejmo*. Variants: *Semaiya, Shmaya* [P], *Simok* [L]

Shemariya \Shemar'e\ {II Chronicles 11:19} Kinnuim: *Makhraz, Shmeril, Shmerka* [V], *Shmerki, Szmerek* [P], *Zalman, Zel'kind, Zeligin, Zeligman, Zelik, Zelikman, Zelkin, Zelko*. Variants: *Samariya* [B], *Shemar'ya, Shemarie* [L], *Shemario, Shmir'ya* [V], *Shmorak* [V], *Smarko* [L]

Sheppel' [P]

Sheshan \Shejshon\ {I Chronicles 2:31} Variants: *Sasan, Shejshon, Shojshon*

Shevakh {Ohalei Shem} Variant: *Shejvakh* [V] This name can also be a kinnui of Solomon.

Shibsoi {Bet Shmu'el}

Shigmund [L] Distorted form of the Polish Zygmund.

Shillem {Genesis 46:24} Kinnuim: *Mshalejm, Mshilejm*. Variants: *Sellim, Shilim* [V]

Shiman {Shulkhan Gama'arekhet} Could have derived from either

Shimon (I Chronicles 4:20) or Simeon (Sh. Gam.).

Shimon \Shimojn\ {I Chronicles 4:20} *Shejmon* [V]

Shimriya \Shimri\ {I Chronicles 4:37} Kinnuim: *Shmeril, Shmerke, Zalmon*. Variant: *Simriya*

Shimshaj {Ezra 4:17}

Shimsia [P]

Shimsid [P]

Shiniur \Shiniir\ {Shemot Gittin}

Shiza \Shizo\ {I Chronicles 11:42}

Shlojmli {Kav Nuki}

Shlojmtsiejl' {Kav Nuki}

Shmechko [L]

Shmur [V]

Shneur \Shnejir\ {Bet Shmu'el} Kinnuim: *Vajvish, Vajvl, Zalman, Zel'kind, Zeligin, Zeligman, Zelik, Zelikin, Zelikman, Zelkin, Zelkind, Zelko, Ziskind, Zusa, Zushkin*. Variants: *Shneer,*[25] *Shneor, Sneer* [B]

Shnum [V]

Shokhojr \Shukhojr\ {Bet Shmu'el} Kinnui: *Shvartsman*. Variant: *Shokher*

Sholojm \Shulojm\ {Yerushalmi Demai 12:4} Kinnuim: *Fridman, Shakhne, Shul'man, Vridman*. Variants: *Salom* [L], *Sholaim* [L], *Sholem, Sholeme* [L], *Sholom* [L], *Sholomets* [L], *Shulajm* [L], *Shulem* [B, L], *Shulim* [L], *Solem*

Shopel' [V]

Shoval \Shojvol\ {I Chronicles 4:1} Kinnui: *Shevil'*. Variant: *Seval*

Shrago {Shulkhan Gama'arekhet} Kinnuim: *Fajvel', Fajvesh, Fevel'* [L]. Variants: *Shraga, Shrage*

Shrants \Shrentsil'\ {Kav Nuki}

Shtrojlan \Shtrojlin\ {Bet Shmu'el}

Shual \Shiol\ {I Chronicles 7:36} Kinnui: *Fuks*. Variant: *Suan*

Shulimo {Shulkhan Gama'arekhet}

Shulom {Kav Nuki}

Shunko {Bet Shmu'el}

Shunlajn {Bet Shmu'el}

Sid {Shulkhan Gama'arekhet}

Sigizmund [P]

Simeon \Shimojn\ {Genesis 29:33} Kinnuim: *Bajkh', Shejma, Shejnman, Shenko, Shinka* [L], *Shmel'ko, Viblin, Vilblin, Zimel, Zimlik, Zimlin, Zuml,*

Zumlin. Variants: *Semen* [V], *Semion* [V], *Shiman* [L], *Shimel'* [P, V], *Shimenko, Shimojn, Shimon* [V], *Shimontso* [L], *Shimshejn, Shimshon, Shmonko* [L], *Shmun'* [V], *Shmunya* [V], *Shomon* [V], *Siman* [L], *Simen* [B, L, P], *Simok, Simon* [L, V], *Zimen, Zimon* [L]

Simkho {Bet Shmu'el} Kinnuim: *Binem, Bunmo, Bunom, Frejdman, Vrejdman.* Variants: *Shimkhe, Simkhe*

Simma \Shimo\ {I Chronicles 2:13}

Simon-Tov \Simen-Tojv\ {Bet Shmu'el} Kinnui: *Samed*

Simyan [L]

Sinaj {Bet Shmu'el}, [L]

Siva \Tsiva\ {II Samuel 9:2}

Sivan [V]

Siyabuziya [P]

Slama {Shulkhan Gama'arekhet} Used by Jews in Eretz Yisrael (Sh. Gam.).

Sliman {Shulkhan Gama'arekhet}

Smokhno [L]

Smonko [L]

Sobol' [V]

Sofonia \Tsfan'e\ {Zephaniah 1:1} Kinnui: *Gilibi*

Solomon \Shlojmoj\ {II Samuel 5:14} Kinnuim: *Blankugi, Khimojn, Muli, Salamon, Salemon* [L], *Salmon, Shalmon, Shlioma, Shliome, Shliomka, Shlojma, Shlojme, Shlojmikhil, Shlojmitsl, Shlojmitso, Shlojmko, Shlojmshi, Shlojmtsil, Sholomon* [B], *Sholumko, Solamon* [P], *Solemon, Sulem, Valk, Velklin, Zal'kind, Zale* [P], *Zali, Zalko, Zalman, Zalo, Zel'kin, Zel'kind, Zeli, Zelig, Zeligin, Zeligman, Zelik, Zelikin, Zelikman, Zelko.* Variants: *Salomej* [P], *Salomo* [L], *Shlejma* [L], *Shlema* [L, V], *Shliom* [B], *Shlomo, Shloume* [B], *Szlama* [P], *Szlami* [P], *Szloma* [P]. The Spanish version of Solomon is Salamun.

Stanislaw [P]

Stefan [P]

Strozhan [L]

Suliman {Shulkhan Gama'arekhet}

Sumor \Isumor\ {Exodus 6:23} Variant: *Sumer*

Szczensnyj [P]

Szlam [P]

Tais {Shulkhan Gama'arekhet}

Takhlifo {Bet Shmu'el} Variants: *Takhlif, Takhlif*

Tal'ko [L]

Talman \Talmojn\ {I Chronicles 9:17}

Tam {Shulkhan Gama'arekhet}

Tamrij {Ohalei Shem}

Tanis {Shulkhan Gama'arekhet}

Tankha [P]

Tankhum \Tankhim\ {Bet Shmu'el} Variant: *Tankhel'* [L]

Tankhumo \Tankhimo\ {Ohalei Shem}

Tanokh [P]

Tarfon {Shulkhan Gama'arekhet} Variant: *Trifon*

Tavejl' \Tovejl\ {Isaiah 7:6} Kinnui: *Tevel'*

Teofil [P]

Tevaliya \Tval'yugi\ {I Chronicles 26:11} Kinnui: *Tevele*

Tikva \Fikvo\ {II Kings 22:14} Variant: *Fekuev*

Timro {Bet Shmu'el}

Tishbi {Shulkhan Gama'arekhet}

Tishko [L]

Tiviumi {Shulkhan Gama'arekhet} Variant: *Tivium*

Todros {Bet Shmu'el} Variants: *Feodor, Tadeusz* [P]. Derived from Menachem (Zh.R.), *Tavder, Teodor* [L, P], *Teodrus, Tevder* [B], *Tivium, Todres* [L], *Todris* [V], *Todrus* [B], *Todya* [V]. Todros may also be a folk name.

Tomasz [P]

Tov \Tojv\ {II Chronicles 17:8} This name is commonly used in conjunction with another word, for example, Shem-Tov, Yom-Tov, Simon-Tov (Sh. Gam.).

Tovi {Shulkhan Gama'arekhet}

Toviya \Tojvie\ {Nehemiah 2:10} *Tojvi.* Kinnuim: *Bonsineur, Guterman* [P], *Gutkind,*[26] *Gutman, Gutokind.* Variants: *Tabiyash* [L], *Tav'ya* [V], *Tev'e, Tev'ya* [V], *Tevel'* [L], *Tevele* [P], *Tobias* [L], *Tobiya, Tobiyash* [L], *Tov'e* [B], *Tov'eri* [P], *Tov'ya, Tovij* [L, V], *Tovit* [V], *Toviya* [V], *Tub'ya* [L], *Tubias* [B], *Tubiash* [L], *Tubiya* [L],

Tuv'ya [L], *Tuvie* [P]. Yiddish
translation of the adopted name
Gutman (Get Pashut), *Tuviya* [B, L]
Tovus {Kav Nuki}
Trojsh {Shulkhan Gama'arekhet}
Kinnui: Zalman
Tsadik {Bet Shmu'el} Kinnui: *Bibl'man*.
Variant: *Sadik* [P]
Tsalakh {Shulkhan Gama'arekhet}
Tsdoko {Bet Shmu'el}
Tsedek {Ohalei Shem}
Tselek {I Chronicles 11:39}
Tsemakh {Zakhariah 3:8} Kinnui:
Tsempl
Tsenik [P]
Tsezar [P]
Tshuo \Tshio\ {Shulkhan Gama'arekhet}
Furigo
Tshuvo \Tshivo\ {Shulkhan
Gama'arekhet}
Tsil'faj \Tsilsoj\ {I Chronicles 12:21}
Tsine [P]
Tsion \Tsiojn\ {Bet Shmu'el} Kinnui:
Vinturo
Tsisho {Bet Shmu'el}
Tsiviya \Tsivio\ {I Chronicles 8:9}
Tsogejl' {Shulkhan Gama'arekhet}
Tsur {Numbers 25:15} Variant: *Sur*
Tsuri {Bet Shmu'el}
Tsuriil \Tsuriejl\ {Numbers 3:35}
Tsurishaddaj \Tsurishadoj\ {Numbers
1:6}
Tsvi {Bet Shmu'el} Kinnuim: *Georgij*
[V], *Gershel'* [L], *Gershk* [P], *Gershko*,
Gershlik [P], *Gerts*, *Gertsik* [L],
Gertsko, *Gertsl*, *Gertso*, *Gesha*, *Girsh*
[B, L], *Girshko*, *Girshl*, *Girts*, *Girtsko*,
Girtsl, *Girtso*, *Grigorij* [B, P, V],
Grzegorz [P]. Variants: *Savi*, *Sevij*,
Tsevi
Ulla \Ilo\ {I Chronicles 7:39} Variants:
Ulan, *Ulo*
Uriil \Uriejl\ {I Chronicles 6:9} Variants:
Uriel, *Uriel'* [B, V], *Uriil*, *Uriil'*
Uriim [V]
Urij \Iri\ {Exodus 31:2} Kinnuim:
Fajbush, *Fajvis*, *Fajvish*, *Fajvl*, *Feul*
[B], *Gilibi*, *Gimplin*, *Gumo*, *Gumplin*,
Libman, *Lipa*. May have derived from
Lipman (O.R.), *Lipman*. This name
was also used by Christians in the

Middle Ages (O.R.), *Vajfesh*, *Vajvish*,
Vajvl, *Vibel'man*, *Viblamu*, *Viblan*.
Variants: *Ur'e*, *Ur'e* [P], *Ura* [L],
Urchik [L], *Ure* [P], *Urele* [P], *Urik*
[B], *Urish* [P], *Uriyash* [L], *Urka* [L],
Uryash [L], *Yurdko* [V], *Yuri* [B, L, P]
Urshrago \Irshrago\ {Bet Shmu'el}
Kinnuim: *Fab'yus* [V], *Fabian* [B],
Fajbusz [P], *Fajsh*, *Fajtel'* [B], *Fajve*
[B], *Fajvel'* [P, V], *Fajvish*, *Fajvl*,
Fajvus [B], *Fajvush* [P, V], *Fejbus* [P],
Filipp [B], *Vajvish*, *Vajvl*, *Valk*
Uziil \Uziejl\ {Exodus 6:18} Kinnui:
Labush. Variants: *Aziel'* [P], *Oziil*,
Uziel, *Zil'* [P], *Zil'ka* [P]
Uziya \Oziya\ {II Kings 15:30} Kinnui:
Enzil
Valentij [P]
Valerij [P]
Vaneya \Bnuyugi\ {I Chronicles 16:5}
Vani \Bani\ {I Chronicles 6:31} Kinnui:
Boni
Varak \Burok\ {Judges 4:6} Variant:
Barak
Varakhiya \Everekhyugi\ {Isaiah 8:2}
Varukh \Borukh\ {Jeremiah 32:12}
Abbreviation: *Bnoio*. Kinnuim: *Banet*,
Barukh [P], *Bash*, *Bendet* [V], *Bendid*,
Bendit. This name was also used by
Christians in the Middle Ages (O.R.),
Benedikt [P], *Benet*, *Bindit*, *Borek* [P],
Bundit. Variants: *Barukh* [P], *Borekh*
[V], *Borokh* [V], *Burakh* [V], *Burukh*
[V]. Varukh means blessed, which has
the same meaning as Benedict
(Russian), or Bendet (Jewish-Russian),
or Benedictus (Roman languages). It is
incorrect to translate this name as
Boris (Pg.).
Vasilij [P]
Veniamin {Genesis 35:18} Kinnuim:
Bajnim [V], *Bajnus* [L], *Bejnash* [L],
Bejnes [B, L], *Bejnus* [L], *Bena* [L],
Benes [B, L], *Beni* [L], *Benish* [P],
Beniyamin, *Benjomin*, *Benyash* [L],
Bima, *Bimla*, *Bina* [L], *Binash* [L],
Binim [V], *Binlajn*, *Binlin*, *Binom*,
Binush, *Binyash*, *Bishka*, *Bonek* [P],
Bunam, *Bunash*, *Buni*, *Bunim*,
Bunish, *Bunmo*, *Lubu*, *Nyuma*, *Valbil*,
Valblain, *Valchko* [L], *Valko* [V],

Valvlajn, Vavila, Vejlka [L], *Vejlo,*
Vel'vish, Vele, Veli, Velva [B], *Velvil,*
Velvish, Velvul, Veniyamin, Vilf [V],
Voftsi, Vol'ka, Vol'ko, Volf, Volflajn,
Volfo, Volle, Volvish [L], *Vova, Vovi,*
Vovtsi, Vul'f, Vulf [B, L], *Zeev, Zejv,*
Zev, Ziv. Variants: *Bejomin* [V],
Ben'yamin [L, V], *Ben'yomin,*
Benyumen [V], *Benyumin* [V],
Biniomin, Ven'yamin [B, L, V],
Venyamin [B]

Veria \Brio\ {I Chronicles 23:11}
Variant: *Beria*

Verzellij \Barzilaj\ {II Samuel 17:27}

Veseliil \Betsale'jl\ {Exodus 31:2}
Kinnuim: *Btsalke, Btshulka, Btsulka,*
Ptshulka, Tsal' [V], *Tsejl'io, Tsale,*
Tsalek, Tsalel, Tsalel' [L, P], *Tsalik,*
Tsalka [V], *Tsalko* [L, P], *Tsalya,*
Tsejlio, Tsylka [P]. Variants: *Betsalel*
[V], *Betsalel'* [V], *Veseleil, Veseliil*

Vikentij [P]

Vil'gel'm [B, L, P]

Vil'khel'm [B, L, P]

Villiam [L]

Vilyam [L, P]

Vintsent [P] From Polish: Wincent

Virgo {Shulkhan Gama'arekhet}

Vitoshin [L]

Vits {Shulkhan Gama'arekhet}

Vladislav [P] From Polish: Wladislaw

Vooz \Bojaz\ {Ruth 2:1} Variants: *Beez*
[V], *Bejaz* [V], *Boyaz* [V], *Vaaz*

Vyacheslav [P]

Yakhod [V]

Zael [B]

Zakar {Shulkhan Gama'arekhet} *See*
Zakhariya.

Zakhariya \Zkhar'e\ {II Kings 14:29}
Kinnuim: *Mendl, Mendlan, Mendlin,*
Menlin, Zvedl. Variants: *Skhar'e,*
Skhariya, Zahkar, Zakhariash [B, L],
Zakharij, Zehkar'ya, Zekhariash [P],
Zekhariya [V], *Zkharia* [P], *Zkhario*

Zakkaj {Ezra 2:9} Variant: *Zakhej*

Zakkur \Zakir\ {Numbers 13:4} *See*
Zakhariya.

Zamel [P]

Zamiru {Shulkhan Gama'arekhet}

Zara \Zerakh\ {Genesis 38:30} Variants:
Zarakh [L], *Zhurakh* [L, V], *Zora,*

Zorakh [L], *Zorokh* [L, V], *Zorukh* [P],
Zurakh [V]

Zavdi {Nehemiah 11:17}

Zavdiil \Zavdiejl\ {I Chronicles 28:2}

Zavulon \Zvilin\ {Genesis 30:20}
Variants: *Zebulon, Zebulun* [P],
Zevilin [P], *Zevulon, Zevulun, Zvulon*

Zdislav [P]

Zegfried [L]

Zejn {Shulkhan Gama'arekhet} Means
beautiful in Turkish.

Zenokh [P]

Zenon \Zelik\ [L]

Zerakhya \Zrakhie\ {I Chronicles 5:32}

Zevadiya \Zvad'e\ {Ezra 8:8} Kinnui:
Zvedil'. Variant: *Zvadio*

Zevel' [L]

Zhanno [B]

Zigbor [V]

Zigmun [P]

Zikhri {Exodus 6:21} *See* Zakhariya.

Zima \Zimo\ {Pg.} *Zimel'*

Zimri {Numbers 25:14}

Zimro {Shulkhan Gama'arekhet}

Ziv \Zejv\ {Judges 7:25} *Vilf* [V], *Vul'f,*
Vulf [B, L]. Variants: *Zeev, Zev*

Ziza \Zizo\ {I Chronicles 4:37}

Zukhen [P]

Zunlin \Zulin\ {Bet Shmu'el} Variant:
Zilin [V]

Zus'a {Bet Shmu'el} *Ziza, Zizel'*

Zutra {Shulkhan Gama'arekhet}

Zuza {Talmud}

Zvul \Zvil\ {Judges 9:30} Kinnuim:
Sanvil',[27] *Zavel, Zibel'*

Notes

1. Bintsi, Buntse, Bune derive from Bona (German for kind). The Old Germanic forms of this name, Gutor and Gurlein gave rise to the German-Jewish variants Gite, Gitl and Gise, and to the Russian Dobrish (O.R.).
2. Derived from Iudif' (O.R.).
3. Calque of Iokhvedunya.
4. May have also derived from Gela (Pg.).
5. Misspelled Lidiya.
6. May have derived from Bess—abbreviated Elisabeth (O.R.).
7. Jewish and Chaldean name. Phonetically, the sound *ab* is strange in the Russian language and is often transliterated as *av*.
8. This name was also used by Christians in the Middle Ages (O.R.).
9. Also pronounced Zishkind; the proper form is Zyus'kind. The name was used in Russia paired with Alexander (Alexander-Ziskind). In actuality it is a spoiled translation of the German Siegeskind—a child of victory. (O.R.).
10. From the Greek, Alexandros, meaning protector of men. According to the Talmud (Tamid 31b), when Alexander the Great concurred Palestine in 333 B.C.E., he demanded that a statue of himself be erected in the Temple.
11. According to Pogorel'skij, Khanon is a root name, see II Samuel 10:1.
12. Means God's mercy, the form is a reverse of Elhanan.
13. A distorted form of the German Lowe. Arye was used by Russian Jews only to communicate with Gentiles. During religious ceremonies, the name was used only in its Hebrew version or in combination with other sacred names (e.g. Iuda- Ariya, Iuda-Lejb, Ariya-Lejb, Iud, Iuda-Lejb, Lejb).
14. According to Genesis 49:9, it was Judah's nickname. It translates into Russian as Lion, Leo, Lev, Leontij (Pg.).
15. The Italian version was Diofatto (Pg.).
16. This name was also used by Christians in the Middle Ages (O.R.).
17. Diminutive form of Hans/Johannes; it corresponds to the biblical Yohanan and the Russian Ioann, Ivan.
18. Asriel should not be confused with Azriel.
19. Bejbe was also considered as a pet form of Lejb (Pg.).
20. Nickname of Solomon; it means beloved of the Lord. When translated into other languages, it gave rise to Feofil (Greek), Amadeus (Roman), Gottlib (German), and Bogolyub, Bogomil, Bogumil (Russian).
21. Khokhom is not related to Isaac etymologically. It was used as a pet name of a newborn named officially after a deceased father or grandfather. Sacred name would be forgotten and the boy was called to read the Torah as Abraham or Isaac (Tuv Gittin).
22. Means love in Russian; it is used primarily as a feminine name.
23. Mendl derives from Man, analogous to the formations Fan-Fendl and Kan-Kendl.
24. The name Tsakhrajm most likely is a scribe's error; the correct spelling is Tsakhrajs, which also has been used for Issachar and Zachariah by non-Jews (N.Sh.).
25. According to one legend, Shneer (which means two flames) once was the nickname of a young bridegroom whose father was called Meer (one who shines) and father-in-law—Ur (flame). (S. ben D. Halevi, Nikhmat Shiva).
26. Gutkind is derived from the German translation of the root T'ov of the name Toviya (B.Sh.).
27. Sanvil' may have also derived from Samuel.

List of Secular Names and Their Root Names

Listed below are the everyday secular names—*kinnuim*—that were used in Russia at the turn of the twentieth century. The first list is of feminine names, the second of masculine names. The first name in every entry is the *kinnui*; the second is the root name. Where the two names are identical, it means the *kinnui* is a root name. For example, it shows that Adasa is a variant of Gadassa. When a *kinnui* has more than one root, it is listed more than once; each line representing a different root name. For example, Adelya is a *kinnui* of both Aida and Ejda. A list of all root names appears in Section II—Jewish Names Used in Russia, Including Known Derivations, Abbreviations and Distortions.

Feminine Names

Ada=Ada
Adaliya=Adaliya
Adasa=Gadassa
Adeliya=Ajda
Adeliya=Ejda
Adelya=Ajda
Adelya=Ejda
Adina=Adina
Afidra=Afidra
Afidupula=Afidupula
Afinda=Afinda
Afru=Afru
Afundupula=Aureliya
Agaf'ya=Agaf'ya
Agar'=Agar'
Agata=Agata
Aiola=Aiola
Ajda=Ajda
Ajdil=Ejda
Ajdla=Ejda
Ajdlya=Ejda
Akhinoam=Akhinoama
Akhinoama=Akhinoama
Akhrudupla=Akhrudupla
Akhsa=Akhsa
Aleksandra=Aleksandra
Alfdina=Alfdina
Alfguta=Buntse
Algugr=Algugr
Aligra=Aligra
Alika=Ela
Alisa=Alisa
Alitsiya=Alitsiya

Alojzu=Alojzu
Alta=Alta
Altaduna=Altaduna
Altaruna=Altaruna
Aluna=Aluna
Alzguta=Guta
Alzgute=Dobra
Ama=Ama
Amado=Amado
Amata=Amata
Amato=Amado
Ameliya=Ameliya
Amgutsha=Amgutsha
Amina=Emino
Amira=Amira
Amiro=Amira
Amitala=Khumutal'
Amna=Amna
Anashta=Anashta
Anastasi=Anastasiya
Anastasiya=Anastasiya
Andza=Andza
Anelya=Anna
Aneta=Anna
Angila=Angila
Anna=Anna
Anne=Anna
Annelya=Anna
Anneta=Anna
Ansta=Ansta
Antonina=Antonina
Antoniya=Antoniya
Antsha=Antsha

Anyuta=Anna
Arandra=Arandra
Araviana=Araviana
Arduinaia=Arduinaia
Arginti=Arginti
Arkhudu=Arkhudu
Arkhundu=Arkhundu
Asa=Asa
Ashpiransha=Esperansa
Ashruga=Ashruga
Ashtapla=Ashtapla
Asila=Asila
Asila=Gofoliya
Askhan'=Akhsa
Asma=Asnefa
Asna=Asnefa
Asnat=Asnefa
Asnefa=Asnefa
Aster=Esfir'
Astna=Asnefa
Astru=Astru
Ataduna=Ataduna
Ataliya=Ataliya
Atara=Atara
Aureliya=Aureliya
Avgali=Avigeya
Avgusta=Avgusta
Avgusti=Avgusta
Aviga=Avigeya
Avigeya=Avigeya
Avisaga=Avisaga
Avtala=Avtala
Azibuina=Azibuina

Aziza=Aziza
Baba=Baba
Babe=Baba
Babetli=Babetli
Babtsi=Baba
Babuk=Babuk
Badyana=Badyana
Bagdana=Begodna
Bagdana=Bogodna
Bajla=Valla
Bajlya=Valla
Bajn=Bajn
Bajni=Bontsie
Bal'bina=Bal'bina
Bal'cha=Valla
Balgusha=Virsasiya
Balita=Balita
Balshojn=Balshojn
Barojna=Barojna
Bas-Sheva=Bas-Sheva
Bas'e=Bif'ya
Bas'e=Virsaviya
Bas'ka=Eirsaviya
Bas'ka=Virsaviya
Base=Bif'ya
Bash-Sheva=Virsaviya
Basha=Virsaviya
Basheva=Virsaviya
Bashiva=Virsaviya
Bashke=Bif'ya
Basi=Bif'ya
Basio=Bif'ya
Basiya=Bif'ya
Bassheva=Virsaviya
Bastsion=Bastsion
Bastsiya=Bif'ya
Basya=Bif'ya
Basya=Villa
Batsheva=Virsaviya
Baya=Valla
Baza=Baza
Beatrisa=Beatrisa
Bebagani=Bebagani
Begodna=Begodna
Beilaki=Beilaki
Bejla=Iezavel'
Bejla=Nezabel'
Bejla=Valla
Bejlaj=Valla
Bejle=Valla
Bejlka=Valla
Bejlo=Valla

Bejltsi=Valla
Bele=Valla
Belkha=Belkha
Bella=Valla
Bella=Villa
Belle=Villa
Belta=Valla
Belta=Villa
Bentsya=Bentsya
Berakha=Berakha
Berakha=Berakha
Berin=Berin
Berta=Berta
Berte=Berta
Bess=Bess
Bessa=Pesa
Besya=Bif'ya
Betshil=Bas-Sheva
Betshil=Virsaviya
Betshl=Virsaviya
Betti=Betti
Bezya=Bif'ya
Bif'ya=Bif'ya
Bilajda=Bilajda
Bilkhya=Valla
Bilkovo=Bilkovo
Billya=Valla
Bilta=Valla
Bine=Bontsie
Bingi=Bingi
Bintsya=Bontsie
Binya=Bontsie
Bisio=Bif'ya
Bitsha=Vita
Blanka=Blanka
Blima=Bluma
Blimche=Bluma
Blimkhen=Bluma
Bliml=Bluma
Blimla=Bluma
Bliomo=Bluma
Bluma=Bluma
Blumlin=Bluma
Bnida=Eanda
Bogdana=Bogodno
Bogodna=Bogodna
Bogodno=Bogodno
Boigdana=Bogodna
Bontsie=Bontsie
Bootsie=Bootsie
Brajna=Brana
Brajndel'=Brana

Brajndla=Brana
Brajne=Brana
Brajntsha=Branf
Brajntsya=Brana
Brana=Brana
Brandl=Brana
Brandlya=Brana
Branf=Branf
Brendlin=Brana
Brendlya=Brana
Brenya=Brana
Brigida=Brigida
Brikha=Brikha
Brina=Brina
Briva=Briva
Brojna=Brina
Brojneta=Brana
Brojnita=Brojnita
Brojnlajn=Brana
Brojnlin=Brana
Brokha=Berakha
Bronislava=Bronislava
Broniya=Brana
Bronka=Brana
Bru=Bru
Brukha=Berakha
Brukhche=Berakha
Bruna=Brana
Brunilin=Brana
Brunlin=Brana
Bryukha=Berakha
Bshajtsa=Bshajtsa
Bstsion=Bstsion
Budina=Budina
Buelan=Bootsie
Buga=Luna
Buina=Bontsie
Bujna=Bontsie
Bukha=Bukha
Bula=Bula
Bulada=Bulada
Bulisa=Bulisa
Bulitsa=Bulisa
Bulta=Bulta
Bulu=Bula
Bun'ka=Bontsie
Buna=Bontsie
Bunanv=Bontsie
Bundaga=Bundaga
Bunguo=Bunguo
Bunila=Bontsie
Bunkhin=Bontsie

Bunla=Bontsie
Bunlajn=Bontsie
Bunlin=Bontsie
Buntse=Buntse
Buntsya=Bontsie
Bunuza=Bunuza
Bunya=Bontsie
Charna=Charna
Cherna=Charna
Chesa=Chesa
Chicha=Chisha
Chidzana=Tsisha
Chila=Sepfora
Chillo=Tsilla
Chinya=Chinya
Chisha=Chisha
Chiza=Tsisha
Chizha=Chisha
Dagavaj=Dagavaj
Dajamanti=Dajamanti
Dajkha=Dajamanti
Dajkha=Dajkha
Dajla=Dajamanti
Dajla=Dajla
Dajna=Dajamanti
Dajna=Dajna
Dakha=Dajamanti
Dakha=Dajkha
Dakhe=Iegudifa
Dana=Dana
Danya=Dana
Danya=Dona
Dar'cha=Dariya
Dariya=Dariya
Darna=Darna
Dashka=Dariya
Dasya=Gadassa
Daube=Doba
Debora=Devora
Debosya=Devora
Deiorya=Deiorya
Dejra=Devora
Denya=Dina
Devora=Devora
Did'ya=Iedidia
Didiya=Didiya
Dilikada=Dilikada
Dimanti=Dajamanti
Din'che=Dina
Din'ka=Dina
Dina=Dina
Dine=Dina

Dintsya=Dinya
Dinya=Dina
Dinya=Dinya
Dishiada=Dishiada
Dishka=Dariya
Dissa=Dissa
Doba=Devora
Doba=Doba
Dobar=Dobra
Dobche=Doba
Dobka=Doba
Dobra=Dobra
Dobre=Dobra
Dobrish=Devora
Dobrush=Devora
Dobrusha=Devora
Dobrusha=Dobra
Dobrusya=Devora
Dobtsi=Doba
Dojkhana=Dojkhana
Dojltsa=Dojltsa
Doltse=Toivsa
Doltse=Tol'tsa
Domanya=Domanya
Dona=Dona
Donka=Dina
Dora=Dora
Dorota=Dorotea
Dorotea=Dorotea
Doshe=Doshe
Dovsa=Devora
Drashna=Drazna
Drasna=Drazna
Drasne=Drazna
Drazil=Drezil'
Drazna=Drazna
Drejza=Drezil'
Drejzel'=Drezil
Drejzya=Drezil'
Drezel'=Drezil'
Drezil'=Drezil'
Drezil=Drezil
Drezlya=Drezil'
Drezya=Drezil'
Drobna=Drobna
Duinaya=Duinaya
Dul'sa=Dul'sa
Dul'tsa=Dul'sa
Duna=Dona
Dunaj=Dona
Duni=Dona
Duntsya=Dina

Dunya=Dina
Dunya=Iokhaved
Duranta=Duranta
Dushil'=Dushil'
Dushl'=Dushl'
Dushna=Dushna
Dutsl'=Dutsl'
Duziadu=Duziadu
Dvejra=Devora
Dvera=Devora
Dveril'-Bina=Devora
Dvesya=Devora
Dvora=Devora
Dvorka=Devora
Dvorsha=Devora
Dvosha=Devora
Dvosya=Devora
Dyshlya=Dushil'
Eanda=Eanda
Ede=Eida
Ede=Ejda
Edel'=Ejda
Edel'=Ejda
Edisa=Eida
Edit=Edit
Edzha=Ejda
Egla=Khogla
Eida=Eida
Eiea=Eiea
Eirsaviya=Eirsaviya
Eizhel'=Eizhel'
Ejda=Ejda
Ejda=Ejda
Ejde=Ejda
Ejdi=Eiea
Ejdi=Ejda
Ejdl=Ejda
Ejdla=Ejda
Ejdlya=Ejda
Ejdsha=Ejdsha
Ejdya=Ejdya
Ejga=Ejga
Ejgila=Ejga
Ejgle=Ejga
Ejlka=Ela
Ejzhel'=Ejzhel'
Ekaterina=Ekaterina
Ekhlin=Iokhaved
Ekuta=Ekuta
El'cha=Elta
El'frida=El'frida
El'ka=Ela

El'za=El'za
Ela=Ela
Elainor=Eleonora
Elena=Elena
Eleonora=Eleonora
Elina=Elina
Elisa=Elisa
Elisaveta=Elisaveta
Elisheva=Elisaveta
Eliza=Liya
Elizaveta=Elisaveta
Elize=Liya
Elka=Ela
Elke=Ela
Elke=Elle
Elkla=Ela
Ella=Ela
Elle=Elle
Ellya=Ela
Elta=Elta
Elzbieta=Elisaveta
Em-Barakha=Em-Barakha
Em-Saad=Em-Saad
Emalie=Emiliya
Emiliya=Emiliya
Emino=Emino
Emira=Emira
Emma=Emma
Emme=Emma
Endya=Endya
Eniga=Eniga
Enta=Enta
Ente=Enta
Entil'=Enta
Entl'=Enta
Entlin=Enta
Erish=Erish
Erka=Erka
Erl=Erl
Erna=Ernestina
Ernestina=Ernestina
Erusa=Erusha
Erusa=Ierusha
Erusha=Erusha
Esfir'=Esfir'
Esli=Asila
Esperansa=Esperansa
Esperanza=Esperansa
Essel'=Essel'
Ester=Esfir'
Estrula=Esfir'
Estusha=Estusha

Et'ka=Eta
Eta=Eta
Ete=Esfir'
Eti=Eta
Etil=Eta
Etis=Eta
Etka=Eta
Etki=Eta
Etl'=Esfir'
Etl=Eta
Etlya=Eta
Etta=Ita
Ette=Eta
Eva=Eva
Eva=Eva
Evel'=Evel'
Evelina=Evelina
Evgenie=Evgenie
Evgeniya=Evgeniya
Evva=Eva
Evzel'=Evzel'
Faga=Fejga
Fajga=Fejga
Fajna=Fajna
Fale=Feliksa
Fane=Fanni
Fanni=Fanni
Fanya=Fanni
Fejcha=Fejcha
Fejga=Fejga
Fejge=Fejga
Fejgi=Fejga
Fejgl=Fejga
Fejgla=Fejga
Fejgu=Fejga
Fekuev=Fikva
Fel'ka=Feliksa
Fela=Feliksa
Feliksa=Feliksa
Felitsie=Feliksa
Felitsiya=Feliksa
Feliya=Feliksa
Felya=Feliksa
Fenya=Fanni
Feofila=Feofiliya
Feofila=Teofiliya
Feofiliya=Feofiliya
Feofilya=Feofilya
Ferka=Ferka
Fersa=Tirtsi
Fiala=Fiala
Fikva=Fikva

Fil'ka=Feliksa
Filipina=Filipina
Fimna=Fimna
Finaj=Finaj
Finklya=Finklya
Firmuza=Firmuza
Fishel'=Fishel'
Flora=Flora
Fluma=Fluma
Flumu=Fluma
Fojgil=Fejga
Fojgl=Fejga
Fojgla=Fejga
Fomar=Fomar
Frade=Fradi
Fradelya=Fradi
Fradi=Fradi
Fradi=Fradi
Fradka=Fradi
Fradsya=Fradi
Fradya=Fradi
Frajdl=Fradi
Frajdl=Vrajda
Frajdlya=Fradi
Frajna=Frajna
Frajndlya=Frajna
Fralya=Fralya
Framet=Frima
Franka=Frantsiska
Frantsiska=Frantsiska
Franya=Frantsiska
Frasha=Frasha
Freda=Frederika
Frederika=Frederika
Frejda=Fradi
Frejda=Simkha
Frejda=Vrajda
Frejdal'=Simkha
Frejdl'=Fradi
Frejna=Frejna
Frekha=Frekha
Frendlya=Frajna
Fridya=Fralya
Frima=Frima
Frimet=Frima
Frimeta=Frima
Frinejt=Frajna
Frineta=Frajna
Frineta=Frejna
Frome=Frima
Fronishka=Frantsiska
Fronya=Frajna

Frume=Frima
Frumt=Frima
Fula=Feliksa
Gadasa=Gadasa
Gadase=Gadasa
Gadassa=Gadassa
Gadasse=Gadasse
Gadassya=Gadassya
Gadesa=Gadasa
Gagara=Agar'
Gaila=Gela
Gajdi=Gajdi
Gajl'=Gajl'
Gajl=Gajl
Gajl=Gajl
Gajla=Gela
Gajla=Gelya
Gajn=Gajl
Gal=Gal
Gala=Gala
Galaj=Galaj
Gale=Gela
Gali=Gali
Galia=Galia
Galya=Gala
Galya=Gela
Gamila=Gamila
Gandel'=Gandel'
Gane=Anna
Ganele=Anna
Ganka=Anna
Ganku=Anna
Ganla=Anna
Ganna=Anna
Gannya=Anna
Gantil'=Gantil'
Gantsya=Anna
Ganuna=Anna
Garieta=Garieta
Gavriela=Gavriela
Gazila=Gazila
Gazla=Gazla
Gebora=Gebora
Gedviga=Gedviga
Geidel'khin=Geni
Gejdya=Gejdya
Gejela=Gejla
Gejla=Gejla
Gekhl=Gekhl
Gela=Gela
Gele=Khela
Geli=Gela

Gelkhi=Gelkhi
Gelya=Elena
Gelya=Gelya
Gena=Anna
Gena=Gena
Genda=Ginda
Gendil=Ginda
Gendl'=Gena
Gendla=Gena
Gendli=Gena
Gendlya=Gena
Gene=Gena
Geni=Gena
Geni=Geni
Geniya=Gena
Genka=Anna
Genrieta=Genrieta
Genrika=Genrika
Gerta=Gerta
Gertruda=Gertruda
Gertsega=Gertsega
Geruna=Gruna
Gesa=Gesa
Gesha=Gesa
Gesha=Gisa
Gesha=Gisa
Gesha=Gusiya
Geshka=Gesa
Gesko=Gisa
Gesko=Gusiya
Gesn=Gesa
Gestera=Esfir'
Gesya=Gesa
Gesya=Gisa
Gesya=Gusiya
Geta=Geta
Getaskhen=Gadasse
Geti=Geti
Gil'tsya=Gela
Gilo=Gilo
Gilya=Gilo
Gima=Gima
Gimel'trojt=Gima
Giml=Gima
Gimla=Gima
Gina=Gina
Ginandl=Ginandl
Ginda=Ginda
Gindale=Ginda
Ginde=Ginda
Gindel'=Ginda
Gindl=Ginda

Gindlajgin=Ginda
Gindlajkhin=Ginda
Gindlajn=Ginda
Gindlin=Ginda
Gindlya=Ginda
Ginedla=Ginandl
Ginenda=Ginandl
Ginenden=Ginandl
Ginendil=Ginandl
Ginendlya=Ginandl
Ginesa=Ginesa
Ginesya=Ginesa
Ginesya=Gnesa
Ginka=Anna
Ginka=Anna
Gintil'=Gantil'
Ginya=Gina
Girana=Girana
Girasa=Girasa
Girglaj=Girglaj
Giri=Giri
Giriya=Giri
Girmuza=Girmuza
Gis'e=Gisa
Gis'e=Gusiya
Gisa=Gesa
Gisa=Gisa
Gisa=Guttsya
Gisha=Gusya
Giska=Gesa
Giska=Gesa
Gissa=Gisa
Gissa=Gusiya
Gisse=Gesa
Gisse=Gisa
Gisse=Gusiya
Gissya=Gesa
Gissya=Gisa
Gita=Gita
Gita=Guta
Gitel'=Dobra
Gitl=Guta
Gitla=Guta
Gitli=Guta
Gitlin=Guta
Gitlya=Guta
Gitsla=Gmul
Gitslya=Guttsya
Gitsya=Guttsya
Gitta=Guta
Gitte=Guta
Gitul=Guta

Glaj=Gela
Glik=Glika
Glika=Glika
Glikel'=Glika
Glikkhen=Glika
Glikkhin=Glika
Gliklya=Glika
Glikman=Glika
Gluk=Glika
Gmul=Gmul
Gnana=Gnana
Gnedl=Ginandl
Gnejdil=Ginandl
Gnendel'=Ginandl
Gnendil=Gnese
Gnendl=Ginandl
Gnesa=Gnesa
Gnese=Gnesa
Gnese=Gnese
Gnesha=Gnesa
Gnesya=Gnesya
Gnesya=Gnesya
Gnishe=Gnesa
Gnondel'=Ginandl
Gnoshe=Gnesa
Godes=Gadassya
Godil=Gudl
Godla=Gudl
Godlya=Gudl
Godya=Gudl
Gofoliya=Gofoliya
Goga=Goga
Gogor=Agar'
Gojka=Gojka
Gojldkhen=Golda
Gol'd'yana=Golda
Golda=Golda
Golde=Golda
Golya=Gela
Gomera=Gomera
Gosiya=Gisa
Gosya=Gisa
Gosya=Gusya
Gotfrida=Gotfrida
Gotlya=Guta
Grant=Grant
Grasal=Grasya
Grasayuza=Gratsiya
Grasil'za=Grasya
Grasiuza=Gratsiya
Grasya=Grasya
Gratsiya=Gratsiya

Gratsya=Gratsiya
Gresil=Grasya
Grine=Grine
Gritshl'=Gritshl'
Griva=Griva
Grone=Gruna
Grukha=Grukha
Gruna=Gruna
Grune=Gruna
Grunt=Grant
Grunya=Grunya
Grunya=Grunya
Gudajkha=Gudajkha
Gudajkhi=Gudajkha
Gudel=Gudl
Gudes=Gadassa
Gudesl=Gadassa
Gudessa=Gadassa
Gudi=Gadassa
Gudi=Gudl
Gudl=Ejda
Gudl=Gudl
Gudlya=Gudl
Gudya=Gudl
Guej=Guej
Gugara=Gugara
Gugorkhen=Agar'
Gugorl=Agar'
Gugr=Algugr
Gulda=Golda
Gulda=Gudl
Gulin=Gulin
Guni=Guni
Gurdikhen=Gurdikhen
Gushta=Gushta
Gusiya=Gusiya
Gusta=Gustava
Gustava=Gustava
Gusya=Gisa
Gusya=Gusya
Guta=Guta
Gute=Dobra
Gutel'=Dobra
Guti=Guta
Gutil'=Guta
Gutkhin=Guta
Gutlajn=Gita
Gutliba=Gutliba
Gutlya=Guta
Gutrejd=Dobra
Gutrid=Gutrid
Gutsya=Kutsa

Guttsya=Guttsya
Gyugo=Gyugo
Gzala=Gzala
Iaad=Iaad
Iakhaved=Iakhaved
Ial=Ejdya
Ianna=Ioganna
Ida=Iegudifa
Idessa=Iegudifa
Idesso=Iegudifa
Iedidia=Iedidia
Iegojsheva=Iegojsheva
Iegoshavas=Iosavef
Iegudifa=Iegudifa
Iegudifya=Iegudifya
Iegudit=Iegudifa
Iekholiya=Iekholiya
Ierka=Ierka
Ierl'=Ierusha
Ierusha=Ierusha
Iese=Iese
Iezabel'=Iezabel'
Iezabel'=Iezabel'
Iezavel'=Iezavel'
Iidasi=Iegudifa
Iides=Iegudifa
Iita=Iegudifa
Iita=Ita
Ioanna=Ioganna
Ioganna=Ioganna
Iojkha=Iokhaved
Iojtlin=Iokhaved
Iokha=Iokhaved
Iokhaved=Iokhaved
Iokhaveda=Iokhaved
Iokhebed=Iokhaved
Iokhejl'=Iokhl'
Iokhil'=Iokhl'
Iokhl'=Iokhl'
Iokhla=Iokhaved
Iokhlin=Iokhaved
Iokhved=Iokhaved
Iokhvedunya=Iokhaved
Iokhvet=Iokhaved
Iola=Aiola
Ionta=Enta
Ior=Ior
Iora=Iora
Iore=Ierusha
Iosavef=Iosavef
Iosfa=Iosfa
Iospa=Iospa

Ioveta=Ioveta
Iozefa=Iospa
Ira=Ira
Iras=Ira
Iras=Iras
Ire=Ire
Irena=Ira
Irina=Irina
Irinaj=Irina
Irma=Irma
Irmut=Irmut
Isabela=Iezabel'
Ishklavuna=Ishklavuna
Ishkluna=Ishkluna
Ishruga=Ashruga
Ishtrima=Ishtrima
Ishtruga=Ashruga
Ishtruna=Ishtruna
Ismiralada=Ismiralada
Ispiransa=Ispiransa
Istajso=Istajso
Istamta=Istamta
Istarupula=Istarupula
Isterlaj=Isterlaj
Istmu=Istmu
Istrungila=Istrungila
Ita=Ita
Ita=Ita
Itale=Ita
Ite=Ita
Itel'=Ita
Iti=Ita
Itil=Ita
Itka=Ita
Itkis=Ita
Itkoshe=Ita
Itla=Ita
Itle=Ita
Iudasa=Iegudifa
Iudel'=Ejdya
Iudif'=Iegudifa
Iudis=Iegudifya
Iyudaliya=Iyudaliya
Iyudita=Iegudifa
Iyura=Iyura
Izabela=Iezabel'
Izabela=Izevel'
Izevel'=Izevel'
Izmirilada=Izmirilada
Kachka=Kachka
Kadina=Kadina
Kagana=Kagana

Kaila=Kejla
Kailya=Kejla
Kajle=Kejla
Kajrasa=Girasa
Kalaj=Kalu
Kali=Kalu
Kalu=Kalu
Kamarida=Kamarida
Kamiliya=Kamiliya
Kara=Kara
Karna=Karna
Karolina=Karolina
Karolya=Karolina
Kasena=Kasena
Kasha=Kasha
Kashina=Kashina
Kashtu=Kashtu
Katerina=Ekaterina
Katlya=Katlya
Kazina=Kazina
Kejla=Kejla
Kenda=Kenya
Kende=Kenya
Kendil'=Kenya
Kendl=Kenya
Kentsina=Kentsina
Kenya=Kenya
Ketsina=Ketsina
Kha=Kha
Khada=Khada
Khaf'che=Eva
Khajcha=Khaya
Khajenko=Anna
Khajka=Khaya
Khajke=Anna
Khajma=Khajmo
Khajma=Khojvo
Khajmo=Khajmo
Khajnke=Anna
Khajtsya=Khaya
Khakhnashik=Anna
Khalu=Khalu
Khalvo=Khela
Khamama=Khamama
Khamutala=Khumutal'
Khana=Anna
Khancha=Anna
Khanele=Anna
Khanie=Anna
Khaninashum=Anna
Khanka=Anna
Khankhin=Anna

Khanna=Anna
Khanne=Anna
Khanne=Anna
Khantsi=Anna
Khanuko=Mariam
Khanula=Anna
Khanuna=Anna
Khanuna=Khanuna
Khanush=Anna
Khanusha=Anna
Khanya=Anna
Khas'ka=Anna
Khasa=Anna
Khase=Anna
Khasha=Anna
Khasha=Khaya
Khasida=Khasida
Khasna=Khasna
Khasya=Anna
Khat=Khat
Khava=Khava
Khave=Eva
Khaviva=Khaviva
Khavka=Eva
Khavke=Eva
Khavu=Khavu
Khaya=Khaya
Khejna=Anna
Khekha=Khekha
Khekhomo=Khekhomo
Khela=Khela
Khena=Anna
Khenke=Anna
Kheva=Eva
Khevcha=Iokhaved
Kheved=Iokhaved
Khiena=Anna
Khiese=Khaya
Khimula=Khimula
Khina=Anna
Khinda=Khinda
Khine=Anna
Khiner=Khiner
Khinka=Anna
Khinkhe=Anna
Khintsa=Anna
Khintsya=Anna
Khinya=Anna
Khirana=Khirana
Khisse=Anna
Khisya=Anna
Khiva=Eva

Khlata=Khlata
Khogla=Khogla
Khojvo=Khojvo
Khona=Anna
Khova=Eva
Khristina=Khristina
Khudesa=Khudesa
Khudi=Khudi
Khuma=Khekhomo
Khuma=Nekhomo
Khumutal'=Khumutal'
Khundi=Khundi
Khunke=Anna
Khunya=Khunya
Khurshea=Khurshea
Khursi=Khursi
Khusha=Anna
Khusya=Anna
Khuva=Eva
Khvalet=Khvalet
Khvolesa=Khvalet
Kina=Kina
Kina=Kunigunda
Kiratsa=Kiratsa
Kirna=Kirna
Kirtsu=Kirtsu
Kisha=Kushi
Klara=Klara
Klarisa=Klara
Klarisi=Klara
Klavdiya=Klavdiya
Klementa=Klementina
Klementina=Klementina
Klera=Klara
Kleril=Klara
Klerkhen=Klara
Klerl=Klara
Klumira=Klumira
Klura=Klara
Klutivi=Klutivi
Klyara=Klara
Knina=Knina
Kojla=Kejla
Kojna=Kojna
Konstantsiya=Konstantsiya
Kostsina=Kostsina
Krajnchale=Kirna
Krajndl=Kirna
Krajndlya=Atara
Krajne=Kirna
Krandlya=Kirna
Krasha=Krasha

Krasna=Krasha
Krejndel'=Atara
Krejndel'=Kirna
Krejndel'khen=Kirna
Krejne=Atara
Krejnkhen=Kirna
Krejnlan=Kirna
Krejntsa=Kirna
Krejntsya=Kirna
Krejse=Kresel'
Krejsl=Kresel'
Krendl=Kirna
Kreschiya=Kresel'
Kresel'=Kresel'
Kresil'=Kresel'
Kreskiya=Kresel'
Kreslajn=Kresel'
Kreslya=Kresel'
Krida=Krida
Krisa=Krisa
Krishpulya=Krishpulya
Kritsu=Kritsu
Krojn=Kirna
Krojna=Kirna
Krojnlin=Kirna
Krouna=Atara
Kudojn=Kudojn
Kukina=Kukina
Kuna=Kunigunda
Kunigunda=Kunigunda
Kunitsa=Kunigunda
Kuntse=Kunigunda
Kunya=Kunigunda
Kupa=Kupa
Kurshidmu=Kurshidmu
Kusha=Kushi
Kushi=Kushi
Kushya=Kushi
Kutsa=Kutsa
Kutsya=Guttsya
Kuza=Kuza
Laie=Leni
Lana=Liya
Lane=Liya
Lata=Lata
Laya=Liya
Lea=Lea
Ledka=Ledka
Leitsa=Liya
Lejbel'=Lejbel'
Lejbel=Lejbel
Lejbla=Lejbel

Lejcha=Liya
Lejche=Liya
Lejka=Lya
Lejke=Liya
Lejku=Liya
Lejol'ka=Liya
Lejole=Liya
Lejshka=Liya
Lejtsa=Liya
Lejtsi=Liya
Lejtsil'=Liya
Lejya=Liya
Leni=Leni
Leol=Liya
Leonche=Leonniya
Leonniya=Leonniya
Leonora=Leonora
Leontina=Leonniya
Lesha=Lesha
Leslya=Leslya
Levi=Levi
Leya=Liya
Liba=Liba
Libe=Liba
Libisha=Liba
Libka=Liba
Libke=Liba
Libsha=Liba
Libsha=Liba
Libshe=Liba
Libusha=Liba
Libushe=Liba
Lideya=Lidiya
Lidisiya=Lidisiya
Lidiya=Lidiya
Lif'cha=Liba
Lifshchits=Liba
Likhanka=Likhanka
Lilli=Lilli
Limut=Limuta
Limuta=Limuta
Lina=Lina
Linka=Lina
Lipa=Lipa
Lipka=Liba
Lishiva=Lishiva
Lisru=Lisru
Lista=Lista
Liya=Liya
Liyaba=Liba
Liz'beta=Elisaveta
Liz=Liya

Liza=Liya
Lojtsa=Liya
Lolya=Lolya
Lota=Lota
Lotta=Sharlotta
Lotte=Sharlotta
Ludka=Ludka
Luiza=Liya
Luna=Aluna
Luna=Luna
Lushcha=Lushcha
Lvio=Leni
Lya=Lya
Lyaska=Lyaska
Lyuba=Liba
Lyubka=Liba
Lyubka=Liba
Lyubov'=Liba
Lyudvika=Lyudvika
Lyupka=Liba
Maakha=Maakha
Madzha=Madzha
Magda=Magda
Maja=Maja
Majmlin=Majmlin
Majnka=Majnka
Majt'e=Majta
Majta=Majta
Majte=Majte
Majte=Majte
Majti=Majta
Majti=Majta
Majtin=Majta
Majtl'=Majta
Majtlin=Majta
Makhla=Melkhola
Makhluf=Makhluf
Makhlya=Melkhola
Mal'e=Malka
Mal'vina=Mal'vina
Malikhe=Malka
Maliya=Malka
Malka=Malka
Malle=Malka
Mamel'=Mamel'
Mamla=Mamel'
Mamli=Mamel'
Mamtsi=Mamtsi
Mamush=Mamush
Man'cha=Mariam
Man'tsi=Mariam
Mani=Mariam

Manis=Manis
Manka=Mariam
Manna=Mariam
Manya=Mariam
Mar'em=Mariam
Mar'm=Mariam
Mar'ya=Mariam
Mar'yam=Mariam
Mar'yanka=Mariam
Mar'yasya=Mariam
Mar'yasya=Mir'em
Marasha=Mariam
Marem=Mariam
Maresa=Mariam
Margala=Margolis
Margalit=Margolis
Margola=Margolis
Margoli=Margolis
Margolis=Margolis
Margolisa=Margolis
Margolish=Margolis
Margosha=Margozhata
Margozhata=Margozhata
Margule=Margolis
Mariam'=Mariam'
Mariam=Mariam
Mariam=Mariam
Mariamma=Mariam
Mariamma=Mariam'
Marianka=Mariam
Marianna=Mariam
Mariasha=Mariam
Mariashe=Mariam
Marie=Mariam
Mariem=Mariam
Marietta=Mariam
Marietta=Mriim
Mariim=Mariam
Marim=Mariam
Marim=Mariam'
Mariom=Mariam
Mariya=Mariam
Mariyasya=Mariam
Marl=Mariam
Marlin=Mariam
Marta=Marta
Masa=Mariam
Masha=Mariam
Masha=Mariam'
Mashe=Mashe
Masi=Mariam
Masuda=Masuda

Masya=Mariam
Mata=Majta
Mate=Majta
Matil'da=Matil'da
Matil=Majta
Matl=Majta
Matla=Majta
Matlya=Majta
Matsa=Matsa
Matula=Matula
Matvel'da=Matvel'da
Mayur=Mayur
Mazi=Mariam
Mazya=Mariam
Mechislava=Mechislava
Meita=Meita
Mejkhush=Melkhola
Mejna=Mejna
Mejshulemes=Mejshulemes
Mejta=Majta
Mejte=Majta
Mejte=Majte
Mejtl=Majta
Mekhli=Melkhola
Mekhlya=Melkhola
Mel'che=Mel'che
Mele=Malka
Melkhola=Melkhola
Mema=Mema
Memil=Mema
Meni=Menukha
Menikha=Menukha
Mentsya=Mindel'
Menukha=Menukha
Meojros=Meojros
Mere=Mariam'
Meri=Mariam
Meri=Mariam'
Merim=Mariam'
Merka=Mariam
Merka=Mariam'
Merlya=Mariam'
Merova=Merova
Merush=Mariam'
Mervyasya=Mariam'
Meryam=Mariam'
Mesa=Mariam
Mesa=Mariam'
Mesha=Mariam
Mesha=Mariam'
Meshullemee=Meshullemee
Messe=Mariam

Messe=Mariam'
Messolam=Mejshulemes
Mesya=Mariam
Mesya=Mariam'
Meza=Mariam'
Mezi=Mariam'
Mida=Mida
Midlajn=Mida
Midlin=Mida
Mieta=Mieta
Mikhala=Melkhola
Mikhalina=Mikhalina
Mikhl'=Melkhola
Mikhla=Melkhola
Mikhlajn=Melkhola
Mikhlin=Melkhola
Mikhlya=Melkhola
Mikri=Mikri
Milka=Milka
Min'cha=Mariam'
Min'hci=Mariam'
Min'tsi=Mariam'
Mina=Melkhola
Mincha=Mindel'
Minchla=Mariam'
Minda=Mindel'
Mindel'=Mindel'
Mindi=Mindel'
Mindl=Mindel'
Mindlin=Mindel'
Mindlya=Mindel'
Mindya=Mindel'
Mindzha=Mindel'
Mingit=Mingit
Mini=Mindel'
Minka=Melkhola
Minka=Mindel'
Minklin=Minklin
Minlin=Mindel'
Minsa=Mindel'
Mintla=Mindel'
Mintsa=Mindel'
Mintsla=Mariam'
Mintsla=Mindel'
Mintsya=Mindel'
Minya=Mindel'
Mir'em=Mir'em
Mir'yam=Mariam'
Mira=Amira
Mira=Emira
Mira=Mariam'
Miranda=Miranda

Miras=Miras
Mirel'=Mariam
Mirel'=Mariam'
Miriam=Mariam
Miriam=Mariam'
Miriam=Miriam
Mirka=Mariam'
Mirlin=Mariam'
Mirlya=Mariam'
Mirsh=Mariam'
Mirukhna=Mariam'
Mirule=Miras
Mirush=Mariam'
Mirusha=Mariam'
Mirushka=Mariam'
Mirushka=Miriam
Mishelina=Mishelina
Mishket=Mushkut
Mitil'=Majta
Mitshya=Mindel'
Mitsya=Mitsya
Miva=Miva
Miza=Mariam'
Mizya=Mariam'
Mnojro=Mnojro
Mnukha=Menukha
Model=Model
Moemin'=Moemin'
Mojdl'=Majta
Mojdl=Model
Molli=Molli
Monna=Mariam
Motlya=Majta
Motya=Majta
Mriim=Mriim
Muda=Muda
Mulhajra=Mulhajra
Mulina=Mulina
Mulom=Mulom
Munkha=Munkha
Muntsya=Mindel'
Murina=Murina
Musa=Mariam
Muse=Mariam'
Musha=Mashe
Mushe=Mashe
Mushka=Mashe
Mushkru=Mushkru
Mushkut=Mushkut
Mushla=Mashe
Mushle=Mashe
Muska=Mariam'

Muslya=Mashe
Musya=Mariam'
Mutil'=Majta
Mutsha=Mindel'
Muzula=Mariam'
Muzya=Mariam'
Naama=Naama
Naara=Naara
Nadezhda=Nadezhda
Nadzieja=Nadzieja
Nagama=Nagama
Nakha=Nekhomo
Nakhama=Nekhomo
Nakhe=Nekhomo
Nakhema=Nekhomo
Nakhmanki=Nakhmon
Nakhmon=Nakhmon
Nan'cha=Nena
Nata=Nataliya
Nataliya=Nataliya
Nekha=Nekhomo
Nekhama=Nekhomo
Nekhamka=Nekhomo
Nekhana=Nekhomo
Nekhe=Nekhomo
Nekhil'=Menukha
Nekhil=Nekhomo
Nekhlajn=Nekhomo
Nekhlin=Nekhomo
Nekhma=Nekhomo
Nekhomo=Nekhomo
Nekhuma=Nekhomo
Nekhushta=Nekhushta
Nena=Nena
Nenash=Nena
Nendl=Nena
Nendla=Nena
Neni=Nena
Nenkhin=Nena
Nenla=Nena
Nenlin=Nena
Nesa=Nesa
Nesha=Nesa
Neshka=Nesa
Nessa=Nesa
Netl'=Netl'
Netta=Nataliya
Nezabel'=Nezabel'
Nikha=Menukha
Nikha=Menukha
Nina=Nina
Nishka=Nekhomo

Nisil'=Nisli
Nisli=Nisli
Nislya=Nisli
Nisya=Nisli
Noemin=Noemin
Nojemi=Moemin'
Nojemi=Noemin
Nojma=Moemin'
Nojma=Noemin
Nojmi=Moemin'
Nojmi=Noemin
Nokhama=Nekhomo
Nokhame=Nekhomo
Nokhnyu=Nokhnyu
Noma=Moemin'
Noma=Noemin
Nomka=Moemin'
Nomka=Noemin
Nora=Nora
Nukha=Menukha
Nukha=Nukha
Nukhl=Menukha
Nusil'=Nisli
Odo=Ada
Ofeliya=Ofeliya
Ogusha=Ogusha
Ol'ga=Ol'ga
Olya=Ol'ga
Pajsya=Pesa
Pajvis'=Sepfora
Palkuna=Palkuna
Paluma=Paluma
Palumba=Paluma
Palunba=Paluma
Palya=Palya
Papusa=Papusa
Pasha=Pasha
Pasna=Pasna
Patsha=Patsha
Paulina=Paulina
Pavis'=Sepfora
Pavsh=Sepfora
Paya=Paya
Pazi=Pazi
Pel'ka=Pel'ka
Pela=Anna
Pepa=Pepa
Pera=Pera
Peral=Perl
Peril=Margolis
Peril=Perl
Perka=Pera

Perl=Margolis
Perl=Perl
Perla=Margolis
Perlajn=Perl
Perle=Perl
Perlo=Perl
Perlya=Perl
Pesa=Pesa
Peshka=Pesa
Peshka=Pesya
Peshu=Peshu
Pesil=Pesya
Pesile=Pesa
Peska=Pesa
Peskhen=Pesa
Pesl=Pesya
Peslajn=Pesya
Peslin=Pesya
Pesse=Pesa
Pessi=Pesa
Pesya=Pesa
Pesya=Pesya
Peurlkhin=Peurlkhin
Pilya=Pilya
Pinsha=Pinsha
Pinshkha=Pinsha
Pintsa=Pintsa
Pintsi=Pintsa
Pintska=Pintsa
Pinya=Pinya
Pirna=Pirna
Pisla=Pesa
Pisya=Pesa
Pizi=Pazi
Pojra=Sepfora
Pojri=Pojri
Pojza=Pojza
Pojzerl=Sepfora
Pojzr=Sepfora
Porelo=Pojri
Poriya=Pojri
Pozi=Pazi
Prashtura=Prashtura
Prikha=Prikha
Priva=Briva
Priva=Griva
Priva=Priva
Priva=Sepfora
Puerlan=Puerlan
Pujza=Pazi
Pul'kheriya=Pul'kheriya
Puna=Puna

Puni=Puna
Punsha=Pinsha
Punshikha=Pinsha
Puntsa=Puntsa
Puntska=Pintsa
Puntska=Puntsa
Pur'ya=Pojri
Puza=Pazi
Puza=Puza
Puzi=Pazi
Rada=Rada
Radesh=Roda
Radish=Roda
Radl=Roda
Raisa=Rosa
Rajcha=Rajtse
Rajkha=Rakhil'
Rajkhe=Ketsina
Rajkhil'=Rakhil'
Rajkhl=Ketsina
Rajkhl=Rakhil'
Rajla=Rala
Rajna=Rajna
Rajna=Rona
Rajntsla=Rajna
Rajts=Rajtsa
Rajtsa=Rajtsa
Rajtse=Rajtse
Rajtsl'=Rajtse
Rajtslin=Rajtse
Rajtsva=Rajtse
Rajvtsa=Revekka
Rajzel=Rejza
Rajzla=Rejza
Rajzli=Rejza
Rajzol=Rejza
Rajzol=Rojzya
Rajzya=Rejza
Rakhal'=Rakhal'
Rakhel'=Rakhil'
Rakhelya=Rakhil'
Rakhenya=Rakhil'
Rakhil'=Rakhil'
Rakhil=Rakhil
Rakhil=Rakhil'
Rakhlya=Rakhil'
Rakhma=Rokhmo
Rakhmo=Rakhmo
Rakhna=Rakhna
Rakhyl=Rakhil'
Rala=Rala
Rale=Rale

Ranya=Rona
Rasel'=Rosa
Rasha=Rosa
Rashel'=Rakhil'
Rashel'=Rosa
Rasheli=Rakhil'
Rasheli=Rosa
Rashka=Rakhil'
Rashka=Rosa
Rashke=Rosa
Rashki=Rakhil'
Rashya=Rosa
Raska=Rosa
Ratsya=Rajtse
Rebeka=Revekka
Rebekka=Revekka
Redl=Roda
Reitsa=Reitsa
Rejkha=Rakhil'
Rejla=Rala
Rejna=Rejna
Rejnusha=Rejna
Rejse=Rejza
Rejtsa=Rajtsa
Rejtslan=Rajtse
Rejtsva=Rajtse
Rejza=Rejza
Rejze=Rejza
Rejzha=Rejza
Rejzkhen=Rejza
Rejzl=Rejza
Rejzlin=Rejza
Rejzlya=Rejza
Rejzlya=Rejza
Rekhama=Rakhmo
Rekhama=Rokhmo
Rekhana=Rokhmo
Rekhe=Rokhmo
Rekhil=Rakhil
Rekhil=Rakhil'
Rekhlajn=Rakhil'
Rekhlya=Rakhil'
Rekhuma=Rokhmo
Rela=Rala
Rela=Rale
Renata=Renata
Reshna=Reshna
Ressa=Rosa
Reuma=Reuma
Reveka=Revekka
Revekka=Revekka
Revr=Revr

Rez'ka=Rejza
Rez'ka=Rejza
Rida=Rada
Rifka=Revekka
Rika=Ketsina
Rika=Revekka
Rikel'=Rikl
Rikhila=Rikhila
Rikl=Rikl
Riklajn=Rikl
Rikli=Revekka
Riklin=Rikl
Riklya=Rikl
Rinusha=Rajna
Risa=Risa
Rise=Revekka
Risha=Rosa
Riska=Rosa
Rislya=Rosa
Ritsh=Ritsh
Ritshel'=Ritsh
Ritshil'=Ritsh
Riva=Revekka
Rivele=Revekka
Rivkele=Revekka
Rivlya=Revekka
Rivshe=Revekka
Rivtsa=Revekka
Rivtse=Revekka
Rivtsi=Revekka
Rivtsya=Revekka
Rkhama=Rakhmo
Roda=Roda
Rodi=Roda
Rodya=Roda
Rojza=Rejza
Rojzel=Rejza
Rojzula=Rejza
Rojzvan=Rojzvan
Rojzya=Rejza
Rojzya=Rojzya
Rokha=Rakhil'
Rokhama=Rokhmo
Rokhcha=Rakhil'
Rokhchya=Rakhil'
Rokhe=Rakhil'
Rokhil=Rakhil'
Rokhl'=Rakhil'
Rokhliya=Rakhil'
Rokhlya=Rakhil'
Rokhma=Rokhmo
Rokhmo=Rokhmo

Rokhtsya=Rakhil'
Ron'ya=Rajna
Rona=Rona
Ronya=Rona
Roozla=Rejza
Ros'e=Rosa
Rosa=Rakhil'
Rosa=Rosa
Rosha=Rosa
Roshe=Rosa
Roshya=Rosa
Rosi=Rosa
Rosya=Rakhil'
Rouza=Rejza
Rouza=Rejza
Roza=Rejza
Rozaliya=Rejza
Rozaliya=Rejza
Roze=Rejza
Rozlya=Rejza
Ruda=Roda
Ruda=Roda
Rude=Roda
Rudisha=Roda
Rudlya=Rala
Rudlya=Roda
Rudya=Roda
Ruf'=Ruf'
Rukhejl=Rukhejl
Rukhla=Rakhil'
Rukhlya=Rakhil'
Rukl'=Rikl
Rulya=Rala
Rulya=Rulya
Rusa=Rosa
Rusha=Rosa
Rusha=Shakra
Rushka=Rosa
Rushya=Rosa
Rusya=Rosa
Rut=Ruf'
Ruzha=Reitsa
Ruzha=Rejza
Ruzya=Reitsa
Ruzya=Rejza
Ryfka=Revekka
Ryl'tsya=Ryl'tsya
Rynya=Rona
Rysha=Rosa
Sabdki=Sabdki
Sabina=Sabina
Sabol'=Sabol'

Sabtka=Sabdki
Safira=Safira
Sakhna=Sakhna
Sal'ka=Sul'
Sal'va=Slava
Sala=Sala
Salamanda=Salamanda
Saliya=Gofoliya
Salma=Salma
Salomeya=Salomeya
Saltana=Saltana
Saltana=Shultana
Salva=Salva
Samarifa=Shimrafa
Saro=Sarra
Sarra=Sarra
Sarro=Sarro
Saruiya=Saruiya
Sas=Sas
Sasalbanas=Sasalbanas
Saviya=Tsvio
Sejna=Shejna
Sejsej=Sejsej
Selima=Selima
Sella=Tsilla
Semakh=Semakh
Semeafa=Shimeafa
Semeara=Shel'effa
Senda=Aleksandra
Sendla=Shejna
Senla=Shejna
Sepfora=Sepfora
Serafima=Serafima
Seril'=Sarra
Serka=Sarra
Serke=Sarra
Serkhen=Sarra
Serl=Sarra
Serlya=Sarra
Serlya=Suro
Sertsa=Sarra
Shabsiya=Shabsiya
Shabsu=Shabsu
Shabsule=Shabsule
Shaj=Shaj
Shajna=Shejna
Shajna=Shejna
Shakhna=Shakhna
Shakra=Shakra
Shal'va=Esfir'
Shal'va=Slava
Shalomif'=Shalomif'

Shalvo=Shalvo
Sharlotta=Sharlotta
Shatl'=Shatl'
Shchera=Shchera
Sheiva=Sheva
Shejka=Shejka
Shejna=Shejna
Shejndil'=Shejna
Shejndl=Shejna
Shejndle=Shejna
Shejne=Shejna
Shejniurula=Shejniurula
Shejnla=Shejna
Shejntsha=Shejna
Shejntsya=Shejna
Shejze=Shejze
Shel'effa=Shel'effa
Shelomif=Shelomif
Shendl=Shejna
Shendla=Shejna
Shendlin=Shejna
Shene=Shejna
Shenka=Shejka
Shenka=Shenkha
Shenkha=Shenkha
Shenkhl=Shejka
Shenkhl=Shenkha
Shenva=Shenva
Shera=Sarra
Sheril'=Sarra
Sherke=Sarra
Sherlin=Sarra
Sheva=Sheva
Shidana=Shidana
Shifka=Shifra
Shifra=Shifra
Shima=Shimo
Shime=Shimo
Shimeafa=Shimeafa
Shimka=Shimo
Shimkha=Simkha
Shimo=Shimo
Shimrafa=Shimrafa
Shinajrula=Shinajrula
Shira=Shira
Shishvojna=Shishvojna
Shitl=Shatl'
Shiva=Sheva
Shlima=Shlima
Shlojmis=Shlojmis
Shloumis=Shelomif
Shloumis=Shlojmis

Shlova=Slava
Shnerra=Shnerra
Shojnlin=Shejna
Shora=Sarra
Shorke=Sarra
Shosa=Sarra
Shosha=Sarra
Shosya=Sarra
Shprintsa=Esperansa
Shprintsa=Ispiransa
Shprintsl=Esperansa
Shprintsl=Ispiransa
Shrentsa=Shrentsa
Shretsa=Shretsa
Shtamta=Shtamta
Shtera=Shtera
Shterna=Esfir'
Shterna=Shterna
Shterne=Shtera
Shtersi=Shtersi
Shtilya=Shtilya
Shul'=Shul'
Shul'ka=Shul'
Shultana=Shultana
Shundlajn=Shejna
Shundlin=Shejna
Shunlin=Shunlin
Shunya=Shunya
Shura=Sarra
Shuya=Shuya
Shvartsa=Shvartsa
Sil'ka=Sul'
Sil'viya=Sil'viya
Silka=Sul'
Sima=Serafima
Sima=Simkha
Simkha=Simkha
Simme=Simkha
Sina=Sinaj
Sinaj=Sinaj
Sireta=Sireta
Sirka=Sarra
Sirla=Tsiral
Sirle=Tsiral
Sirpianna=Sirpianna
Slatka=Slatka
Slatka=Zlata
Slava=Slava
Slova=Slava
Slova=Slava
Slove=Slava
Slove=Slava

Slovea=Slava
Sobe=Sabol'
Sobee=Sobol'
Soblya=Sabol'
Soblya=Sobol
Sobol'=Sobol'
Sobol=Sobol
Sofiya=Sofiya
Soflya=Sofiya
Soja=Soja
Sojbl'=Sabol'
Sojbl=Sobol'
Soje=Sarra
Sokhna=Sokhna
Solomif'=Shalomif'
Solomif=Shelomif
Solomoniya=Solomoniya
Soniya=Sarra
Sonya=Sarra
Sorka=Sarra
Sorke=Sarra
Sorlya=Sarra
Sorra=Sorra
Sos'e=Sarra
Sos'ki=Suro
Sosha=Sarra
Soshka=Sarra
Soshya=Sarra
Sosya=Sorra
Soya=Soya
Sperantsa=Esperansa
Sperantza=Esperansa
Sprintsya=Esperansa
Sprintsya=Ispiransa
Srejba=Srejba
Sruve=Sruve
Stamta=Istamta
Stashek=Stashek
Stefaniya=Stefaniya
Stekhna=Stekhna
Sterluba=Sterluba
Sterne=Shterna
Stira=Stira
Stirka=Shterna
Stirka=Stira
Stirlya=Stira
Stisya=Tishl'
Stru=Astru
Stru=Stru
Strungila=Istrungila
Strupula=Istarupula
Strupula=Strupula

Stusya=Stusya
Styrkel'=Stira
Styrlya=Stira
Sukhna=Sakhna
Sukhna=Sokhna
Sul'=Shul'
Sul'=Sul'
Sul'ka=Shul'
Sul'ka=Sul'
Sul'ke=Sul'
Sul'ko=Sul'
Sula=Shuya
Sulamit=Sulamita
Sulamita=Sulamita
Sura=Sarra
Sure=Sarra
Suro=Suro
Susanna=Susanna
Svitlya=Svitlya
Syuzanna=Susanna
Taberlajn=Tojba
Tabl=Tojba
Tabul=Tojba
Taburla=Tojba
Tafaf=Tafaf
Tajbelin=Tojba
Tajbl=Tojba
Tajblain=Tojba
Tajblin=Tojba
Tajblin=Tojba
Tajya=Tajya
Taklin=Rakhil'
Tamara=Thamar
Tamaril'=Thamar
Tana=Tana
Tani=Tana
Tanina=Tanina
Tanya=Tatiyana
Taranta=Taranta
Tatiyana=Tatiyana
Tatsdzina=Tsisha
Tauba=Tojba
Taube=Tojba
Tauns=Tauns
Tefas=Tafaf
Tejejna=Tana
Tejna=Tana
Tejno=Tejno
Tekea=Tekea
Tekhterlajn=Tekhterlajn
Tekla=Tekla
Tel'tsa=Tol'tsa

Tel'tsya=Tela
Tela=Tela
Teltsl=Tela
Tema=Tema
Temchlin=Tema
Temeril'=Thamar
Temerl=Thamar
Temerlin=Thamar
Temirl=Thamar
Temna=Fimna
Temril=Thamar
Temtsa=Tema
Temtsi=Tema
Temuil'=Tela
Tena=Tena
Teni=Teni
Tenya=Tana
Teodora=Teodora
Teofila=Teofiliya
Teofiliya=Teofiliya
Tereza=Tereza
Tetsdzina=Tetsdzina
Thamar=Thamar
Tiklin=Rakhil'
Tiklip=Rukhejl
Tikva=Tikva
Tila=Tela
Tile=Nekhushta
Tile=Tela
Tilya=Tela
Tircha=Tirtsi
Tirtsa=Tirtsa
Tirtsi=Tirtsi
Tirua=Tirua
Tis'ya=Tisa
Tisa=Tisa
Tishl'=Tishl'
Tishpe=Tishpe
Tislaba=Tisa
Tislava=Slava
Tislojba=Tishl'
Tisluba=Tisa
Toba=Tojba
Toivsa=Toivsa
Toivtsa=Toivtsa
Tojba=Tojba
Tojbelin=Tojba
Tojvo=Tojba
Tokl=Rakhil'
Tol'tsa=Tol'tsa
Tol'tsi=Tol'tsa
Tol'tsya=Tol'tsa

Toltsa=Dul'sa
Toltse=Dojltsa
Toltse=Toivtsa
Toltse=Tol'tsa
Tomor=Fomar
Tomor=Thamar
Tona=Tana
Tone=Tana
Tortsya=Tirtsa
Tovba=Tojba
Trajna=Trajna
Trajndlya=Trajna
Trajnuna=Trajna
Trana=Trajna
Trandlya=Trajna
Tranu=Trajna
Tranuna=Trajna
Tranya=Trajna
Trushel'=Trushel'
Tsajpa=Sepfora
Tsalka=Tsalka
Tsapa=Sepfora
Tsarit=Tsart
Tsarka=Tsarka
Tsarkhil'=Tsarkhil'
Tsarne=Charna
Tsarne=Tsarne
Tsarnil'=Charna
Tsarnil'=Tsarnil'
Tsart=Tsart
Tsartil=Tsart
Tsartl=Tsart
Tsatdzina=Tsisha
Tsejtlya=Tsejtlya
Tsemakh=Tsemakh
Tsena=Tsena
Tserka=Tsarka
Tserka=Tserka
Tserlya=Tsiril'
Tserna=Charna
Tserta=Tserta
Tsertlya=Tsart
Tsertlya=Tserta
Tsesha=Tsesya
Tsesya=Tsesya
Tsetsiliya=Tsetsiliya
Tseviya=Tsvio
Tsherna=Brana
Tshitel'=Tshitsha
Tshitl=Shatl'
Tshitsha=Tshitsha
Tshiza=Tshiza

Tsif'ya=Tsvio
Tsif'ya=Tsvio
Tsil'te=Tsil'te
Tsile=Sepfora
Tsilka=Tsalka
Tsilke=Tsalka
Tsilla=Tsilla
Tsima=Simkha
Tsima=Tsemakh
Tsimel'=Tsimel'
Tsiml'=Tsemakh
Tsimlya=Tsemakh
Tsimpa=Simkha
Tsimpkha=Tsimpkha
Tsina=Finaj
Tsina=Kentsina
Tsina=Sinaj
Tsina=Tsina
Tsine=Ketsina
Tsine=Tsina
Tsini=Sinaj
Tsini=Tsina
Tsinka=Ketsina
Tsinka=Tsina
Tsipa=Sepfora
Tsipe=Sepfora
Tsipejra=Sepfora
Tsipera=Sepfora
Tsipora=Sepfora
Tsipoura=Sepfora
Tsipra=Tsipra
Tsiral=Tsiral
Tsirasha=Girasa
Tsirasha=Tsirasha
Tsirel'=Tsiril'
Tsiril'=Tsiril'
Tsiril=Tsiril
Tsirl=Sarro
Tsirl=Tsiril
Tsisha=Tsisha
Tsistya=Tsistya
Tsita=Tsita
Tsitra=Tsitra
Tsiv'che=Tsvio
Tsiv'e=Tsvio
Tsiv'ya=Tsvio
Tsiv'ya=Tsvio
Tsiva=Tsvio
Tsiza=Tsisha
Tsizani=Tsisha
Tslava=Slava
Tsluva=Slava

Tsrit=Tsruio
Tsrit]=Saruiya
Tsruio=Tsruio
Tsuftlya=Tsuftlya
Tsumpa=Tsumpa
Tsuril'=Saruiya
Tsuril'=Tsiril
Tsurli=Tsiril
Tsurlin=Tsiril
Tsurtlya=Tsart
Tsvetl'=Tsvetl'
Tsvia=Tsvio
Tsvie=Tsvio
Tsvio=Tsvio
Tsyupa=Sepfora
Tuba=Tojba
Tukal'=Rakhal'
Tukil'=Rakhil'
Tukl=Rakhil'
Tukl=Rukhejl
Tuklajn=Rakhil'
Tuklan=Rakhil'
Tul'tsa=Tol'tsa
Tumorl=Thamar
Tunoril=Thamar
Turkaya=Turkaya
Tushna=Dushna
Tushna=Tushna
Tyl'tsya=Tela
Udel'=Ejda
Udele=Ejda
Udil=Ejda
Udl=Ejda
Udliya=Ejda
Udlua=Ejda
Udlya=Udlya
Umgustu=Umgustu
Umrufya=Umrufya
Umya=Umya
Unglin=Devora
Ura=Ura
Urarusho=Urarusho
Urdunanina=Urdunanina
Urulajdu=Urulajdu
Urusul=Urusul
Uziala=Uziala
Valentina=Valentina
Vali=Vali
Valla=Valla
Vanda=Vanda
Varda=Varda
Varvara=Varvara

Vefiya=Vif'ya
Vejlka=Vejlka
Veli=Veli
Velkova=Vejlka
Velkova=Vejlka
Vena=Vena
Vera=Vera
Vida=Vida
Vif'ya=Vif'ya
Vikhna=Vikhna
Viktoriya=Viktoriya
Vilajda=Vilajda
Vilgelmina=Vilgelmina
Villa=Villa
Vilnu=Vilnu
Vintura=Vintura
Virsasiya=Virsasiya
Virsaviya=Virsaviya
Virtuaza=Virtuaza
Vita=Vita
Vitil=Vita
Vitka=Vida
Vitka=Vita
Vitl=Vita
Vitla=Vita
Vitlya=Vita
Vitsha=Vita
Vitul=Vita
Vitush=Vita
Vitya=Vita
Vnida=Vanda
Vrajda=Vrajda
Vrajdel'khen=Vrajda
Vrajdkhen=Vrajda
Vravda=Vravda
Vrejda=Vrajda
Vrejde=Simkha
Vrejdkhen=Vrajda
Vrimt=Vrimt
Vrojda=Vrojda
Vrumit=Vrimt
Vrumut=Vrimt
Vruna=Brana
Vruna=Vruna
Yadviga=Yadviga
Yakha=Iokhaved
Yakhat=Yakhat
Yakhe=Iokhaved
Yakhet=Yakhet
Yakhit=Yakhat
Yakhle=Iekholiya
Yakhnat=Yakhnat

Yakhne=Iokhaved
Yakht=Iakhaved
Yakhud=Yakhat
Yakhvod=Iokhaved
Yakuta=Iokhaved
Yalsa=Yalsa
Yanina=Ioganna
Yanta=Enta
Yares=Iras
Yudashka=Iegudifa
Yudes=Iegudifa
Yudsa=Iegudifa
Yudsa=Yudsa
Yudsya=Iegudifa
Yukl'=Yukl'
Yuli=Yuliya
Yuliya=Yuliya
Yustina=Yustina
Yuta=Ita
Yute=Ita
Zabella=Iezavel'
Zafira=Zafira
Zaftya=Zaftya
Zagra=Zagra
Zajna=Zajna
Zakhra=Zakhra
Zanda=Zanda
Zara=Zagra
Zara=Zara
Zarakh=Zara
Zashka=Zusa
Zefir=Zafira
Zel'cha=Zel'da
Zel'da=Zel'da
Zel'ma=Zel'ma
Zelfa=Zelfa
Zempl'=Zempl'
Zenftil'=Zenftil'
Zgovis=Zgovis
Zhanne=Ioganna
Zhanneta=Ioganna
Zharzheta=Zharzheta
Zhenni=Evgeniya
Zhenya=Evgeniya
Zhivnitsa=Zhivnitsa
Zhvi=Zhvi
Zigfrid=Zigfrid
Zilka=Sul'
Zina=Zinaida
Zinaida=Zinaida
Zindel'=Zindel'
Zisa=Zusa

Zisel'=Zusa
Zisel=Zusa
Ziskel'=Zusa
Zisla=Zusa
Zislya=Zusa
Zisya=Zusa
Zlat'=Zlata
Zlata=Zlata
Zlatka=Zlata
Zmojrida=Zmojrida
Zoza=Zoza
Zul'ka=Sul'
Zusa=Zusa
Zushta=Zushta
Zusl=Zusa
Zusla=Zusa
Zuslin=Zusa
Zusya=Zusa

Masculine Names

Aaron=Aaron
Aba=Abo
Abada=Abada
Abadalkrim=Abadalkrim
Abadalshalom=
 Abadalshalom
Abadrakhman=Abadrakh-
 man
Abaej=Abaej
Abali=Abo
Abarlima=Avraam
Abarlipa=Avraam
Abbo=Abo
Abdalrakhum=Abdalrakhum
Abduelelem=Abduelelem
Abdula=Abdula
Abel'=Abo
Abele=Abo
Abele=Avel'
Aberl'=Avraam
Aberlan=Avraam
Aberle=Avraam
Aberman=Avraam
Aberman=Avraam
Abesh=Abo
Abigdor=Avigdor
Abigedor=Moisej
Abil'=Abo
Abish=Abo
Abish=Avraam
Abisha=Avraam
Abisooh=Moisej
Abizoog=Moisej
Abli=Avraam
Abner=Avenir
Abo Shoul=Abo Shoul
Abo=Abo
Abo=Avraam
Abomori=Abomori
Abragam=Avraam
Abram=Avraam
Abrash=Avraam
Abrashka=Avraam
Abril'=Avraam
Abrul'=Avraam
Abrumchik=Avraam
Abrush=Avraam

Abrushka=Avraam
Abrushke=Avraam
Absalom=Avesalom
Abtsi=Avraam
Abualkhir=Abualkhir
Abulfaragu=Abulfaragu
Abulkhsin=Abulkhsin
Abus=Abo
Abusaad=Abusaad
Abush=Ar'ej
Abush=Avraam
Abusia=Avishu
Adad=Oded
Adam=Adam
Addon=Addon
Adnaj=Adnaj
Ado=Ado
Adol'f=Avraam
Adol'fo=Avraam
Adonim=Adonim
Adoniya=Adoniya
Afida=Afida
Afir=Efer
Afrash=Efrem
Afroim=Efrem
Agarojn=Aaron
Agaron=Aaron
Agavo=Agavo
Age=Age
Aggej=Aggej
Aggej=Aggej
Aggij=Aggej
Agiman=Agiman
Agrele=Aaron
Agrojnko=Aaron
Agron=Aaron
Aguvij=Aguvio
Aguvio=Aguvio
Ajid=Ajid
Ajtel'khen=Moisej
Ajza=Isaak
Ajzik=Iokor
Ajzik=Isaak
Ajzik=Salafiel
Ajzik=Selafijl
Ajzika=Isaak
Ajzl=Iokor

Ajzman=Isaak
Akasriel'=Akasriel'
Akavio=Akavio
Akhiezer=Akhiezer
Akhinaam=Akhinoam
Akhinoam=Akhinoam
Akhinoam=Akhinoam
Akhiya=Akhiya
Akhiyazer=Akhiezer
Akho=Akho
Akhso=Akhso
Akiva=Akiva
Aksel'rud=Aksel'rud
Akshil'rod=Akshil'rod
Akuv=Akuv
Al'bert=Avraam
Al'brekht=Al'brekht
Al'fred=Al'fred
Aleksa=Aleksa
Aleksandor=Aleksandr
Aleksandr=Aleksandr
Alfej=Khalifa
Aliko=Elkana
Alkon=Elkana
Alkuna=Elkana
Alzguto=Alzguto
Amasaj=Amshej
Amashsaj=Amshej
Amasiya=Amasiya
Amato=Amado
Ameram=Amram
Amessaj=Amshej
Aminadov=Aminadov
Aminodov=Aminadov
Ammieil=Ammiile
Ammiile=Ammiile
Ammiud=Ammiud
Amniel=Emmanuil
Amnon=Amnon
Amos=Amos
Amram=Amram
Amron=Amron
Amsel'=Asir
Amshej=Amshej
Amsl=Asir
Amush=Amshej
Amushaj=Amshej

Anameil=Anameil
Anan=Anan
Ananeil=Ananeil
Ananiya=Ananiya
Ananyail=Ananyail
Anastas=Eliakim
Anastazij=Eliakim
Anatol'=Anatol'
Anatolij=Anatolij
Anboaz=Anboaz
Anbonit=Anbonit
Anchel'=Asir
Anchil=Anchil
Andrej=Andrej
Andzej=Andrej
Andzel=Asir
Anmojshe=Anmojshe
Anruvin=Anruvin
Ansel'm=Asir
Anshel'=Anchil
Anshel'=Asir
Anshil'=Asir
Anshl=Asir
Anshlojma=Anshlojma
Anskhin=Asir
Anten=Anten
Antonij=Antonij
Antsel=Asir
Antshil=Asir
Ar'e=Ar'ej
Ar'ej=Ar'ej
Ar'ya=Ar'ej
Aral=Aaron
Arche=Aaron
Are=Aaron
Arel=Aaron
Arele=Aaron
Aria=Ar'ej
Ariam=Ar'ej
Arij=Ar'ej
Ariya-Lejb=Ar'ej
Ariya=Ar'ej
Ariyash=Ar'ej
Arkadij=Aaron
Arkadiush=Aaron
Arkadiya=Aaron
Arke=Aaron
Arkhudupula=Arkhudu
Arkhundupula=Arkhundu
Arko=Aaron
Arn=Aaron
Arngol'd=Aaron

Arnojn=Aaron
Arnol'd=Aaron
Arnun=Aaron
Aro=Aaron
Arojn=Aaron
Aron=Aaron
Artsi=Aaron
Artur=Artur
Aru=Aaron
Asail=Asail
Asar=Asar
Asher=Asir
Ashkar=Ashkar
Ashlan=Ashlan
Ashman=Iuda
Ashoel=Asail
Ashtruk=Ashtruk
Asir=Asir
Askhan'=Akhso
Aslan=Iuda
Asniel=Gofoniil
Asriejl=Asriejl
Asriel'=Asriejl
Assir=Asir
Assur=Asir
Atsel=Atsel
Atslan=Iuda
Auzer=Ozer
Avadia=Avadia
Avadia=Avraam
Avadia=Ovadia
Avdenago=Azariya
Avdia=Avadia
Avdiil'=Avdiil'
Avdij=Ovadia
Avdiya=Ovadia
Avdon=Avdon
Avel'=Avel'
Avenir=Avenir
Avesaj=Avessa
Avesalom=Avesalom
Avessa=Avessa
Avgali=Avigeja
Avi Goezer=Avi Goezer
Aviezer=Aviezer
Aviezro=Aviezro
Avigdor=Avigdor
Avigdour=Avigdor
Avigeja=Avigeja
Avirlin=Iuda
Avisalom=Avesalom
Avishir=Avishir

Avisholoum=Avisholoum
Avishu=Avishu
Avishua=Avishua
Avishur=Avishur
Avraam=Avraam
Avragam=Avraam
Avrakam=Avraam
Avram=Avraam
Avram=Avram
Avramets=Avraam
Avremchij=Avraam
Avremij=Avraam
Avrogam=Avraam
Avrogom=Avraam
Avromko=Avraam
Avrum=Avraam
Avrumchik=Avraam
Avrumko=Avraam
Avrunko=Avraam
Avsej=Iisus
Avsholoum=Avesalom
Avtuli=Naffalim
Avva=Abo
Avvakum=Avvakum
Ayid=Ayid
Azario=Azariya
Azariya=Azariya
Aziel'=Iziil
Aziel'=Uziil
Azon=Azon
Azreil'=Azriil
Azriel'=Azriil
Azriel=Azriil
Azriil=Azriil
Azril'=Azriil
Azur=Ozer
Azyas=Azyas
Baboku=Baboku
Baer=Dov
Bagbag=Bagbag
Bajkh'=Simeon
Bajnim=Beniamin
Bajnim=Veniamin
Bajnus=Beniamin
Bajnus=Veniamin
Bajrakh=Bebaj
Bajras=Iom-Tov
Bakhram=Iom-Tov
Banet=Varukh
Barak=Varak
Barche=Dov
Bardalo=Bardalo

Barkhiel'=Barkhiel'
Barukh=Varukh
Bash=Varukh
Bati=Bati
Batko=Batko
Bdaus=David
Bebaj=Bebaj
Beez=Vooz
Bejaz=Vooz
Bejbe=Bebaj
Bejnash=Veniamin
Bejnes=Veniamin
Bejnus=Veniamin
Bejomin=Veniamin
Bejrakh=Bebaj
Bejrakh=Berekhiya
Bejrish=Dov
Beliklajn=Iokor
Ben-Tsion=Bentsion
Ben'yamin=Veniamin
Ben'yomin=Veniamin
Bena=Beniyamin
Bena=Veniamin
Bendavid=Bendavid
Bendet=Akshil'rod
Bendet=Iom-Tov
Bendet=Varukh
Bendid=Akshil'rod
Bendid=Iom-Tov
Bendid=Varukh
Bendit=Akshil'rod
Bendit=Iom-Tov
Bendit=Varukh
Benedikt=Varukh
Benes=Veniamin
Benet=Varukh
Beni=Veniamin
Beniamin=Beniamin
Benish=Veniamin
Beniyamin=Beniyamin
Beniyamin=Veniamin
Benjomin=Veniamin
Bension=Bentsion
Bentsa=Bentsion
Bentsel'=Bentsion
Bentsen=Bentsion
Bentsian=Bentsion
Bentsio=Bentsion
Bentsion=Bentsion
Benyash=Veniamin
Benyumen=Veniamin
Benyumin=Veniamin

Ber=Dov
Ber=Isaak
Ber=Issakhar
Bera=Dov
Berakh'ya=Berekhiya
Berakhie=Berekhiya
Berek=Dov
Berekhio=Berekhiya
Berekhiya=Berekhiya
Berel'=Dov
Berend=Dov
Beria=Veria
Beril'=Isaak
Beril=Issakhar
Berish=Dov
Berka=Dov
Berkhen=Berekhiya
Berkhen=Dov
Berkhen=Issakhar
Berkhin=Isaak
Berko=Dov
Berl=Dov
Berlin=Dov
Berlin=Isaak
Berlin=Issakhar
Berman=Berekhiya
Berman=Dov
Berman=Isaak
Berman=Issakhar
Bernard=Dov
Bernat=Dov
Berngard=Dov
Bero=Isaak
Bero=Issakhar
Bersh=Dov
Bertgol'd=Bertgol'd
Bertol'd=Dov
Bertsya=Dov
Berush=Dov
Besaliil=Besaliil
Beseliil=Beseliil
Betsalel'=Besaliil
Betsalel'=Veseliil
Betsalel=Beseliil
Betsalel=Veseliil
Bibenshits=Bibenshits
Bibl'man=Tsadik
Bima=Veniamin
Bimla=Veniamin
Bina=Veniamin
Binash=Veniamin
Bindit=Akshil'rod

Bindit=Iom-Tov
Bindit=Samuil
Bindit=Varukh
Binekh=Binekh
Binem=Simkho
Binet=Binet
Binim=Veniamin
Biniomin=Veniamin
Binlajn=Veniamin
Binlin=Veniamin
Binom=Veniamin
Binush=Veniamin
Binyash=Veniamin
Birakh=Bebaj
Bishka=Beniyamin
Bishuf=Akshil'rod
Bishuf=Iakov
Bishuf=Samuil
Bkhaj=Bkhaj
Bkhor=Avraam
Blankugi=Solomon
Bnet=Iom-Tov
Bnoio=Varukh
Boaz=Boaz
Bogdan=Bogdan
Boleslav=Boleslav
Bonaventura=Bonaventura
Bonek=Veniamin
Bonfant=Samuil
Boni=Vani
Bonsineur=Toviya
Borek=Varukh
Borekh=Varukh
Boris=Dov
Borokh=Varukh
Boyaz=Vooz
Brakhia=Berekhiya
Bronislav=Bronislav
Brukha=Berakha
Brukhche=Berakha
Bruno=Bruno
Brushan=Brushan
Bryukha=Berakha
Btsalke=Veseliil
Btshulka=Veseliil
Btsulka=Veseliil
Buan-Gojren=Iom-Tov
Budan=David
Budin=David
Bukhsh=Eliezer
Bukish=Eleazar
Bukish=Eliezer

Buks=Eleazar
Buksh=Eleazar
Buksh=Eliezer
Bulakhsin=Bulakhsin
Buna=Buna
Bunash=Veniamin
Bundio=Iom-Tov
Bundit=Iakov
Bundit=Samuil
Bundit=Varukh
Bundiun=Bundiun
Bundyan=Bundyan
Bunem=Samuil
Bunet=Iom-Tov
Bunfant=Akshil'rod
Bunfant=Iakov
Bunfat=Akshil'rod
Bunfat=Iakov
Bunfat=Samuil
Bunfet=Bunfet
Bunfil'=Iakov
Buni=Iekhiil
Buni=Veniamin
Bunian=Iekhiil
Bunim=Veniamin
Bunin=Iekhiil
Bunish=Veniamin
Buniun=Iekhiil
Bunmo=Simkho
Bunmo=Veniamin
Bunom=Simkho
Bunvet=Bunvet
Bunya=Iofoniya
Burakh=Varukh
Burgel'=Avraam
Burukh=Barukh
Burukh=Varukh
Buva=Buva
Chanko=Chanko
Dafan=Dafan
Dalo=Dalo
Dan'el'=Daniil
Dan=Dan
Danel'=Daniil
Daniil=Daniil
Danil=Daniil
Danila=Daniil
Dankhel=Daniil
Danki=Daniil
Danun=Iom-Tov
Dasan=Dasan
Daud=David

Dav'yu=David
David=David
Davidko=David
Davitka=David
Davitki=David
Dejsha=Dejsha
Demyan=Demyan
Denil=Dan
Denzajl=Dan
Did'ya=Iededia
Dionizij=Dionizij
Dliaksiv=Eleashiv
Dode=David
Dodi=David
Dodl=David
Dodo=Dodo
Donki=Dan
Donki=David
Dov=Dov
Dov=Issakhar
Dovetki=David
Dovid=David
Dovidil=David
Dovidl=David
Dovitki=David
Duda=David
Dudi=David
Dudil=David
Duida=David
Dujnika=Dov
Dun'ka=David
Dun'ki=David
Dunika=David
Duran=Duran
Durant=Isaak
Durant=Meshuilam
Durant=Moisej
Duse=Dafan
Duse=Dasan
Duvidl'=David
Eber=Avraam
Eber=Eber
Eber=Moisej
Eberl'=Avraam
Eberlajn=Avraam
Eberlan=Avraam
Eberlin=Avraam
Ebermajn=Avraam
Eberman=Avraam
Ebril'=Avraam
Ebrush=Avraam
Edid'ya=Iededia

Edidia=Edidia
Edidiyash=Iededia
Edmund=Edmund
Eduard=Eduard
Eejnokh=Genokh
Efer=Efer
Efim=Khaim
Efraim=Efrem
Efrashka=Efrem
Efrem=Efrem
Efroim=Efrem
Egide=Iuda
Egon=Egon
Egoshiya=Iisus
Egoshua=Iisus
Eguda=Iuda
Eididio=Iededia
Ejber=Avraam
Ejded=Oded
Ejdidio=Iededia
Ejkev=Iakov
Ejkhel'=Iekhiil
Ejkhen=Ejkhen
Ejkhor=Ejkhor
Ejlik=Ioil
Ejna=Iona
Ejshua=Iisus
Ejz=Ejz
Ejzep=Iosif
Ejzer=Ozer
Ejzhen=Ejzhen
Ejzik=Isaak
Ejzil'=Asir
Ejzyk=Isaak
Ekalets=Iakov
Ekef=Iakov
Ekev=Eliakim
Ekhezkel=Iekufiil
Ekhezkel=Iezekiil'
Ekhfiil=Iekufiil
Ekhiel'=Iekhiil
Ekhiel=Iekhiil
Ekhio=Ekhio
Ekir=Iakov
Ekisiel=Iekufiil
Ekl=Fliakim
Ekl=Iakov
Ekufiil'=Iekufiil
Ekufiil=Ekufiil
Ekutiel'=Iekufiil
Ekutiel=Iekufiil
El'kon=Elkana

El'noson=Elnafan
El'noson=Elnofan
El'tsofon=Elitsafan
El'ya=Il'ya
El'yu=Il'ya
El'yukim=Eliakim
El=Il'ya
Elanasfan=Elnafan
Elanassan=Elnafan
Elash=Il'ya
Elazar=Eleazar
Elazar=Eliezer
Eldod=Eldod
Eleanan=Elkhanan
Eleasa=Eleasa
Eleashiv=Eleashiv
Eleazar=Eleazar
Elezer=Eliezer
Elezerek=Eliezer
Eli=Il'ya
Elia=Il'ya
Eliakim=Eliakim
Eliakim=Eliakim
Elian=Il'ya
Elias=Il'ya
Eliash=Il'ya
Eliashiv=Eleashiv
Eliazar=Eliezer
Eliazer=Eliezer
Elie=Il'ya
Elieaveta=Elieaveta
Eliejnaj=Elioenaj
Eliezer=Eliezer
Eliezer=Eliezer
Elij=Il'ya
Elik=Il'ya
Elimalakh=Elimelekh
Elimelekh=Elimelekh
Elioenaj=Elioenaj
Eliogu=Il'ya
Eliokim=Eliakim
Eliokim=Eliokim
Eliokum=Eliakim
Elionaj=Elioenaj
Elios=Il'ya
Elioshiv=Eleashiv
Elisafan=Elitsafan
Elisej=Elisej
Elisej=Elisej
Elisha=Elisej
Elishe=Elisej
Elitsafan=Elitsafan

Elitsfan=Elitsafan
Eliya=Il'ya
Eliyagu=Il'ya
Eliyas=Il'ya
Eliyu=Il'ya
Elkana=Elkana
Elkano=Elkano
Elkhanan=Elkhanan
Elkhanan=Elkhanan
Elkhanon=Elkhanan
Elkhonon=Elkhanan
Elkhune=Elkhanan
Elkhuno=Elkhanan
Elkhunon=Elkhunon
Elkona=Elkana
Elkono=Elkana
Elkune=Elkana
Ellikh=Gillel
Elnafan=Elnafan
Elnofan=Elnofan
Elozor=Eleazar
Eltsafan=Elitsafan
Elyakum=Eliakim
Elyam=Il'ya
Elyash=Il'ya
Eman=Eman
Emaniel'=Emmanuil
Emanuel'=Emmanuil
Emanuel=Emmanuil
Emanuil=Emmanuil
Emil'=Iemuil
Emiliya=Iemuil
Emilyan=Emilyan
Emmanuil=Emmanuil
Emuan=Eman
Enanij=Enanij
Encha=Iakov
Endl=Endl
Eneil=Iuziya
Enokh=Enokh
Enos=Enos
Enshkhin=Asir
Enskhin=Asir
Enzil=Uziya
Enzkhin=Asir
Eorg=Eorg
Eremiya=Eremiya
Eremiya=Ieremiya
Erikh=Erikh
Erikhem=Ierukham
Erma=Eremiya
Erma=Ieremiya

Ermash=Ieremiya
Ernest=Ernest
Erukhim=Ierukham
Erukhom=Erukhom
Erzhij=Erzhij
Es'ka=Iosif
Eshaia=Isaia
Eshia=Iisus
Eshiel'=Iisus
Eshii=Iisus
Eshij=Iisus
Eshua=Iisus
Eshuj=Iisus
Eshuya=Iisus
Esko=Iosif
Eslo=Iosif
Esua=Iisus
Eten=Eten
Etio=Etio
Eugen=Eugen
Evad'ya=Ovadia
Evadij=Ovadia
Evadio=Ovadia
Evadiya=Ovadia
Evats=Khalfon
Evdij=Ovadia
Evdokim=Evdokim
Evel'=Ioil
Ever=Ever
Evgenij=Evgenij
Evidi=Evidi
Evits=Moisej
Evna=Iona
Evnos=Iona
Evsej=Iisus
Ezaes=Isaia
Ezdra=Ezdra
Ezekhil=Iezekiil'
Ezekie=Ezekie
Ezekiil'=Ezekiil'
Ezekiil=Ezekiil
Ezel'=Ezel'
Ezif=Iosif
Eziz=Eziz
Ezkhea=Ezkhea
Ezra=Ezdra
Ezro=Ezdra
Fab'yus=Urshrago
Fabian=Fabian
Fabian=Urshrago
Fabil=Samson
Fabul=Samson

Fabuli=Eleazar
Fabuli=Eliezer
Fabuli=Samson
Fadassur=P'datsur
Fajbus=Irshrago
Fajbush=Eleazar
Fajbush=Irij
Fajbush=Irshrago
Fajbush=Irshrago
Fajbush=Urij
Fajbusz=Urshrago
Fajbuzia=Fajbuzia
Fajfel'=Fajfel'
Fajsh=Irshrago
Fajsh=Urshrago
Fajtel'=Iokor
Fajtel'=Urshrago
Fajtel=Irshrago
Fajtsh=Fajtsh
Fajve=Irshrago
Fajve=Urshrago
Fajvel'=Shrago
Fajvel'=Urshrago
Fajvel'=Urshrago
Fajvel=Eliakim
Fajvesh=Shrago
Fajvis=Urij
Fajvish=Eliakim
Fajvish=Eliezer
Fajvish=Ezekie
Fajvish=Iezekiil
Fajvish=Ioil
Fajvish=Irshrago
Fajvish=Khaim
Fajvish=Meshuilam
Fajvish=Neemiya
Fajvish=Samson
Fajvish=Samuil
Fajvish=Urij
Fajvish=Urshrago
Fajvl=Eliezer
Fajvl=Ezekie
Fajvl=Iezekiil
Fajvl=Ioil
Fajvl=Iri
Fajvl=Irshrago
Fajvl=Khaim
Fajvl=Neemiya
Fajvl=Samson
Fajvl=Samuil
Fajvl=Urij
Fajvl=Urshrago

Fajvuli=Samuil
Fajvus=Urshrago
Fajvush=Urshrago
Fakhul'=Samson
Faleg=Faleg
Falek=Faleg
Falek=Iisus
Falk=Iisus
Falk=Ionafan
Fallu=Fallu
Falma=Falma
Faltiil=Faltiil
Famakh=Famakh
Fares=Fares
Fargon=Ieshuo
Fatsejk=Mardokhej
Feb=Feb
Fedaia=Fedaia
Fedassur=P'datsur
Feesiya=Paseakh
Fefeiya=Petakhiya
Fejbus=Irshrago
Fejbus=Urshrago
Fejle=Refail
Fekuev=Fikva
Feliks=Feliks
Fendel'=Fendel'
Feodor=Tiviumi
Ferdinand=Ferdinand
Feul=Irij
Feul=Urij
Fevel'=Shrago
Fihsl=Moisej
Filill=Irshrago
Filipp=Filipp
Filipp=Urshrago
Finees=Finees
Fish=Efrem
Fishel=Ierukham
Fishel=Samuil
Fisher=Fisher
Fishka=Efrem
Fishko=Efrem
Fishl=Efrem
Flem=Flem
Fliakim=Fliakim
Fole=Refail
Folmaj=Falma
Foltiil=Foltiil
Fomakh=Famakh
Fraden=Ruvim
Fraim=Efrem

Frajko=Efrem
Frajmush=Efrem
Franek=Efrem
Frants=Frants
Frantsisk=Frantsisk
Frederik=Frederik
Frefir=David
Frejdman=Simkho
Friderik=Friderik
Fridl=Ruvim
Fridman=Sholojm
Fridrik=Fridrik
Frika=Frika
Frimt=Frimt
Froim=Efrem
Frojka=Efrem
Fua=Fua
Fuks=Eliezer
Fuks=Shuil
Furigo=Tshuo
Futiil=Futiil
Gabor=Gabor
Gabriel'=Gavriil
Gabusia=Gabusia
Gad=Gad
Gadala=Godoliya
Gadala=Igdal
Gaddail=Giddel'
Gadi=Gavriil
Gadoliya=Gadoliya
Gadriel'=Gadriel'
Gaiman=Eman
Gaj=Gaj
Gajman=Gajman
Gakkatan=Gakkatan
Gamaliil'=Gamaliil'
Gamaliil'=Gamaliil'
Gamliel'=Gamaliil'
Gandl=Manoj
Ganir=Daniil
Gankhin=Samuil
Ganko=Ganko
Garol'd=Garol'd
Garrik=Garrik
Garsh=Naffalim
Garts=Naffalim
Gartvig=Gartvig
Gaskiel'=Iezekiil
Gavriel'=Gavriil
Gavriil=Gavriil
Gavril'=Gavriil
Gavrila=Gavriil

Gdal'=Godoliya
Gdal'yash=Godoliya
Gdal'yu=Godoliya
Gdale=Godoliya
Gdale=Igdal
Gdaliya=Godoliya
Gdush=Godoliya
Gdush=Igdal
Gdushman=Godoliya
Gebel=Nakhman
Gebel=Nakhmon
Gedal'e=Godoliya
Gedal'e=Igdal
Gedaliya=Godoliya
Gedaliya=Igdal
Gedalya=Godoliya
Gedalya=Igdal
Gedil=Gotoliya
Geidel'=Manoj
Gejman=Eman
Gejnokh=Enokh
Gejnrikh=Genrik
Gejshil=Osia
Gejvel'=David
Gel'man=Samuil
Gelias=Gelias
Gemali=Gemali
Gemerlin=Aaron
Genakh=Enokh
Gendil'=Shavfaj
Gendzel'=Asir
Genek=Genek
Genokh=Enokh
Genokh=Genokh
Genrik=Genrik
Genrikh=Genrik
Gensl=Asir
Gentshil=Asir
Genukh=Enokh
Georg=Georg
Georgij=Tsvi
Gerasim=Gerasim
Gerbert=Gerbert
Gerford=Gerford
Gerig=Gerig
Germam=Germam
German=German
Geronim=Samuil
Gersh=Naffalim
Gershel'=Tsvi
Gershk=Tsvi
Gershko=Tsvi

Gershl=Naffalim
Gershlik=Tsvi
Gershom=Girshon
Gershon=Girson
Gershun=Girson
Gerson=Gillel
Gerson=Girson
Gerts=Naffalim
Gerts=Tsvi
Gertsik=Tsvi
Gertsko=Naffalim
Gertsko=Tsvi
Gertsl=Naffalim
Gertsl=Tsvi
Gertso=Naffalim
Gertso=Tsvi
Ges=Ezekie
Ges=Iezekiil
Gesel'=Osiya
Gesha=Tsvi
Geshel'=Iisus
Geshel'=Osiya
Geshika=Iisus
Geshil'=Iisus
Geshil=Osiya
Geshka=Iisus
Geshl=Iezekiil
Geshl=Osiya
Gesikis=Gesikis
Gesikis=Iezekiil
Gesiya=Osiya
Gets=Eliakim
Getshlik=Eliakim
Getsil'=Eliakim
Getsil=Eliakim
Getsko=Eliakim
Getsl=Eliakim
Getsla=Eliakim
Getsli=Eliakim
Gezl=Iosif
Gid'on=Gideon
Gidajl=Godoliya
Giddel'=Giddel'
Giddel'=Giddel'
Gidel'=Gad
Gidel=Giddel'
Gideon=Gideon
Gidol=Godoliya
Gieronim=Gieronim
Gil'=Gillel
Gil'ejl'=Gil'ejl'
Gil'ka=Gillel

Gil'ko=Gillel
Gil'man=Samuil
Gil'mar=Gil'mar
Gila=Gillel
Gilarji=Gilarji
Gile=Gillel
Gilel'=Gillel
Gilel=Gillel
Giler=Gillel
Gilibi=Mardokhej
Gilibi=Sofonia
Gilibi=Urij
Gilibun=Gilibun
Gilik=Iosif
Gillel=Gillel
Gimlil'=Efrem
Gimmerlin=Aaron
Gimpel'=Mardokhej
Gimpikht=Efrem
Gimpli=Mardokhej
Gimplin=Uraj
Gimplin=Urij
Gimtsel'=Mordokhaj
Ginokh=Enokh
Gipolit=Gipolit
Giroriya=Giroriya
Girsh=Naffalim
Girsh=Tsvi
Girshil=Naffalim
Girshko=Tsvi
Girshl=Tsvi
Girshon=Girshon
Girshon=Girson
Girsom=Girshon
Girson=Girson
Girson=Girson
Girts=Tsvi
Girtsil=Nafaalin
Girtsil=Naffalim
Girtsko=Tsvi
Girtsl=Naffalim
Girtsl=Tsvi
Girtso=Naffalim
Girtso=Tsvi
Girtsship=Naffalim
Gis=Gesikis
Gisikis=Ezekiil
Gisikis=Gesikis
Gisikis=Iezekiil'
Gisikis=Isikis
Gitlin=Aguvio
Glebko=Glebko

Gmalin=Gmalin
Gniva=Gniva
Godajl=Godoliya
Gode=Gad
Godel'=Godoliya
Godfrid=Godfrid
Godil=Gad
Godil=Godoliya
Godl=Gad
Godl=Godl
Godli=Gad
Godol=Godoliya
Godoliya=Godoliya
Godush=Godoliya
Godya=Godl
Gofoniil=Gofoniil
Gojshia=Iisus
Gojshika=Osiya
Gojshika=Osiya
Gojshil=Iisus
Gojshil=Osiya
Gojshka=Osiya
Gojshko=Iisus
Gojshl=Iisus
Gojshla=Iisus
Gojshma=Osiya
Gojshman=Osiya
Gojvesh=Ioas
Golibi=Mordokhaj
Golosh=Golosh
Gorko=Gorko
Gorojn=Gorojn
Goroz=Goroz
Gosha=Osiya
Goshaia=Goshaia
Goshaya=Goshia
Goshea=Iisus
Goshia=Goshia
Goshiya=Iisus
Goshki=Osiya
Goshko=Iisus
Goshko=Osiya
Goshma=Osiya
Goshman=Iisus
Goshman=Osiya
Gosko=Osiya
Gotlib=Aguvio
Gotlib=Iedidia
Gotlib=Ioets
Gotlip=Aguvio
Gotlipo=Iosif
Gotoliya=Gotoliya

Govsej=Iisus
Govshiya=Iisus
Goz=Iosif
Gozhko=Osiya
Gozias=Gozias
Grasajanu=Enokh
Grasajanu=Iokhanan
Grigorij=Tsvi
Grojnem=Samuil
Grojno=Samuil
Grojsman=Gadoliya
Grzegorz=Tsvi
Guchlek=Ierakhmeil
Gudl=Iuda
Guglel'mo=Guglel'mo
Gugo=Gugo
Gulek=Iakov
Gulik=Gillel
Gumf=Efrem
Gumo=Irij
Gumo=Mardokhej
Gumo=Urij
Gump=Efrem
Gumpes=Mardokhej
Gumpil=Efrem
Gumpil=Mardokhej
Gumpl'=Efrem
Gumpl=Mardokhej
Gumplajn=Mardokhej
Gumplin=Irij
Gumplin=Mardokhej
Gumplin=Urij
Gumprekht=Efrem
Gumprekht=Mardokhej
Gumprikht=Efrem
Gumprikht=Girshon
Gumprikht=Girshon
Gumprikht=Iakov
Guna=Guna
Gur'yan=Gur
Gur=Gur
Gurij=Gur
Gurion=Gurion
Gushi=Khusij
Gushl=Iisus
Gushma=Iisus
Gushma=Iuda
Gushman=Iisus
Gustav=Gustav
Gutel'=Gutel'
Guter=Guter
Guterman=Toviya

Gutkind=Toviya
Gutlib=Aguvio
Gutlib=Iedidia
Gutlib=Iegidia
Gutlib=Iosif
Gutlif=Aguvio
Gutlif=Iedidia
Gutlif=Iosif
Gutlifo=Aguvio
Gutlipo=Iedidia
Gutlipo=Iosif
Gutman=Moisej
Gutman=Toviya
Gutokind=Toviya
Guts=Eliakim
Gutsel'=Eliakim
Gutska=Iuda
Gutsla=Eliakim
Gutsli=Eliakim
Gutslik=Eliakim
Gutslik=Ierakhmeil
Gutsmak=Eliakim
Guva=Moisej
Gvursman=Godoliya
Gvursman=Igdal
Iafet=Iafet
Iafniil=Iafniil
Iair=Iair
Iakhel'=Iekhiil
Iakim=Iakim
Iakov=Iakov
Iakush=Iakov
Ianaj=Ianaj
Iarma=Ieremiya
Iatsa=Eliakim
Iatsa=Ioil
Iavis=Iavis
Iber=Avraam
Ibragim=Avraam
Id=Iom-Tov
Idel'=Iuda
Idiya=Idiya
Ido=Ido
Idor=Idor
Iedaiya=Iedaiya
Iedidiya=Iedidia
Iefeaj=Iefeaj
Iefuno=Iofoniya
Iegallelel=Iegallelel
Iegidia=Iegidia
Iegojosh=Iegojosh
Iegoshia=Iisus

Ieguda=Iuda
Iejkusiil=Iekufiil
Iejrakhmiel'=Ierakhmeil
Iekel'=Iakov
Iekhezkel'=Iezekiil
Iekhezkiel'=Iezekiil
Iekhiel'=Iekhiil
Iekhiil=Iekhiil
Iekhoniya=Iekhoniya
Iekisiel'=Iekufiil
Iekufiil'=Iekufiil
Iekufiil=Iekufiil
Iekutiel'=Moisej
Iemuil=Iemuil
Ier=Ier
Ierakhmeil=Ierakhmeil
Ierakhmeil=Ierakhmeil
Ierakhmiejl=Ierakhmeil
Ierakhmiil=Ierakhmeil
Ierameil=Ierakhmeil
Iered=Moisej
Ieremiash=Ieremiya
Ieremiya=Ieremiya
Ieremiyash=Ieremiya
Ierokham=Ierukham
Iersi=Iersi
Ierukham=Ierukham
Ierukhem=Ierukham
Ierukhem=Iorukhom
Ieshaje=Isaia
Ieshuo=Ieshuo
Iessej=Iessej
Ieush=Ieush
Iezekhiel'=Iezekiil
Iezekhil=Iezekiil
Iezekiel'=Iezekiil
Iezekiil'=Iezekiil'
Iezekiil=Iezekiil
Iezekiil=Iezekiil
Iezel'=Iosif
Ifamar=Ifamar
Iga=Iga
Igdal=Igdal
Ignat=Isaak
Ignatij=Isaak
Ignatsa=Isaak
Ignatts=Isaak
Iguda=Iuda
Igudko=Iuda
Iirmio=Ieremiya
Iisrael'=Isruel
Iisrael'=Izrail

Iisskher=Issakhar
Iisuj=Iisus
Iisukher=Issakhar
Iisus=Iisus
Iitskhok=Isaak
Ikel'=Menaim
Ikhel'=Iekhiil
Ikhel'=Ikhel'
Ikhel=Iekhiil
Ikhel=Ikhel'
Ikhiel'=Iekhiil
Ikhil'=Iekhiil
Ikhl=Iekhiil
Ikhudko=Iuda
Il'ko=Il'ya
Il'ya=Il'ya
Il'ya=Il'ya
Ilish=Il'ya
Iliyash=Il'ya
Ilko=Elkano
Ilya=Il'ya
Ilyash=Il'ya
Immanuil=Emmanuil
Imonuel'=Emmanuil
Imordokh=Mardokhej
Ina=Iona
Inam=Anan
Invidal=Invidal
Ioach'=Ioets
Ioakhal=Ioakhal
Ioakim=Ioakim
Ioanan=Iokhanan
Ioann=Iokhanan
Ioas=Ioas
Ioav=Ioav
Iodal=Iuda
Ioel'=Ioil'
Ioel=Ioil
Ioen=Iokhanan
Ioets=Ioets
Iofoniya=Iofoniya
Ioil'=Ioil'
Ioil=Ioil
Ioil=Ioil'
Iojel'=Ioil'
Iojkev=Iakov
Iojkhanan=Iokhanan
Iojkhoj=Iokha
Iojkiv=Iakov
Iojl'=Iojl'
Iojnesen=Ionafan
Iojnoson=Ionafan

Iojpl=Iosif
Iojpl=Iosif
Iojs'in=Iosif
Iojsele=Iosif
Iojsha=Iisus
Iojsha=Iojsha
Iojshka=Osiya
Iojsi=Iosif
Iojsif'e=Iosif
Iojsin=Iosif
Iojskhin=Iojskhin
Iojsko=Iosif
Iojslin=Iosif
Iojzefij=Iosif
Iojzel'=Iosif
Iojzik=Iosif
Iojzip=Iosif
Iojzlin=Iosif
Iojzpl=Iosif
Iojzpo=Asir
Iojzpo=Iosif
Iojzzhe=Iojzzhe
Iokel'=Iakov
Iokha=Iokha
Iokhaf=Iokhaf
Iokhan=Iokhanan
Iokhanan=Iokhanan
Iokhanan=Iokhanan
Iokhel'=Iekhiil
Iokhen=Iokhanan
Iokhenen=Iokhanan
Iokhezkiel'=Iezekiil
Iokhna=Iokhanan
Iokhonan=Iokhanan
Iokhonon=Iokhanan
Iokim=Iokim
Iokish=Iakov
Iokonia=Iekhoniya
Iokor=Iokor
Ioktan=Ioktan
Iokush=Iakov
Iokushko=Iakov
Iolets=Ioets
Iom-Tov=Iom-Tov
Iomtl=Iom-Tov
Iona=Iona
Ionafan=Ionafan
Ionas=Iona
Ionash=Iona
Ionatan=Ionafan
Ionik=Iona
Ionikil=Iona

Ionko=Iona
Ionofan=Ionofan
Iontl=Iom-Tov
Ioram=Ioram
Iorosej=Iorosej
Iorukhom=Iorukhom
Ios'=Iosif
Ios'ko=Iosif
Ios'man=Iosif
Iosef=Iosif
Iosek=Iosif
Iosel'=Iosif
Iosele=Iosif
Iosfis=Iosif
Iosh=Iosif
Iosha=Iosif
Ioshi=Iosif
Ioshie=Iosiya
Ioshko=Iisus
Ioshua=Iisus
Ioshuva=Iisus
Iosiaz=Iisus
Iosie=Iisus
Iosif=Iosif
Iosif=Iosif
Iosij=Iosif
Iosil'=Iosif
Iosip=Iosif
Iosiya=Iosif
Iosiya=Iosiya
Ioskhin=Iosif
Iosko=Iosif
Iosl=Iosif
Ioslin=Iosif
Iosya=Iosif
Iovel'=Ioil'
Iozef=Iosif
Iozeppe=Iosif
Iozibl'=Eliezer
Iozibl=Eliezer
Irad=Irad
Iras=Ira
Iri=Iri
Irigrus=Irigrus
Irij=Irij
Irma=Ieremiya
Irshrago=Irshrago
Isaak=Isaak
Isaakij=Isaak
Isachko=Isaak
Isaia=Isaia
Isaj=Isaia

Isak=Isaak
Isakhar=Isakhor
Isakhor=Isakhor
Isakhor=Issakhar
Isakub=Isaak
Isamar=Isamar
Isaya=Isaia
Iser=Izrail
Iserl=Izrail
Ishak=Isaak
Ishia=Iisus
Ishka=Iisus
Ishmaia=Ishmaia
Ishrugu=Ishrugu
Ishtrugu=Ishtrugu
Isidor=Izrail
Isidore=Izrail
Isikis=Isikis
Iskhak=Isaak
Ismael'=Izmail'
Isomor=Isamar
Isor=Izrail
Israil'=Israil'
Israil=Israil
Isroel'=Izrail
Isrol=Izrail
Isruel=Isruel
Isruel=Izrail
Issak=Issak
Issakhar=Issakhar
Issakhor=Issakhor
Isser=Izrail
Issoskhor=Issoskhor
Istrugu=Istrugu
Isukhor=Issakhar
Isumer=Ifamar
Itamar=Ifamar
Itse=Isaak
Itsek=Isaak
Itsekl=Isaak
Itsel=Aksel'rud
Itsel=Atsel
Itsi=Isaak
Itsig=Isaak
Itsik=Isaak
Itsili=Isaak
Itskanko=Isaak
Itskhak=Isaak
Itskhol'=Isaak
Itsko=Isaak
Itskol=Isaak
Itsl=Isaak

Itsli=Isaak
Itsya=Isaak
Ittsig=Isaak
Iud=Iuda
Iuda-Ariya=Ar'ej
Iuda-Lejb=Ar'ej
Iuda=Ar'ej
Iuda=Iuda
Iudel'=Iuda
Iuka=Iakov
Iulin=Iokhanan
Iuliush=Ioil'
Iushko=Iisus
Iuziya=Iuziya
Ivan=Iokhanan
Ivri=Avraam
Iyames=Iyames
Iyukhal=Ioakhal
Iyushke=Iosif
Iza=Isaak
Izak=Isaak
Izar=Izrail
Izash=Isaak
Izayash=Isaia
Izidor=Izrail
Iziil=Iziil
Izlan=Issak
Izlin=Isaak
Izlin=Isaak
Izmail'=Izmail
Izmail'=Izmail'
Izmail=Izmail
Izor=Izrail
Izrael'=Izrail
Izrail'=Izrail'
Izrail=Izrail
Izrajlo=Izrail
Izral'=Izrail
Kaas=Kaas
Kadesh=Kodojsh
Kadish=Kodojsh
Kadosh=Kodojsh
Kaem=Kaem
Kagan=Kogen
Kagane=Kagane
Kaiel'=Kaiel'
Kajaml=Samuil
Kal'vin=Kal'vin
Kaliman=Klojnimus
Kalman=Avraam
Kalman=Klojnimus
Kalmekhin=Klojnimus

Kalmen=Klojnimus
Kalmon=Klojnimus
Kana=Elkano
Kane=Elkano
Karashkat=Shabfaj
Karashkat=Shavfaj
Karl=Karl
Karmi=Karmi
Karmi=Moisej
Karol'=Karol'
Karpil'=Nafan
Karpil=Efrem
Kashriel'=Kashriel'
Kasiel=Iekufiil
Kaspar=Kaspar
Kasriel'=Kasriil
Kasriil=Kasriil
Kasril'=Kasriil
Kaufman=Meshailam
Kaufman=Meshuilam
Kavrill=Kavrill
Kazhen=Kazhen
Kazhimir=Kazhimir
Kazimierz=Kazimierz
Kazimir=Kazimir
Kedorloamer=Kedorloamer
Kel'ma=Klojnimus
Kel'man=Klojnimus
Kel'mon=Klojnimus
Kelmekhin=Klojnimus
Kelugi=Kelugi
Kerpl=Efrem
Kershon=Girson
Kesil'=Iekufiil
Ketsil=Moisej
Kgetsl=Avraam
Kgisel'=Ezekiil'
Kgisl=Kaas
Kgizel'=Iezekiil'
Kgosl=Kaas
Khachko=Zelikman
Khaim=Khaim
Khaj=Khaj
Khajman=Khajman
Khajno=Khajno
Khakhmojn=Khakhmojn
Khakim=Khakim
Khakin=Isaak
Khakinat=Isaak
Khalafta=Khalafta
Khalev=Khalev
Khalfon=Khalfon

Khalfuj=Khalfuj
Khalifa=Khalifa
Khalifo=Khalifo
Khamel'=Khamel'
Khananejl=Ananeil
Khaniil'=Khaniil'
Khanina=Khanina
Khanniil'=Khaniil'
Khanokh=Enokh
Khanon=Ananeil
Khanon=Ananiya
Khanon=Elkhunon
Khanon=Iokhanan
Khanon=Khanun
Khanuka=Khanuka
Khanun=Khanun
Khasan=Khasan
Khaskel'=Iezekiil'
Khaskel'=Zelikman
Khaskho=Zelikman
Khaskiel'=Iezekiil'
Khasmonej=Khasmonej
Khatse=Iezekiil'
Khatskel'=Iezekiil'
Khatskel'=Zelikman
Khatskim=Zelikman
Khatsko=Zelikman
Khazkl'=Iezekiil'
Khechko=Zelikman
Khedkel'=Khedkel'
Khejn=Il'ya
Khelbo=Khelbo
Khelkiya=Khelkiya
Khemia=Neemiya
Khemiya=Neemiya
Khenokh=Enokh
Kheresh=Kheresh
Khermon=Khermon
Khev'e=Khobaiya
Khichko=Zelikman
Khie=Khie
Khiejl=Iekhiil
Khil'=Iekhiil
Khimojn=Solomon
Khis=Gesikis
Khisda=Khisda
Khisil'=Khisil'
Khiz=Gesikis
Khizkiya=Ezekie
Khlafna=Lapidof
Khlavn=Khlavno
Khlavne=Saad'ya

Khlavne=Saad'ya
Khlavno=Khlavno
Khlavo=Khlavo
Khlavun=Khlavun
Khlojna=Khlojna
Khlouno=Khlavno
Khobaiya=Khobaiya
Khojvo=Moisej
Khokhman=Khakhmojn
Khokhom=Avraam
Khokhom=Isaak
Kholef=Kholef
Khone=Khanun
Khonel'=Elkhunon
Khonin=Khonin
Khono=Elkhunon
Khonon=Ananeil
Khonon=Ananiya
Khonon=Ananyail
Khonon=Elkhunon
Khorosk=Khorosk
Khovel'=Rekhavia
Khovij=Khovij
Khoviv=Khoviv
Khrefir=David
Khrefr=David
Khristian=Khristian
Khuna=Elkhunon
Khune=Ananeil
Khune=Ananiya
Khune=Khanun
Khunen=Ananiya
Khuni=Khuni
Khunon=Elkhunon
Khusij=Khusij
Khuts=Neemiya
Kidor=Il'ya
Kirshman=Girson
Kis=Kis
Kishel'=Iekufiil
Kishlak=Iekufiil
Kisiel'=Iekufiil
Kisiel=Iekufiil
Kitin=Isaak
Kitojn=Isaak
Kiva=Akiva
Kive=Akiva
Kivel'=Akiva
Kiviya=Akiva
Klaude=Klaude
Klejnumus=Klojnimus
Klemens=Klemens

Klojkhi=Klojkhi
Klojnimus=Klojnimus
Klonimes=Klojnimus
Kobke=Iakov
Kodojsh=Kodojsh
Kofman=Iakov
Koftse=Meshuilam
Koftsya=Meshuilam
Kogen=Kogen
Kojfan=Iakov
Kojfilman=Meshailam
Kojfilman=Meshuilam
Kojfman=Iakov
Kojfman=Iekufiil
Kojfman=Meshailam
Kojfman=Meshuilam
Kojpa=Iakov
Kokhman=Iakov
Kolev=Khalev
Kono=Kono
Konrad=Konrad
Konstant=Konstant
Konstantin=Konstantin
Konyuk=Elkano
Kop=Iakov
Kopal=Iakov
Kopalman=Iakov
Kopgan=Iakov
Kopil=Iakov
Kopilman=Iekufiil
Kopl=Iakov
Koplman=Iakov
Kornel'=Kornel'
Kosher=Asir
Kosman=Kosman
Kostush=Kostush
Krefr=David
Kreplan=Iakov
Krishkash=Krishkash
Krivon=Krivon
Krivonya=Krivonya
Krojli=Isaak
Kron=Kron
Krula=Isaak
Krumplig=Moisej
Krumpling=Moisej
Krup=Eliezer
Ksaverij=Ksaverij
Ksiel'=Ekufiil
Ksiel'=Iekufiil
Kufin=Iakov
Kuli=Iakov

Kulik=Iakov
Kulo=Kulo
Kulu=Kulo
Kuna=Elkano
Kundejr=Kundejr
Kune=Elkano
Kunfradu=Iuda
Kunfradu=Moisej
Kunfradu=Samuil
Kuni=Elkano
Kupilman=Iakov
Kurshman=Girshon
Kurshman=Girson
Kurshman=Girson
Kurti=Kurti
Kusa=Iekufiil
Kuse=Kushaia
Kusel'=Iekufiil
Kush=Moisej
Kusha=Iekufiil
Kushaia=Kushaia
Kushe=Kushaia
Kushel'=Iekufiil
Kusheliel'=Iekufiil
Kushko=Iekufiil
Kushman=Moisej
Kusht=Moisej
Kusiel'=Iekufiil
Kusiel'=Iekufiil
Kusiil'=Iekufiil
Kuski=Iekufiil
Kusko=Iekufiil
Kusman=Iekufiil
Kusya=Iekufiil
Kuvin=Iakov
Kyadiya=Kyadiya
Laba=Iuda
Labish=Iuda
Labush=Iuda
Labush=Iziil
Labush=Uziil
Lafidof=Lafidof
Lafidof=Lafidof
Lafidof=Lapidof
Lajb=Iuda
Lajbele=Iuda
Lam=Asir
Lambert=Lambert
Lamekh=Lamekh
Lapidejsh=Lapidof
Lapidof=Lapidof
Lava=Iuda

Lava=Moisej
Lavish=Iuda
Laza=Ekufiil
Laza=Eliezer
Laza=Iekufiil
Lazal=Iekufiil
Lazan=Eliezer
Lazar'=Eleazar
Lazar'=Eliezer
Lazar=Eleazar
Lazar=Eliezer
Lazarus=Eliezer
Lazer=Eliezer
Lazl=Eliezer
Lazo=Ekufiil
Lazo=Iekufiil
Lazor=Eliezer
Leb=Iuda
Leba=Iuda
Leber=Iuda
Lebil'=Iuda
Lebl'=Iuda
Lebl=Eliakim
Lebl=Moisej
Leblan=Eliakim
Leblan=Iuda
Leblan=Moisej
Leblang=Isaak
Leblangen=Isaak
Leblin=Eliakim
Leblin=Iuda
Leblin=Moisej
Lebus=Iuda
Lejb=Ar'ej
Lejb=Iuda
Lejb=Moisej
Lejba=Iuda
Lejba=Moisej
Lejbche=Iuda
Lejbel'=Iuda
Lejbesh=Iuda
Lejbi=Iuda
Lejbish=Iuda
Lejbka=Iuda
Lejbko=Iuda
Lejbli=Iuda
Lejblin=Iuda
Lejblin=Moisej
Lejbus=Iuda
Lejbush=Iuda
Lejme=Iuda
Lejshe=Elisej

Lejshekh=Lejshekh
Lejshke=Elisej
Lejv=Lejv
Lejvb=Moisej
Lejvi=Iuda
Lejvik=Levij
Lejvo=Iuda
Lejvo=Moisej
Lejzer=Eliezer
Lejzl=Eliezer
Lejzor=Eliezer
Lemil'=Asir
Lemil'=Lamekh
Lemko=Asir
Leml'=Asir
Leml=Asir
Lemlin=Asir
Lemlin=Azriil
Leo=Iuda
Leojntij=Leojntij
Leon=Iuda
Leonard=Iuda
Leontij=Leojntij
Leontij=Lojntij
Leopol'd=Iuda
Lepol'd=Iuda
Lev=Iuda
Levan=Iuda
Levek=Iuda
Level'=Levij
Levi=Levij
Levi=Moisej
Levie=Levij
Levij=Levij
Levik=Iuda
Levin=Iuda
Levitas=Levitas
Levka=Iuda
Levko=Iuda
Levlin=Levij
Levon=Iuda
Lezer=Eleazar
Lezl=Eliezer
Lib=Eliakim
Liber=Eliezer
Liber=Iuda
Liberl=Liberl
Liberman=Eliezer
Liberman=Iuda
Libertrojt=Meir
Libkind=Libkind
Liblin=Eliakim

Libman=Eleazar
Libman=Urij
Libo=Eliakim
Liman=Iuda
Limo=Iuda
Linman=Linman
Lionush=Iuda
Liovo=Iuda
Lipa=Eliezer
Lipa=Iom-Tov
Lipa=Urij
Lipko=Eleazar
Lipko=Eliezer
Lipman=Eleazar
Lipman=Eliezer
Lipman=Iom-Tov
Lipman=Urij
Lisha=Elisej
Litman=Eliezer
Liv=Iuda
Livb=Eliakim
Livb=Iuda
Livi=Eliakim
Livn=Iuda
Livo=Eliakim
Livo=Iuda
Livts=Livts
Liz'beta=Elieaveta
Lojntij=Lojntij
Loli=Loli
Lorents=Lorents
Louis=Louis
Lozer=Eliezer
Lozon=Eleazar
Lozor=Eliezer
Lubu=Veniamin
Lupis=Iosif
Lutsian=Lutsian
Luzer=Eliezer
Lyajzer=Eliezer
Lyazer=Eliezer
Lyuba=Edidia
Lyuba=Iedidia
Lyuba=Isaak
Lyuba=Iuda
Lyudvig=Lyudvig
Lyuzer=Eliezer
Maassiya=Maassiya
Maes=Maes
Mafnaj=Mafnaj
Mafusal=Mafusal
Magaram=Meir

Maier=Meir
Majer=Meir
Majir=Meir
Majko=Mardokhej
Majko=Meir
Majlekh=Elimelekh
Majmun=Majmun
Majnko=Majnko
Majnshter=Menaim
Majnsterl=Menaim
Majnsterlan=Menaim
Majre=Meir
Majrek=Meir
Majrim=Meir
Majsterl=Noj
Majzil=Mardokhej
Majzish=Moisej
Majzus=Moisej
Makhir=Makhir
Makhola=Makhola
Makhraz=Sh'mariya
Makhraz=Shemariya
Mako=Mardokhej
Maks=Mardokhej
Maksimilian=Maksimilian
Mal'akhiya=Malakhiya
Mal'kiel=Malkhiil
Malakhiya=Malakhiya
Maleiil=Maleiil
Maleleil=Maleleil
Maliku=Izmail
Malkhiil=Malkhiil
Malkiil=Malkhiil
Malko=Elimelekh
Mallukh=Mallukh
Malul=Malul
Mamfl=Mamfl
Mamri=Mamri
Mamu=Avraam
Man'=Manassiya
Man'=Monush
Man=Man
Man=Man
Man=Manassiya
Man=Manoj
Man=Menaim
Man=Monush
Mana=Menaim
Manaim=Menaim
Manasha=Manassiya
Manasse=Manassiya
Manassiya=Manassiya

Mane=Mardokhej
Mane=Menaim
Manel'=Menaim
Manel=Emmanuil
Manes=Menaim
Mangejm=Mangejm
Mani=Asir
Mani=Mani
Mani=Mardokhej
Mani=Menaim
Manik=Menaim
Manil=Menaim
Manis=Girson
Manis=Menaim
Manish=Menaim
Manke=Menaim
Mankhen=Menaim
Mankhin=Menaim
Manla=Iosif
Manli=Menaim
Manlo=Menaim
Manoj=Manoj
Manos=Menaim
Manosse=Manassiya
Manp=Asar
Mansa=Iosif
Mansh=Menaim
Manshir=Menaim
Mantsojr=Mantsojr
Manuil=Emmanuil
Manus=Menaim
Mardi=Mardokhej
Mardko=Mardokhej
Mardokaj=Mardokhej
Mardokaj=Mordokhej
Mardokhaj=Mardokhej
Mardokhej=Mardokhej
Mardya=Mardokhej
Marechko=Mardokhej
Marek=Mardokhej
Marenko=Mardokhej
Marian=Marian
Marim=Meir
Mark=Mardokhej
Markaj=Mardokhej
Markelij=Mardokhej
Markhaj=Mardokhej
Marki=Mardokhej
Markil'=Mardokhej
Markl=Mardokhej
Marko=Mardokhej
Markus=Mardokhej

Martin=Martin
Martish=Martish
Marton=Marton
Martselij=Martselij
Martsin=Martsin
Mas'e=Matfifiya
Masej=Moisej
Mashulem=Meshuilam
Masid=Masid
Masur=Masur
Mata=Mata
Matafiya=Matfifiya
Matan=Matfan
Matan=Matfin
Matas'ya=Matfifiya
Matas=Matfifiya
Matash'e=Matfifiya
Matel'=Mardokhej
Mates=Matfifiya
Mates=Motfifiya
Matesh=Matfifiya
Matfafiya=Matfifiya
Matfan=Matfan
Matfej=Matfifiya
Matfifiya=Matfifiya
Matfij=Matfifiya
Matfin=Matfin
Matias=Matfifiya
Matis'ya=Matfifiya
Matis'yaga=Matfifiya
Matit'ya=Matfifiya
Matois=Matfifiya
Matous'=Matfifiya
Matoush=Matfifiya
Matsliakh=Matsliakh
Matso=Matso
Matus=Matfifiya
Matvej=Matfifiya
Matys=Matfifiya
Mauris=Mardokhej
Mauritsij=Mardokhej
Mavrikij=Mavrikij
Mayarka=Meir
Mazis=Moisej
Mazol-Tov=Mazol-Tov
Mechislav=Mechislav
Meer=Meir
Mefantslik=Girshon
Meguyail=Meguyail
Meilikh=Elimelekh
Meir=Meir
Mejcha=Mardokhej

Mejche=Matso
Mejche=Motsa
Mejchik=Meir
Mejer=Meir
Mejir=Meir
Mejke=Motsa
Mejlakh=Elimelekh
Mejlakh=Mallukh
Mejlekh=Elimelekh
Mejlikh=Elimelekh
Mejsha=Moisej
Mejshe=Moisej
Mekhakhem=Mekhakhem
Mekl=Asir
Mekl=Iekhiil
Mekl=Mardokhej
Mel'khiil=Maleiil
Melekh=Elimelekh
Melkhiil=Malkhiil
Melkhiram=Melkhiram
Memuilam=Memuilam
Men'khin=Emmanuil
Menaim=Menaim
Menakhem=Menaim
Menakhim=Menaim
Menas=Menaim
Menash=Manassiya
Menasha=Manassiya
Menashe=Manassiya
Menassa=Manassiya
Mendel'=Manoj
Mendel'=Menaim
Mendko=Menaim
Mendl=Girson
Mendl=Manoj
Mendl=Zakhariya
Mendlan=Girson
Mendlan=Manoj
Mendlan=Menaim
Mendlan=Zakhariya
Mendlin=Girson
Mendlin=Manoj
Mendlin=Zakhariya
Menishan=Menaim
Menkhen=Menaim
Menkhin=Menaim
Menki=Menaim
Menko=Menaim
Menli=Menaim
Menlin=Girson
Menlin=Mardokhej
Menlin=Menaim

Menlin=Zakhariya
Menlo=Menaim
Menshin=Menaim
Mentslin=Girshon
Merel'=Mardokhej
Mergel'=Mardokhej
Merkel'=Mardokhej
Mertkhaj=Mardokhej
Mesa=Motsa
Mesel'=Meshelemiya
Meselemiya=Meshelemiya
Meshailam=Meshailam
Meshalam=Meshalam
Meshel'=Meshelemiya
Meshelemiya=Meshelemiya
Meshezavel=Meshezavel
Meshil'=Moisej
Meshilam=Meshuilam
Meshl=Moisej
Meshuilam=Meshuilam
Meshuilom=Meshuilom
Meshulam=Meshuilam
Meshulam=Mshilom
Meshulem=Moisej
Messolam=Meshuilam
Metsl=Meir
Metso=Meir
Metsu=Meir
Metush=Metush
Mevorakh=Mevorakh
Miiamin=Miyamin
Mijzil=Mardokhej
Mikhl=Iekhiil
Mikhne=Mikhne
Mikhush=Iekhiil
Mikhush=Mikhush
Mikl=Iekhiil
Mikl=Mardokhej
Miklos=Miklos
Mikolaj=Mikolaj
Miksa=Miksa
Milalaj=Milalaj
Miniamin=Miniamin
Minko=Menaim
Minman=Iosif
Minster=Menaim
Mintish=Mardokhej
Mir=Mir
Mirkadu=Avraam
Mirkadu=Khasmonej
Mirku=Mardokhej
Miron=Meir

Mirush=Moisej
Misail=Misail
Mishko=Moisej
Mishl=Moisej
Mishoejl=Misail
Mitsi=Meir
Mitsu=Meir
Miyamin=Miyamin
Mizil=Mardokhej
Mnakhejm=Mnakhejm
Mnakhem=Menaim
Mnuejl=Menaim
Mnuejl=Mnuejl
Mnukha=Mnukha
Modil=Mardokhej
Modl=Mardokhej
Moisej=Moisej
Mojdl=Mardokhej
Mojkhno=Moisej
Mojlekh=Elimelekh
Mojshej=Moisej
Mojshele=Moisej
Mojshl=Moisej
Mojshno=Moisej
Mojsi=Moisej
Mojzesz=Moisej
Mojzis=Moisej
Mojzl=Mardokhej
Mokhir=Makhir
Mokhl=Iekhiil
Mokhno=Moisej
Mol'=Mol'
Mola=Mola
Molo=Molo
Monash=Menaim
Monashko=Manassiya
Moni=Moisej
Monis=Girson
Monish=Girson
Monits=Menaim
Monoakh=Manoj
Monsh=Menaim
Monush=Girshon
Monush=Menaim
Monush=Monush
Morais=Morais
Mordash=Mardokhej
Mordekhaj=Mardokhej
Mordesh=Mardokhej
Mordish=Mardokhej
Mordka=Mardokhej
Mordkhaj=Mardokhej

Mordkhe=Mardokhej
Mordkhel'=Mardokhej
Mordko=Mardokhej
Mordokh=Mardokhej
Mordokhaj=Mordokhaj
Mordokhej=Mordokhej
Mordosh=Mardokhej
Mordukh=Mardokhej
Mordus=Mardokhej
Mordush=Mardokhej
Morejnu=Avraam
Morek=Meir
Moris=Mardokhej
Morits=Mardokhej
Morkha=Mardokhej
Mortek=Mardokhej
Mortkhel'=Mardokhej
Mosa=Mosa
Mosek=Moisej
Mosha=Moisej
Moshe=Moisej
Moshej=Moisej
Moshek=Moisej
Moshekil=Moisej
Moshij=Moisej
Moshke=Moisej
Moshko=Moisej
Moshl=Moisej
Moshno=Moisej
Moshuta=Moisej
Mosko=Moisej
Mosya=Moisej
Mot'=Mardokhej
Mota=Mardokhej
Mote=Mardokhej
Motek=Mardokhej
Motel'=Mardokhej
Motfifiya=Motfifiya
Motka=Mardokhej
Motl=Mardokhej
Motsa=Motsa
Motya=Mardokhej
Movsha=Moisej
Moze=Moisej
Mozes=Moisej
Mozesh=Moisej
Mozez=Moisej
Mozis=Moisej
Mozus=Moisej
Msayejl'=Msayejl'
Mshalejm=Shillem
Mshezavel'=Mshezavel'

Mshilejm=Shillem
Mshilom=Mshilom
Mshulom=Meshuilam
Muejd=Samuil
Muejl=Samuil
Muemin=Majmun
Mukaj=Moisej
Muki=David
Muki=Moisej
Mukil'=Mardokhej
Mukil=Asir
Mukl=Asir
Mulem=Menaim
Muli=Samuil
Muli=Solomon
Mulin=Moisej
Mulo=Samuil
Muna=Moisej
Muna=Samuil
Mune=Moisej
Muni=Asir
Muni=Mardokhej
Muni=Muni
Munie=Samuil
Munish=Menaim
Munkhin=Iosif
Muno=Muno
Murkel'=Mardokhej
Murkil'=Mardokhej
Mushel'=Moisej
Mushi=Mushi
Mushku=Mushku
Mushman=Moisej
Mutin=Samuil
Muts=Iosif
Mutun'=Samuil
Muzes=Moisej
Mvajt=Meshuilam
Mvajt=Moisej
Myukhos=Myukhos
Naason=Naason
Nadav=Nadav
Nafaalin=Nafaalin
Nafalim=Nafalim
Nafan=Matfan
Nafan=Nafan
Nafanejl'=Nafanejl'
Nafaniya=Nafaniya
Nafaniya=Nefaniya
Naffalim=Naffalim
Nafon=Nafon
Naftala=Naffalim

Naftalim=Naffalim
Naftel'=Naffalim
Naftol=Naffalim
Naftola=Naffalim
Naftul'=Naffalim
Naftula=Naffalim
Najlikh=Najlikh
Nakhaf=Nakhaf
Nakhamu=Nakhamu
Nakhim=Naum
Nakhli=Nakhmon
Nakhlifo=Nakhlifo
Nakhlo=Menaim
Nakhlo=Nakhmon
Nakhman=Nakhman
Nakhman=Nakhmanij
Nakhmanie=Nakhmanij
Nakhmanij=Nakhmanij
Nakhmanki=Nakhman
Nakhmanki=Nakhmon
Nakhmen=Nakhmon
Nakhmenke=Nakhmanij
Nakhmias=Neemiya
Nakhmish=Nakhmish
Nakhshon=Naason
Nakhum=Menaim
Napoleon=Napoleon
Nasanmok=Nasanmok
Nasel'=Nafan
Nashka=Manassiya
Natan=Nafan
Natan=Nafon
Natan=Natan
Natanel'=Moisej
Nataniil=Nafanejl'
Natrejn=Natrojno
Natrejne=Natrojno
Natrojno=Natrojno
Natsejr=Natsejr
Naum=Naum
Navin=Navin
Navtal=Nafalim
Navtal=Naffalim
Nazariya=Nazariya
Nedel=Nedel
Neemiya=Neemiya
Nefaniya=Nefaniya
Negojri=Negojri
Nejme=Iuda
Nekhamiyashch=Neemiya
Nekhemia=Neemiya
Nekhemie=Neemiya

Nekhemij=Neemiya
Nekhemiya=Neemiya
Nekhemiyash=Neemiya
Nekhil'=Nakhman
Nekhil'=Nakhmon
Nekhl=Nakhmon
Nekhunio=Nekhunio
Nerio=Niriya
Nesanejl=Nafanejl'
Nesanel=Nafanejl'
Nesel'=Nison
Neus=Neus
Nevakh=Noj
Nikodem=Nikodem
Nikolaj=Nikolaj
Nikomojkhi=Nikomojkhi
Nir=Nir
Niriin=Niriya
Niriya=Niriya
Nis=Nison
Nisale=Nison
Nisek=Nison
Nisim=Nisim
Niska=Nison
Nison=Nison
Noakh=Noj
Noan=Noj
Nodov=Nadav
Noe=Noj
Noim=Menaim
Noj=Noj
Nojm=Mekhakhem
Nokhemiya=Neemiya
Nokhim=Naum
Nokhum=Menaim
Nokhum=Naum
Norbert=Norbert
Nosan=Nafan
Nosel'=Nafan
Nosi=Nafan
Noson=Ionofan
Noson=Nafan
Nota=Nafan
Notel'=Nafan
Notka=Nafan
Notki=Nafan
Novakh=Noj
Nover=Nover
Noyakh=Noj
Nukhem=Naum
Nukhim=Menaim
Nukhim=Mnakhejm

Nukhim=Naum
Nukhimche=Naum
Nus'=Nafan
Nusa=Nafan
Nuse=Nafan
Nusen=Nafan
Nusin=Nafan
Nusya=Nafan
Nute=Nafan
Nutsli=Eliakim
Nutslik=Eliakim
Nutya=Nafan
Nyuma=Veniamin
Oded=Oded
Ogij=Ogij
Ogron=Aaron
Ojshie=Ojshie
Ojvedi=Ojvedi
Ojvedi=Ovadia
Ojvidi=Ojvidi
Ojzer=Ezdra
Ojziro=Ezdra
Okhron=Aaron
Ol'e=Idiya
Ol'e=Il'ya
Olev=Olev
Onezimus=Onezimus
Onuel'=Asir
Orel=Aaron
Orelo=Aaron
Orem=Orem
Orko=Aaron
Orlik=Aaron
Oro=Aaron
Ortchik=Aaron
Orule=Aaron
Orun=Aaron
Oser=Asir
Osha=Osiya
Osher=Asir
Osia=Osia
Osip=Iosif
Osiya=Osiya
Oskar=Oskar
Osof=Osof
Otor=Otor
Otsel=Atsel
Otto=Otto
Ovadia=Ovadia
Ovadia=Ovadia
Ovaia=Khobaiya
Oved=Oved

Ovel'=Ioil'
Ovodia=Ovadia
Ovotsiya=Ovadia
Ovotya=Ovadia
Ovsej=Iisus
Ovshej=Iisus
Ovshij=Iisus
Ovshiya=Iisus
Ovsiej=Iisus
Ovzer=Ozer
Ozer=Ozer
Oziil=Iziil
Oziil=Uziil
P'datsur=P'datsur
Pade=Pade
Paguil=Paguil
Pajlets=Pajlets
Pajsha=Paseakh
Pal'tiel'=Faltiil
Pal'tiel'=Foltiil
Paltij=Faltiil
Paltij=Foltiil
Pandiro=Iosif
Pantelej=Pantelej
Papa=Papa
Papilo=Moisej
Papu=Avraam
Papu=Eliezer
Papu=Iakov
Papulo=Moisej
Parnejs=Parnejs
Paseakh=Paseakh
Pashtir=Samuil
Pashtur=Samuil
Paul=Paul
Pavel=Pavel
Pdochur=P'datsur
Pejlet=Pejlet
Pejsak=Paseakh
Pejsakh=Paseakh
Pejsha=Paseakh
Pejshke=Paseakh
Pejsya=Paseakh
Pekhturts=Pekhturts
Pel'te=Faltiil
Pelter=Pelter
Pelyutka=Pelyutka
Perets=Fares
Perko=Dov
Perlajn=Issakhar
Perman=Issakhar
Permun=Issakhar

Pertsi=Fares
Pertsin=Fares
Pesakh=Paseakh
Peshak=Paseakh
Pesnyj=Pesnyj
Petakh'ya=Pusejakh
Petakh=Paseakh
Petakhiya=Petakhiya
Peter=Peter
Pil'to=Faltiil
Pilte=Elimelekh
Pilu=Moisej
Pina=Finees
Pinel'=Finees
Pinhkus=Finees
Pini=Finees
Pinio=Finees
Pinkas=Finees
Pinkhas=Finees
Pinko=Finees
Pinkus=Finees
Pinkvas=Finees
Pinya=Finees
Pitsa=Isaak
Plit=Elimelekh
Ponkhes=Finees
Potku=Moisej
Prakhiya=Prakhiya
Prejdel'=Prejdel'
Prigrus=Prigrus
Prikhodosh=Prikhodosh
Prisadu=Avraam
Projsferu=Matsliakh
Prosfer=Matsliakh
Prufito=Prufito
Psakh'e=Psakh'e
Psakhiya=Petakhiya
Ptshulka=Veseliil
Pufir=Izrail
Puga=Isaak
Pul'zuto=Iosif
Pulder=Isaak
Pulikhruni=Iuda
Pulikhrunu=Iuda
Pulu=Avraam
Puntsha=Finees
Puntsko=Puntsko
Pupu=Israil'
Pupu=Izrail
Pusejakh=Pusejakh
Puss=Puss
Putsi=Isaak

R'uil=Raguil
Rabej=Rabo
Rabo=Rabo
Rafael'=Refail
Rafail=Refail
Rafal'=Refail
Rafel'=Refail
Rafol'=Refail
Rafuel'=Refail
Raful'=Refail
Raguil=Raguil
Raiya=Raiya
Rakhaiel'=Rakhaiel'
Rakhail=Rakhail
Rakhamim=Rakhamim
Rakhav=Rekhaviya
Rakhaviya=Rekhaviya
Rakhmael=Ierakhmeil
Rakhmel'=Rakhmiil
Rakhmiel=Ierakhmeil
Rakhmiil=Rakhmiil
Rakhmil'=Ierakhmeil
Rakhmil'=Rakhmiil
Rakmhil'=Paguil
Ramiro=Ramiro
Rampa=Rampa
Rasuil=Rasuil
Ravio=Rekhaviya
Ravn=Ruvim
Rechejka=Rechejka
Refael'=Refail
Refael'=Rofail
Refail=Refail
Refoel'=Refail
Refoil=Refail
Refuel'=Refail
Refuo=Refuo
Reiben=Ruvim
Reiven=Ruvim
Rejben=Ruvim
Rejdel'=Roguil
Rejkhum=Rekhum
Rejolo=Rejolo
Rejuel=Raguil
Rejze=Ruvim
Rekhavia=Rekhavia
Rekhavio=Rekhaviya
Rekhaviya=Rekhaviya
Rekhemio=Rekhemio
Rekhovo=Rekhovo
Rekhum=Rekhum
Reum=Rekhum

Revan=Ruvim
Revil=Mardokhej
Riel'=Raguil
Riel'=Rasuil
Rikhard=Rikhard
Rimeon=Rimeon
Rimon=Rimon
Rkhemio=Rkhemio
Robert=Ruvim
Rofail=Rofail
Roguil=Roguil
Rokhval=Rekhaviya
Roman=Roman
Romio=Romio
Romual'd=Romual'd
Rosh=Rosh
Rovel'=Ruvim
Rovn=Ruvim
Rovo=Rovo
Ruban=Ruvim
Rubik=Rubik
Rubin=Ruvim
Rudol'f=Rudol'f
Rul'ke=Raguil
Runi=Runi
Ruvel'=Ruvim
Ruven'=Ruvim
Ruven=Ruvim
Ruvim=Ruvim
Ruvin=Ruvim
Ruzha=Ruzha
Ruzin=Ruzin
Ryven=Ruvim
Saad'ya=Saad'ya
Saad'ya=Saad'ya
Saada=Saada
Saadiya=Isaia
Saadon=Saadon
Sabbataj=Shabfaj
Sabbataj=Shavfaj
Sablika=Sablika
Sadik=Tsadik
Safat=Shafat
Safatiya=Safatiya
Safronij=Safronij
Sagulo=Sagulo
Said=Said
Sak=Isaak
Sakhar=Issakhar
Sakhar=Issoskhor
Sakhno=Shakhno
Sal'nik=Sal'nik

Salafiel=Salafiel
Salam=Salam
Salamon=Solomon
Salemon=Solomon
Salim=Salim
Salmon=Salmon
Salmon=Solomon
Salom=Sholojm
Salomej=Solomon
Salomo=Solomon
Salum=Shalum
Samaa=Shema
Samarij=Sh'mariya
Samariya=Shemariya
Samed=Simon-Tov
Sammaj=Shammaj
Samoil=Samuil
Sampson=Samson
Samshel'=Samshel'
Samson=Samson
Samuel'=Samuil
Samuil=Samuil
Sana=Nafanejl'
Sana=Nefaniya
Sane=Nafanejl'
Sanejl'=Nafanejl'
Sanel'=Nafanejl'
Sani=Nafanejl'
Sani=Nefaniya
Sanii=Nafaniya
Sanio=Nafanejl'
Sanio=Nefaniya
Sanko=Nafanejl'
Sano=Nafanejl'
Santel'=Santel'
Sanvel'=Sanvel'
Sanvil'=Zvul
Sar-Sholojm=Sar-Sholojm
Saraf=Saraf
Sasan=Sheshan
Saul=Saul
Savej=Savej
Savelij=Saul
Savi=Tsvi
Savvafaj=Shabfij
Savvafaj=Shavfaj
Sebast'yan=Sebast'yan
Sebastian=Sebastian
Sebastian=Sebastian
Sedekiya=Sedekiya
Sejman=Sejman
Selafijl=Selafijl

Selemiya=Selemiya
Seliklajn=Iokor
Sellim=Shillejm
Sellim=Shillem
Semaiya=Shemaiya
Semakhiya=Semakhiya
Semej=Semej
Semen=Simeon
Semeon=Semeon
Semion=Simeon
Senda=Aleksandr
Sender=Aleksandr
Sender=Nafanejl'
Senderla=Aleksandr
Senderlajn=Aleksandr
Senderman=Aleksandr
Sendvrla=Aleksandr
Sergej=Sergij
Sergij=Sergij
Sergiusz=Sergij
Seruya=Seruya
Seudi=Seudi
Sevakhiya=Semakhiya
Seval=Shoval
Severin=Severin
Sevij=Tsvi
Sevna=Sevna
Seyabuziya=Seyabuziya
Sh'mar'ya=Sh'mariya
Sh'mario=Sh'mariya
Sh'mariya=Sh'mariya
Shaba=Shavfaj
Shabati=Shavfaj
Shabfaj=Shabfaj
Shabfij=Shabfij
Shabos=Shabos
Shabsa=Shavfaj
Shabse=Shavfaj
Shabsel'=Shavfaj
Shabsil=Shavfaj
Shabso=Shabso
Shabsoj=Shabsoj
Shabsuli=Avraam
Shabsuli=Shavfaj
Shafat=Shafat
Shafmi=Avraam
Shaiya=Isaia
Shajka=Isaia
Shakhna=Shakhno
Shakhne=Shakhno
Shakhne=Sholojm
Shakhno=Shakhno

Shalman=Ioets
Shalmo=Shalmo
Shalmon=Solomon
Shalmun=Samuil
Shalshel'=Shalshel'
Shalum=Shalum
Shame=Shammaj
Shamkhe=Shammaj
Shamkho=Shamkho
Shamkhon=Samson
Shammaj=Shammaj
Shamshel'=Samson
Shamshon=Samson
Shamson=Samson
Shamsuli=Avraam
Shapatan=Shabfaj
Shapatan=Shavfaj
Shapsa=Shavfaj
Shapsel'=Shabfaj
Shapsel'=Shavfaj
Shapsiya=Shabfaj
Shapsiya=Shavfaj
Shar'e=Shar'e
Shaul=Saul
Shaul=Shaul
Shaulko=Saul
Shaulko=Shaul
Shavfaj=Shavfaj
Shavsfaj=Shavsfaj
Shaya=Goshaia
Shaya=Isaia
Sheban=Shavfaj
Shebl'=Shebl'
Shebsel'=Shavfaj
Sheftel'=Iakov
Sheftil=David
Sheftil=Shavfaj
Sheftl=David
Shejl'=Saul
Shejlil=Saul
Shejma=Shema
Shejma=Simeon
Shejmo=Shemaiya
Shejmon=Shimon
Shejnman=Efrem
Shejnman=Semeon
Shejnman=Simeon
Shejshes=Shejshes
Shejshon=Sheshan
Shejvakh=Shevakh
Shem-Tojv=Shem-Tojv
Shema=Shema

Shemaiya=Moisej
Shemaiya=Shemaiya
Shemar'ya=Shemariya
Shemarie=Shemariya
Shemario=Shemariya
Shemariya=Shemariya
Shemiel=Samuil
Shemiuel=Samuil
Shender=Aleksandr
Shenko=Semeon
Shenko=Simeon
Shepe=Shavfaj
Sheppel'=Sheppel'
Sheps=Shavfaj
Shepsel'=Shavfaj
Shepsil=Shavfaj
Shepsyu=Shavfaj
Sheshan=Sheshan
Shevakh=Shevakh
Sheve=Shavfaj
Shevil'=Shoval
Shgalshel=Shgalshel
Shia=Iisus
Shibi=Shavfaj
Shibsoi=Shibsoi
Shiela=Iisus
Shigmund=Shigmund
Shika=Iisus
Shikar=Aaron
Shilim=Shillem
Shillejm=Shillejm
Shillem=Shillem
Shima=Shema
Shiman=Moisej
Shiman=Shiman
Shiman=Simeon
Shimel'=Simeon
Shimenko=Simeon
Shimkhe=Simkho
Shimoitso=Simeon
Shimojn=Simeon
Shimon=Shimon
Shimon=Simeon
Shimontso=Simeon
Shimriya=Shimriya
Shimshaj=Shimshaj
Shimshejn=Samson
Shimshejn=Simeon
Shimshojn=Shimshojn
Shimshon=Samson
Shimshon=Simeon
Shimsia=Shimsia

Shimsid=Shimsid
Shiniur=Shiniur
Shinka=Simeon
Shiskin=Aleksandr
Shiza=Shiza
Shlejma=Solomon
Shlema=Solomon
Shlemkhaj=Moisej
Shliman=Moisej
Shliom=Solomon
Shlioma=Solomon
Shliome=Solomon
Shliomka=Solomon
Shlojme=Solomon
Shlojmikhl=Solomon
Shlojmitsl=Solomon
Shlojmitso=Solomon
Shlojmko=Solomon
Shlojmli=Shlojmli
Shlojmshi=Solomon
Shlojmtsiejl'=Shlojmtsiejl'
Shlojmtsil=Solomon
Shlomo=Solomon
Shloume=Solomon
Shmaiya=Shmaiya
Shmarie=Sh'mariya
Shmaya=Shemaiya
Shmechko=Shmechko
Shmel'ko=Simeon
Shmelko=Samuil
Shmerek=Sh'mariya
Shmerik=Sh'mariya
Shmeril=Shemariya
Shmeril=Shimriya
Shmerka=Sh'mariya
Shmerka=Shemariya
Shmerke=Sh'mariya
Shmerke=Shimriya
Shmerki=Shemariya
Shmiel=Samuil
Shmil=Samuil
Shmilik=Samuil
Shmir'ya=Sh'mariya
Shmir'ya=Shemariya
Shmojlo=Samuil
Shmonko=Simeon
Shmorak=Sh'mariya
Shmorak=Shemariya
Shmuejlo=Samuil
Shmuejlo=Samuil
Shmuel'=Samuil
Shmuel=Samuil

Shmuil=Samuil
Shmul'=Samuil
Shmul'ke=Samuil
Shmul'ko=Samuil
Shmuli=Samuil
Shmulik=Samuil
Shmulo=Samuil
Shmun'=Simeon
Shmun=Rimeon
Shmunya=Simeon
Shmur=Shmur
Shneer=Shneur
Shneor=Shneur
Shneur=Shneur
Shniur=Moisej
Shnum=Shnum
Shoel'=Saul
Shoel=Saul
Shojejl=Saul
Shojl=Saul
Shojshon=Sheshan
Shokher=Shokhojr
Shokhojr=Shokhojr
Sholaim=Sholojm
Sholem=Sholojm
Sholeme=Sholojm
Sholojm=Sholojm
Sholom=Sholojm
Sholomets=Sholojm
Sholomon=Solomon
Sholumko=Solomon
Shomon=Simeon
Shopel'=Shopel'
Shotur=Moisej
Shoturl=Moisej
Shoul=Saul
Shoval=Shoval
Shraga=Shrago
Shrage=Shrago
Shrago=Shrago
Shrants=Shrants
Shtajr=Samuil
Shteuglin=Eliakim
Shtir=Samuil
Shtiur=Moisej
Shtrojlan=Shtrojlan
Shua=Iisus
Shual=Shual
Shuela=Iisus
Shueli=Iisus
Shuil=Shuil
Shul'man=Iokhanan

Shul'man=Sholojm
Shulajm=Sholojm
Shulem=Sholojm
Shulim=Sholojm
Shulimo=Shulimo
Shulman=Ioets
Shulom=Shulom
Shuman=Natrojno
Shunko=Shunko
Shunlajn=Shunlajn
Shunman=Menaim
Shvartsman=Shokhojr
Shvartsmon=Nafan
Sid=Sid
Sigizmund=Sigizmund
Sima=Saraf
Siman=Simeon
Simen=Simeon
Simeon=Simeon
Simkhe=Simkho
Simkho=Simkho
Simma=Simma
Simok=Shemaiya
Simok=Shmaiya
Simok=Simeon
Simon-Tov=Simon-Tov
Simon=Simeon
Simoon=Simoon
Simriya=Shimriya
Simson=Samson
Simuil=Samuil
Simyan=Simyan
Siva=Siva
Sivan=Sivan
Siyabuziya=Siyabuziya
Skhar'e=Zakhariya
Skhariya=Zakhariya
Slama=Slama
Sliman=Sliman
Smakhio=Semakhiya
Smarko=Sh'mariya
Smarko=Shemariya
Smokhno=Smokhno
Smonko=Smonko
Smuel'=Samuil
Sneer=Shneur
Soferl=Moisej
Sofonia=Sofonia
Soid=Saad'ya
Sokhor=Issakhar
Solamon=Solomon
Solem=Sholojm

Solemon=Solomon
Solomon=Solomon
Soskher=Issakhar
Sosojn=Moisej
Srol'=Izrail
Srul'=Izrail
Srulik=Izrail'
Stanislaw=Stanislaw
Stefan=Stefan
Strozhan=Strozhan
Suan=Shual
Sukher=Issakhar
Sulem=Solomon
Suliman=Suliman
Sumer=Ifamar
Sumer=Ifamar
Sumer=Sumor
Sumor=Sumor
Sumshin=Samson
Sur=Tsur
Suse=Aleksandr
Susi=Moisej
Svechki=Il'ya
Szczensnyj=Szczensnyj
Szlam=Szlam
Szlama=Solomon
Szlami=Solomon
Szloma=Solomon
Szmerek=Shemariya
Tabiyash=Toviya
Tadeusz=Todros
Tais=Tais
Takhlif=Takhlifo
Takhlif=Takhlifo
Takhlifo=Takhlifo
Tal'ko=Tal'ko
Talman=Talman
Tam=Tam
Tamrij=Tamrij
Tanis=Tanis
Tankha=Tankha
Tankhel'=Tankhum
Tankhimo=Tankhimo
Tankhum=Tankhum
Tankhumo=Tankhumo
Tanokh=Tanokh
Tarfon=Tarfon
Taus=Issakhor
Tav'ya=Toviya
Tavder=Todros
Tavejl'=Tavejl'
Tejbel'=David

Tejvel'=David
Temerlin=Avraam
Teodor=Todros
Teodorus=Neemiya
Teodorus=Nefaniya
Teodrus=Todros
Teofil=Teofil
Tev'e=Toviya
Tev'ya=Toviya
Tevaliya=Tevaliya
Tevder=Todros
Tevel'=David
Tevel'=Tavejl'
Tevel'=Toviya
Tevele=Tevaliya
Tevele=Toviya
Tevil'=David
Tevla=David
Timro=Timro
Tishbi=Tishbi
Tishko=Tishko
Tiviomi=Ojshie
Tivium=Todros
Tiviumi=Tiviumi
Tobias=Toviya
Tobiya=Toviya
Tobiyash=Toviya
Tod'=Nafaniya
Tod=Nefaniya
Tode=Nafaniya
Tode=Nefaniya
Todres=Todros
Todris=Todros
Todros=Todros
Todrus=Todros
Todya=Todros
Tojvi=Toviya
Toli=Naffalim
Tomasz=Tomasz
Tov'e=Toviya
Tov'eri=Toviya
Tov'ya=Toviya
Tov'ya=Toviya
Tov=Tov
Tovi=Tovi
Tovij=Moisej
Tovij=Toviya
Tovit=Toviya
Toviya=Toviya
Toviya=Toviya
Tovus=Tovus
Trajt=Iuda

Trajt=Ojshie
Trajtl=Ojshie
Tratl=Iuda
Trejstlajn=Neemiya
Trifon=Tarfon
Trishtal'=Manoj
Trojsh=Trojsh
Trojshtam=Menaim
Truslin=Neemiya
Tsadik=Tsadik
Tsaduk=Sadok
Tsakhrajm=Petakhiya
Tsakhrajs=Issakhar
Tsal'=Veseliil
Tsalakh=Tsalakh
Tsale=Veseliil
Tsalek=Beseliil
Tsalel'=Veseliil
Tsalel'=Veseliil
Tsalik=Veseliil
Tsaliya=Veseliil
Tsalka=Veseliil
Tsalko=Veseliil
Tsdoko=Tsdoko
Tsedek=Tsedek
Tsejl'io=Veseliil
Tselek=Tselek
Tsempl=Tsemakh
Tsenik=Tsenik
Tsevi=Tsvi
Tsezar'=Tsezar'
Tshuo=Tshuo
Tshuvo=Tshuvo
Tsil'faj=Tsil'faj
Tsine=Tsine
Tsion=Tsion
Tsisho=Tsisho
Tsiviya=Tsiviya
Tsodik=Sadok
Tsoduk=Sadok
Tsogejl'=Tsogejl'
Tsudek=Sadok
Tsudik=Sadok
Tsudya=Sadok
Tsur=Tsur
Tsur=Tsur
Tsuri=Tsuri
Tsuriil=Tsuriil
Tsurishaddaj=Tsurishaddaj
Tsvi=Tsvi
Tsylka=Veseliil
Tub'ya=Toviya

Tubias=Toviya
Tubiash=Toviya
Tubiya=Toviya
Tuki=Iakov
Tuv'ya=Toviya
Tuvie=Toviya
Tuviya=Toviya
Ulan=Ulla
Ulla=Ulla
Ulo=Ulla
Ur'e=Urij
Ur'e=Urij
Ura=Urij
Uraj=Uraj
Urchik=Urchik
Urchik=Urchik
Urchik=Urij
Ure=Urij
Urele=Urij
Uriel'=Uriil
Uriel=Uriil
Uriil'=Uriil
Uriil=Uriil
Uriil=Uriil
Uriim=Uriim
Urij=Urij
Urik=Urij
Urish=Urij
Uriyash=Urij
Urka=Urij
Uron=Aaron
Urshrago=Urshrago
Uryash=Urij
Usher=Asir
Ushl=Iisus
Uziel=Uziil
Uziil=Uziil
Uziya=Uziya
Vaaz=Vooz
Vadia=Ovadia
Vajbus=Samuil
Vajbush=Berekhiya
Vajbush=Meshuilam
Vajdel'=Efrem
Vajdel'=Iokor
Vajfesh=Urij
Vajfish=Urij
Vajl=Ezekiil'
Vajvel=Eliakim
Vajver=Eliakim
Vajvil=Meshuilam
Vajvish=Edidia

Vajvish=Eliakim
Vajvish=Eliezer
Vajvish=Ezekie
Vajvish=Iezekiil'
Vajvish=Ioil'
Vajvish=Iri
Vajvish=Khaim
Vajvish=Moisej
Vajvish=Neemiya
Vajvish=Samson
Vajvish=Samuil
Vajvish=Shimshojn
Vajvish=Shneur
Vajvish=Urshrago
Vajvl=Eliezer
Vajvl=Ezekie
Vajvl=Iezekiil'
Vajvl=Ioil'
Vajvl=Irshrago
Vajvl=Khaim
Vajvl=Neemiya
Vajvl=Samson
Vajvl=Shneur
Vajvl=Urij
Vajvl=Urshrago
Valbil=Veniamin
Valblain=Veniamin
Valblajn=Veniamin
Valchko=Veniamin
Valentij=Valentij
Valerij=Valerij
Valk=Iisus
Valk=Ionafan
Valk=Solomon
Valk=Urshrago
Valko=Veniamin
Vaneya=Vaneya
Vani=Vani
Varak=Varak
Varakhia=Berekhiya
Varakhiya=Varakhiya
Varukh=Varukh
Vasilij=Vasilij
Vavil=Khalev
Vavila=Veniamin
Vedil=Gad
Vejlka=Veniamin
Vejlo=Veniamin
Vel'vish=Veniamin
Vele=Veniamin
Veli=Veniamin
Velklin=Solomon

Velva=Veniamin
Velvil=Veniamin
Velvul=Veniamin
Ven'yamin=Veniamin
Veniamin=Veniamin
Veniyamin=Veniamin
Venyamin=Veniamin
Verendt=Dov
Veria=Veria
Verzellij=Verzellij
Veseleil=Veseliil
Veseliil=Veseliil
Veseliil=Veseliil
Vibel'man=Urij
Viblamu=Urij
Viblan=Eleazar
Viblan=Eliakim
Viblan=Irigrus
Viblan=Prigrus
Viblan=Samuil
Viblan=Urij
Vibli=Eliakim
Viblin=Eliakim
Viblin=Simoon
Vidal=Khaim
Vigdejr=Avigdor
Vikentij=Vikentij
Vil'gel'm=Vil'gel'm
Vil'khel'm=Vil'khel'm
Vilblin=Simeon
Vilf=Ziv
Villiam=Villiam
Vilyam=Vilyam
Vintsent=Vintsent
Vinturo=Shavsfaj
Vinturo=Tsion
Virgo=Virgo
Vish=Efrem
Vishel=Ierukham
Vishl=Efrem
Vishl=Moisej
Vishlajn=Samuil
Vishlan=Samuil
Vishli=Erukhom
Vishli=Ierukham
Vishli=Samuil
Vishlin=Samuil
Vishlin=Samuil
Vitalij=Khaim
Vitoshin=Vitoshin
Vits=Vits
Vivlman=Meir

Vladislav=Vladislav
Vlajshl=Samuil
Voftsi=Veniamin
Vol'ka=Veniamin
Vol'ko=Veniamin
Volf=Veniamin
Volflajn=Veniamin
Volfo=Veniamin
Volle=Veniamin
Volvish=Veniamin
Voniamin=Voniamin
Vooz=Vooz
Vova=Veniamin
Vovtsi=Veniamin
Vrejdman=Simkho
Vridl=Ruvim
Vridman=Sholojm
Vruman=Iuda
Vruman=Moisej
Vruman=Neemiya
Vul'f=Ziv
Vulf=Ziv
Vyacheslav=Vyacheslav
Yaakov=Iakov
Yakar=Iokor
Yakef=Iakov
Yaker=Iokor
Yakhim=Iakim
Yakhod=Yakhod
Yakim=Iakim
Yakim=Iokim
Yakl=Iakov
Yakob=Iakov
Yakov=Iakov
Yakovko=Iakov
Yakub=Iakov
Yan=Iokhanan
Yanash=Iakov
Yanche=Iakov
Yane=Iokhanan
Yanin=Iakov
Yankel'=Iakov
Yankel=Iakov
Yankev=Iakov
Yanos=Iona
Yanot=Iona
Yantsi=Iakov
Yanush=Iakov
Yarmush=Ieremiya
Yaska=Iakov
Yatsi=Iakov
Yatsko=Iakov

Yavnin=Iona
Yavno=Iona
Yazon=Yazon
Yuda=Iuda
Yude=Iuda
Yudka=Iuda
Yudko=Iuda
Yukef=Iakov
Yukel'=Iakov
Yukhno=Iokhanan
Yukir=Iakov
Yul'ius=Ioil'
Yulin=Ioets
Yulius=Ioil'
Yuliyan=Ioil'
Yura=Iair
Yurdko=Urij
Yuri=Urij
Yuro=Iair
Yusko=Iosif
Yuzef=Iosif
Yuzheva=Iosif
Zael'=Zael'
Zahkar=Zakhariya
Zajvel=Samuil
Zajvl=Samuil
Zak=Isaak
Zakar=Zakar
Zake=Zelikman
Zakhariash=Zakhariya
Zakharij=Zakhariya
Zakhariya=Zakhariya
Zakhej=Zakkaj
Zakkaj=Zakkaj
Zakkur=Zakkur
Zaklin=Isaak
Zal'kind=Eleazar
Zal'kind=Eliakim
Zal'kind=Solomon
Zal'men=Efrem
Zal'men=Meshuilam
Zale=Solomon
Zali=Solomon
Zalkin=Eleazar
Zalkin=Eliakim
Zalko=Solomon
Zalman=Avraam
Zalman=Efrem
Zalman=Eleazar
Zalman=Eliakim
Zalman=Eliezer
Zalman=Iekufiil

Zalman=Moisej
Zalman=Shemariya
Zalman=Shemariya
Zalman=Shneur
Zalman=Solomon
Zalman=Trojsh
Zalmen=Avraam
Zalmon=Shimriya
Zalo=Solomon
Zamel'=Zamel'
Zamiru=Zamiru
Zamuel'=Samuil
Zanvel'=Samuil
Zanvil'=Nafan
Zanvil'=Samuil
Zanvl=Samuil
Zarakh=Zara
Zarakh=Zarakh
Zavdi=Zavdi
Zavdiil=Zavdiil
Zavel=Zvul
Zavil=Meshezavel
Zavil=Metush
Zavl=Samuil
Zavlin=Nafan
Zavlin=Nafon
Zavlin=Samuil
Zavulon=Zavulon
Zdislav=Zdislav
Zebulon=Zavulon
Zebulun=Zavulon
Zeev=Voniamin
Zeev=Ziv
Zegfried=Zegfried
Zehkar'ya=Zakhariya
Zejlik=Isaak
Zejn=Zejn
Zekhariash=Zakhariya
Zekhariya=Zakhariya
Zekil'=Isaak
Zekl=Isaak
Zeklin=Isaak
Zel'kin=Avraam
Zel'kin=Solomon
Zel'kind=Avraam
Zel'kind=Efrem
Zel'kind=Eleazar
Zel'kind=Shemariya
Zel'kind=Shneur
Zel'kind=Solomon
Zel'man=Eleazar
Zelek=Iuda

Zeli=Solomon
Zelig=Aaron
Zelig=Asir
Zelig=Aviezer
Zelig=Azriil
Zelig=Finees
Zelig=Girson
Zelig=Iakov
Zelig=Iekufiil
Zelig=Iisus
Zelig=Isaak
Zelig=Iuda
Zelig=Ruvim
Zelig=Solomon
Zeligil=Eliakim
Zeligin=Avraam
Zeligin=Efrem
Zeligin=Eleazar
Zeligin=Iekufiil
Zeligin=Meshuilam
Zeligin=Shemariya
Zeligin=Shneur
Zeligin=Solomon
Zeligman=Aaron
Zeligman=Asar
Zeligman=Asir
Zeligman=Aviezer
Zeligman=Avraam
Zeligman=Azriil
Zeligman=Efrem
Zeligman=Eleazar
Zeligman=Eliakim
Zeligman=Finees
Zeligman=Girson
Zeligman=Iakov
Zeligman=Iekufiil
Zeligman=Iisus
Zeligman=Isaak
Zeligman=Iuda
Zeligman=Meshuilam
Zeligman=Ruvim
Zeligman=Shemariya
Zeligman=Shneur
Zeligman=Solomon
Zelik=Aaron
Zelik=Asir
Zelik=Aviezer
Zelik=Avraam
Zelik=Azriil
Zelik=Efrem
Zelik=Eleazar
Zelik=Eliakim

Zelik=Finees
Zelik=Girson
Zelik=Iakov
Zelik=Iekufiil
Zelik=Iisus
Zelik=Isaak
Zelik=Iuda
Zelik=Meshuilam
Zelik=Nafan
Zelik=Ruvim
Zelik=Shemariya
Zelik=Shneur
Zelik=Solomon
Zelikin=Aaron
Zelikin=Asir
Zelikin=Aviezer
Zelikin=Azriil
Zelikin=Finees
Zelikin=Girson
Zelikin=Iakov
Zelikin=Iekufiil
Zelikin=Iisus
Zelikin=Isaak
Zelikin=Iuda
Zelikin=Ruvim
Zelikin=Shneur
Zelikin=Solomon
Zelikind=Meshuilam
Zelikman=Aaron
Zelikman=Asir
Zelikman=Aviezer
Zelikman=Avraam
Zelikman=Azriil
Zelikman=Efrem
Zelikman=Eliakim
Zelikman=Finees
Zelikman=Girson
Zelikman=Girson
Zelikman=Iakov
Zelikman=Iekufiil
Zelikman=Iisus
Zelikman=Iokor
Zelikman=Iuda
Zelikman=Meshuilam
Zelikman=Ruvim
Zelikman=Shemariya
Zelikman=Shneur
Zelikman=Solomon
Zelikman=Zelikman
Zelka=Eliokim
Zelkin=Efrem
Zelkin=Iekufiil

Zelkin=Memuilam
Zelkin=Meshuilam
Zelkin=Shemariya
Zelkin=Shneur
Zelkind=Iekufiil
Zelkind=Shneur
Zelko=Avraam
Zelko=Efrem
Zelko=Eleazar
Zelko=Iekufiil
Zelko=Iuda
Zelko=Meshuilam
Zelko=Shemariya
Zelko=Shneur
Zelko=Solomon
Zemil'=Meshuilam
Zeml'=Meshuilam
Zeml=Moisej
Zendel=Enokh
Zenokh=Zenokh
Zenon=Zenon
Zerakhya=Zerakhya
Zev=Ziv
Zevadiya=Zevadiya
Zevel'=Zevel'
Zevilin=Zavulon
Zevulon=Zavulon
Zevulun=Zavulon
Zhanno=Zhanno
Zheke=Iokhanan
Zheronim=Samuil
Zhurakh=Zarakh
Zibel'=Zvul.
Zigbor=Zigbor
Zigmun=Zigmun
Zigmund=Asir
Zigmunt=Asir
Zikhel'=Iekhiil
Zikhri=Zikhri
Zil'=Uziil
Zil'ka=Uziil
Zil'man=Eleazar
Zilig=Isaak
Zilin=Zunlin
Zima=Zima
Zimel'=Meshuilam
Zimel'=Zima
Zimel=Simeon
Zimen=Simeon
Ziml=Naffalim
Ziml=Samuil
Zimlik=Simeon

Zimlin=Meshuilam
Zimlin=Simeon
Zimon=Simeon
Zimri=Zimri
Zimro=Zimro
Zindl=Aleksandr
Zindl=Enokh
Zis'e=Meshuilom
Zisa=Aleksandr
Zisa=Ioil'
Zisel'=Meshuilam
Zisel=Iisus
Ziska=Iisus
Ziskind=Aleksandr
Ziskind=Aleksandr
Ziskind=Iekufiil
Ziskind=Ierakhmeil
Ziskind=Mardokhej
Ziskind=Shneur
Zisl=Aleksandr
Zisla=Ioil'
Zislan=Ioil'
Zislin=Ioil'
Zisman=Eliezer
Zisman=Iisus
Ziv=Ziv
Ziza=Ziza
Ziza=Zus'a
Zizel'=Zus'a
Zkharia=Zakhariya
Zkhario=Zakhariya
Zora=Zara
Zorakh=Zara
Zorokh=Zara
Zorukh=Zara
Zrael'=Israil
Zrael'=Izrail'
Zrail'=Israil
Zrail'=Izrail'
Zukhen=Zukhen
Zuml=Samuil
Zuml=Simeon
Zumlin=Meshuilom
Zumlin=Samuil
Zumlin=Simeon
Zumm=Meshuilom
Zundel'=Enokh
Zundel'=Iosif
Zundel'=Iuda
Zunlin=Zunlin
Zunovil'=Nafan
Zunvel'=Natan

Zunvil'=Nafan
Zunvil=Samuil
Zurakh=Zara
Zus'a=Zus'a
Zusa=Aleksandr
Zusa=Azariya
Zusa=Eleazar
Zusa=Eliezer
Zusa=Iekufiil
Zusa=Iisus
Zusa=Ioil'
Zusa=Izrail'
Zusa=Meshalam
Zusa=Meshuilom
Zusa=Shneur
Zuse=Ierakhmeil
Zusel'=Ioil'
Zusel=Iisus
Zushkin=Shneur
Zusi=Iekufiil
Zusi=Iisus
Zuskind=Izrail'
Zuskind=Mardokhej
Zusko=Iisus
Zusl=Aleksandr
Zuslan=Iisus
Zuslin=Aleksandr
Zuslin=Iisus
Zuslin=Ioil'
Zuslin=Isaak
Zusman=Aleksandr
Zusman=Azriil
Zusman=Eliezer
Zusman=Emmanuil
Zusman=Iekufiil
Zusman=Ierakhmeil
Zusman=Iisus
Zusman=Iojl'
Zusman=Meshalam
Zusman=Meshalam
Zusman=Meshuilom
Zusman=Moisej
Zusya=Aleksandr
Zutra=Zutra
Zuza=Zuza
Zvadio=Zevadiya
Zvedil'=Zevadiya
Zvedl=Zakhariya
Zvul=Zvul
Zvulon=Zavulon
Zysha=Aleksandr

Glossary

Ashkenazim. Eastern European Yiddish-speaking Jews.

B.C.E.. Before Common Era.

calque. Loan translation. With regards to names, direct translation of a name from one language into another, for example, Tzipora (bird) into Feiga, Matatiya (God's gift) into Theodore, Hirsch into Tzvi.

C.E. Common Era.

compound name. A name with more than one root.

Diaspora. Dispersion of the Jewish people outside Palestine.

diminutive name. Indicating a high level of familiarity, intimacy and love.

elementary name. A name with one root.

Eretz Yisrael. Term used by Jews to designate the Holyland prior to the founding of the State of Israel.

etymology. The history of a linguistic form, (that is, a word) shown by tracing its development, by tracing its transmission from one language to another, or by analyzing it into its component parts.

folk name. Same as kinnui.

given name. Name given to a child by parents at birth.

Hasidism. Pietistic movement within Judaism that started in Poland about 1750 by Rabbi Israel Baal Shem Tov.

homonym. One of two or more words spelled and pronounced alike, but different in meaning.

hypocoristci name. A familiar or pet form of a given name.

Israelites. Descendant of the Hebrew patriarch Jacob; natives or inhabitants of the ancient northern kingdom of Israel.

kinnui. (Plural *kinnuim*.) Vernacular, everyday secular name.

Levites. Members of the tribe of Levi, descended by tradition from the third son of Jacob.

linguistics. Science or study of language.

Mishna. Codified religious law, of Divine oral origin, based on the Torah.

Mishnaic period. The historical period during which the Mishna was written (about 200 C.E.).

morphology. System of word-forming elements within a word.

nickname. A usually descriptive name used instead of, or along with, an official given name.

onomastics. The science or study of the origins or forms of words.

Pale of Settlement. Territory of the Russian Empire in which Jews were legally allowed to settle.

patronymic. Name derived from paternal ancestors, most commonly a father.

pet name. Same as diminutive.

phonetics. A system of sounds in a language

Prussia. A kingdom, with its capital in Berlin, during the eighteenth and nineteenth centuries.

root name. A name in its traditional form (for example, biblical) that has given rise to other forms and variations.

Russia. A former empire in Eastern Europe.

sacred name. A name, *shem ha-kodesh* in Hebrew, used in the synagogue and in Hebrew documents.

Seleucides period. The historic period named after a dynasty of kings that controlled most of the Asian provinces of the Macedonian empire in the third-first centuries B.C.E.

Sefardim. Jews of southern Spain and the southern Mediterranean rim.

Semites. Peoples who speak Semitic languages, such as Arabs and Jews.

shem kodesh. Hebrew for "holy name." The name used by an individual in association with relgious rituals.

shtetl. Small Jewish village or a town found in eastern Europe.

synonym. One of two or more words or expressions of the same language that have the same or nearly the same meaning in some or all senses.

Talmud. The authoritative body of Jewish tradition comprising the Mishna and Gemara (commentary to Mishna).

Tanakh. An acronym standing for Torah-Nevi'im-K'tuvim. Torah, the Five Books of Moses; Nevi'im, prophets; K'tuvim, writings.

theophoric. A name or a name component of religious nature.

variant. One that exhibits variations from the norm.

variation. The state of being different.

vernacular. A name or a dialect native to a region or country, rather than a literary, cultured or foreign language; in the context of Russian-Jewish names Zelik—instead of Avraam, Solomon, Ruvim—is a vernacular name.

YHWH. The four transliterated Hebrew letters that form the biblical name of God.

Bibliography

Andree, R. 1881. *Zur Volkskunde der Juden*. Bielefeld and Leipzig: Verlag & Klasing.

Arkhiv Yugo-Zapadnoj Rossii. 1869. *Akty, izdavaemye vremennoyu kommissieyu dlya razbora drevnikh aktov*, part 5, vol. 1. Kiev.

Beider, A. 1993. *A Dictionary of Jewish Surnames from the Russian Empire*. Teaneck, N.J.: Avotaynu.

———. 1996. "Jewish Given Names in the Grand Duchy of Lithuania," *Avotaynu* (Summer)

Benson, M. 1964. *Dictionary of Russian Personal Names*. Philadelphia, University of Pennsylvania Press.

Bershadskij, S.A. 1883. *Litovskie evrei*. St. Petersburg.

Brückner, A. 1917. "*Zasady etymologii słowiańskiej.*" *Rozprawy Akademii Umiejętności*, vol. 11. Krakow: Nakładem Akademii Umiejętności.

Bulgakov, S. V. 1900. *Nastol'naya kniga dlya svyashchenno-tserkovno-sluzhitelej*. Kharkov.

Bystron, J. 1936. *Nazwiska Polskie*. Lwów-Warszawa.

Dejch, G.M. 1992. *Sinagogi, Molitvennye Doma I Sostoyashchie pri nikh Dolzhnostnye Litsa v Cherte Evreiskoi Osedlosti i Guberniyakh Kurlyandskoi i Liflyandskoi Rossiiskoi Imperii 1853–1854*. New York.

Dubnov, S.M. 1916–20. *History of the Jews in Russia and Poland*. Philadelphia: Jewish Publication Society. Translation from Russian.

Encyclopaedia Judaica. 1972. Jerusalem.

Evrejskaya Entsiklopedia. 1906–13. St. Petersburg: Brokhaus-Efron.

Gessen, Y. "*Imena sobstvennyya po russkomu zakonodatel'stvu.*" In *Evrejskaya Entsiklopedia*, vol. 8.

Gorr, S. 1992. *Jewish Personal Names*. Teaneck, N.J.: Avotaynu.

Graetz, H. 1891–98. *History of the Jews*. Philadelphia: Jewish Publication Society.

Gross, H. 1897. *Gallia Judaica*. Paris: Librarie Léopold Cerf.

Jacobs, J. 1894. *Studies in Biblical Archaeology*. London: David Nutt.

Jewish Encyclopedia. 1901–9. New York: Funk & Wagnalls.

Kaganoff, B. 1977. *Dictionary of Jewish Names and Their History*. Schocken Books. Reprinted, 1996. Northvale, N.J.: Jason Aronson.

Kerber, G. 1897. *Die Religioonseschichtliche Bedeutung der Hebräischen des Alten Testamentes*. Freiburg: I. B: Verlag von J.C.B. Mohr.

Kolatch, A.J. 1984. *The Complete Dictionary of English and Hebrew First Names*. New York: Jonathan Davis Publishers.

Kuhl, Ferdinand. *Zur Muhrüng des Verständnises Unserer Heimischen Votnamin*.

Kulisher, I. 1911. *Sbornik dlya soglasovaniya raznovidnostej imen*. Zhitomir.

Levanda, L. 1874. *Polnyj khronologicheskij sbornik zakonov i postanovlenij, kasayushchikhsya evreev*. St. Petersburg.

Munitz, B. 1972. "Identifying Jewish Names in Russia." *Soviet Jewish Affairs*,

No. 3 (May).

Mysh, M. 1904. *Rukovodstvo k Russkim zakonam o evreyakh*. St. Petersburg.

Otrebski, J. 1935. *O Najdawniejszych Polskich Imionach Osobowych*. Wilno.

The Pentateuch and Haftorah. 1966. London: Soncino Press.

Pogorel'skij, M. 1893. *Evrejskiya imena sobstvennyya*. St. Petersburg.

Prostonarodnyya evrejskiya imena. 1878. St. Petersburg.

Rabinovich, Osip. 1858. "On Moshkas and Ioskas."

Regesty i nadpisi. 1899–1913. *Svod materialov dlya istorii evreev Rossii*. 80–1800. Extracts from Russian documents and chronicles related to Jews. St.Petersburg.

Shternberg, L. 1924. *"Rol' Sokhraneniya imeni v evrejskom levirate."* In *Evrejskaya Starina* 5(9). Leningrad.

Singerman, R. 1977. *Jewish and Hebrew Onomastics*. New York: Garland Publishing.

Stankiewicz, E. 1969. "Derivational Pattern of Yiddish Personal (Given) Names." In *The Field of Yiddish: Third Collection*. The Hague.

Tanakh 1985. Philadelphia: Jewish Publication Society.

Taszycki, W. 1924. *Polskie Nazwy Osobowe*. Krakow: Gebethner i Wolff.

Unbegaun, B.O. 1989. *Russkie familii*. Moscow (translation from English).

Vajsenberg, S. 1914. *"Prozvishcha Yuzhno-Russkikh evreev."* In *Etnograficheskoe obozrenie*, vols. 101–2. Moscow.

Weissenberg, S. 1913. *"Mitteilungen zur Jüdischen Volkskunde."* *Heft*, No. 45.

Zunz, Leopold. 1837. *Die Namen der Juden*. Leipzig.

Sources Cited by Kulisher

Azulay, Chaim Yosef David (–1765). *Shem Hagedolim.*   שם הגדולים

Balcher, Aryeh, of Zaslov. *Shem Aryeh.*   שם אריה

Benvenisti, Chaim ben Yisrael (1603–73). *Kneset Hagedolah.*   כנסת הגדולה

Chabib, Moshe ben (15th–16th century). *Ezrat Nashim*   עזרת נשים

———. *Get Pashut.*   גט פשוט

Chaim of Tsantz. *Teshuvot Divrei Chaim.*   תשובות דברי חיים

Eibenschütz, David Shlomo (–1812). *Ne'ot Deshe—Responsa.*   נאות דשא—תשובות

Ezra, Avraham ibn. *Ibn Ezra.*   אבן עזרא

Frenkel, Yechezkel. *Kuntres Hashemot.*   קונטרס השמות

Gantzfried, Shlomo (1800–86). *Ohalei Shem.*   אהלי שם

Gantzfried, Yosef. *Shem Yosef.*   שם יוסף

Ha-Kohen, Moshe Yequtiel Kaufman. *Khukei Derekh.*   חוקי דרך

Ha-Kohen, Simcha. *Sefer Shemot.*   ספר שמות

Ha-Levi, Shmuel ben David. *Nakhlat Shiv'ah.*   נחלת שבעה

Heilprin, Yechiel ben Solomon (1660–1746). *Seder Hadorot.*   סדר הדורות

Kohen, Chaim. *Teshuvot.*   תשובות

Lavat, Avraham David (Moreh Tsedek of Nikolaev). *Kav Nuki.*   קו נקי

Margaliot, Avraham Zalman. *Shevilei Leket.*   שבלי לקט

Margaliot, Ephrayim Zalman (1762–1828). *Bet Efrayim—Responsa.* בית אפרים
———. *Lekutei Shemot.* לקוטי שמות
———. *Tuv Gittin.* טוב גיטין
———. *Yad Efrayim.* יד אפרים
Menachem Mendel of Lubavitch. *Tsemakh Tsedek Hechadash.* צמח צדק החדש
Mendil, Zekhariyah. *Be'er Heitev 'Al Shulchan Arukh.* באר היטב על שלחן ערוך
Moshe, Rabbi Ba'al Penei. *Shemot Gittin.* שמות גטין
Rabbi Barukh (Moreh Tsedek of Zhitomir). *Mekor Barukh.* מקור ברוך
Rabinovich, O.A. *1880-1888. O sobstvennykh imenakh evreev.* St. Petersburg.
RAM"A. *Darkei Moshe.* דרכי משה
Rapaport, Chaim Ha-Kohen (–1839). *Teshuvot Mayim Chaim.* תשובות מים חיים
Ravich, Yitzchak. *Avnei Zikaron.* אבני זכרון
———. *Be'er Yitzchak.* באר יצחק
———. *Ma'agalei Teshuvah.* מגלי תשובה
Sofer, Moshe (1763–1839). *Chatam Sofer.* חתם סופר
Yaffe, Mordechai ben Avraham. *Levush.* לבוש
Zhurakovskij, K.S. and Rabinovich, E.S. 1874. *Polnoe sobranie evrejskikh imen.*
    Suvalki.

Babylonian Talmud
Bet David בית דוד
Bet Shmu'el בית שמואל
Choshen Mishpat חשן משפט
Hapisgah הפסגה
Imrei Esh—Responsa אמרי אש
Jerusalem Talmud
Kuntres Hashemot—Pitchei Teshuva קונטרס השמות—פתחי תשובה
Lekach Tov לקח טוב
Midrash Rabah מדרש רבה
Ot Letovah אות לטובה
Pitchei Teshuvah Even Ha'ezer פתחי תשובה אבן העזר
Rash"al רש"ל
Seder Mahar"am סדר מהר"ם
Shem Hagedolim Hechadash שם הגדולים החדש
Shoel U-meshiv—Responsa שואל ומשיב—תשובות
Shulchan Arukh Even Ha'ezer שלחן ערוך אבן העזר
Ta"z (Turei Zahav) Yoreh De'ah and Even Ha'ezer ט"ז יורה דעה ואבן העזר
Tosefta תוספתא
Zohar זהר

Archival Sources
Lithuanian State Historical Archives, Vilnius, Lithuania
Vital records, fiscal census records (*revizskiya skazki*). Various collections for

Vilna, Kovno and Suwalki provinces. 1795–1910s.

Central Archives of Kaunas. Kaunas, Lithuania.

Vital records, tax census records. Various collections for Kovno province. Early 1800s–1910s.

National Archives of the Republic of Belarus. Minsk, Belarus.

Vital records. Various collections for Minsk and Mogilev Provinces. Mid-1800s–1910s.

Kiyev State Historical Archives. Kiyev, Ukraine.

Vital records. Various collections for Kiev Province. Mid-1800s–1910s.

State Archive of Kiyev Oblast. Kiyev, Ukraine.

Tax census records. Various collections for Kiev Province. Mid-1800s.

State Archive of Zhitomir Oblast. Zhitomir, Ukraine.

Vital records (1850s–1890s), tax census records (1811–58). Various collections for the city of Zhitomir and Volhyn province.

State Archive of Odessa Oblast. Odessa, Ukraine.

Vital records. Various collections for the city of Odessa. Mid-1800s–1910s.